AF559764

Ambigious Alternative Tourism in Small Developing Countries

Ambigious Alternative Tourism in Small Developing Countries

Jung Bahadur Gupta

RANDOM PUBLICATIONS
NEW DELHI (INDIA)

Ambigious Alternative Tourism in Small Developing Countries

ISBN 978-93-5111-542-7

Published in 2015 in India by

RANDOM PUBLICATIONS

4376-A/4B, Gali Murari Lal, Ansari Road
New Delhi-110 002
Phone : +9111-43580356, 011-23289044, 011-43142548
e-mail: sales@randompublications.com,
info@randompublications.com, randomexports@gmail.com

Type Setting by : Friends Media, Delhi-110089
Printed at : Thomson Press (I) Ltd.

Preface

Tourism is a vital part of the global economy. Generating roughly $1 trillion in global receipts in 2013, international tourism ranked as the fourth-largest industry in the world, after fuels, chemicals, and automotive products. The breadth of international travel also has greatly expanded in recent years to encompass the developing world. In 1950 just fifteen destinations-primarily European-accounted for 98 percent of all international arrivals. By 2013 that figure had fallen to 57 percent.

Once essentially excluded from the tourism industry, the developing world has now become its major growth area. Tourism is a key foreign exchange earner for 83 percent of developing countries and the leading export earner for one-third of the world's poorest countries. For the world's forty poorest countries, tourism is the second-most important source of foreign exchange after oil.

I would like to thank my team for standing beside me throughout my career and writing this book. My special thanks go to "Random Publications" who have published the book.

– Jung Bahadur Gupta

Contents

Preface .... *v-vi*

1. **The Emergence of Alternative Forms of Tourism** **1**

   Economic Trends and Byproducts In Mainstream Tourism 6
   Conceptual Basis for Mainstream and Alternative Tourism 9

2. **Lessons from Development for Tourism** **12**

   Alternative Development 13
   Authenticity In Tourism and Meaning in Development 15
   Modifying the Analytical Tools 24

3. **Selecting and Attracting the Right Customers** **39**

   Task of Creating and Delivering Superior Customer Value 39
   Guests Value Experience Over Location and Price 43

4. **Third World Critique of Tourism** **69**

   A Negative Model 71
   Top-Down Approach 72
   The Political Economy of Third World Tourism 80

5. **State-Civil Society Relations and Tourism** **92**

   Tourism and Politics 93
   Political Socialization and Responses from Civil Society 94
   State-Society Relations and Tourism in Singapore 95

6. **The Rise of Indigenous Cultural Tourism** **107**

   Local Claims on an Australian Legend 121

7. **The Tourist Industry** **132**

   Travel Elements 133

8. **Tourism Policy and International Organizations** **180**

   Globalization and Tourism: the New Age 181

9. **Tourism Demand and Competitiveness** **200**
Tourism Demand trends and Globalisation 201
Ecology and Environmental Concern 205
10. **Global Policies and the Tourism Industry** **220**
Private Sector Policy Challenges221
The growth of Eco-Labels in the Tourism Industry230
11. **Tourism Industry in India** **236**
The Booming Tourism Industry 236
Indian Tourism 2001 237
12. **Tourism in Afghanistan** **241**
13. **Tourism in Australia** **244**
14. **Tourism in Botswana Tourism** **247**
15. **Tourism in Bulgaria** **248**
Tourism in Bulgaria 248
16. **Tourism in Burundi** **250**
17. **Tourism in Chile** **251**
18. **Tourism in China** **252**
19. **Tourism in Costa Rica** **254**
20. **Tourism in Cote d'Ivoire** **255**
21. **Tourism in Croatia** **256**
22. **Tourism in Cuba** **258**
23. **Tourism in Germany** **259**
24. **Tourism in Greece** **261**
25. **Tourism in Italy** **262**
26. **Tourism in Malaysia** **264**
Bibliography **266**
Index **268**

1

The Emergence of Alternative Forms of Tourism

The latter half of the twentieth century has been marked with amazing changes in technology, transportation, and communication and, in varying degrees, a spread of geo-political stability that has accompanied economic affluence for many citizens in industrialized and developing countries throughout the world. These changes have triggered the development of a number of new industries and the substantial evolution of existing industries to address the needs of increasingly prosperous, educated, and sophisticated post-industrial societies. One of these industries, tourism, has quietly emerged to become an important force in many societies and economies in various parts of the world.

Though not usually thought of as a single cohesive industry, the growth of tourism since World War II has nonetheless been dramatic. Higher discretionary incomes, smaller family size, changing demographics, lower transportation costs, improved public health standards, infrastructure development, and hospitable environments for tourists in many destinations have made tourism, especially long-distance tourism, an activity within the reach and desires of many members of many nations.

Furthermore, developments in marketing, management, vertical and horizontal integration, pricing, and tour packaging, as well as capital investments in physical facilities — "bricks and mortar" — and public infrastructure, have provided tourism with the necessary framework to allow the tremendous growth it has experienced over the past half century. Thus, tourism has indeed emerged as an "industry" which, according to the World Tourism Organization, in 1989 gener ated approximately 74 million jobs in its direct and service-related industries, such as airlines, hotels, travel services, and publications.

At least at the international level, the growth and extent of tourism activity can be appreciated by examining the volume and expenditures of international travelers; data from the period 1950 to 1990 are presented. Though these data include many who are traveling for other reasons, a good portion of the growth is attributable to tourism.

Table. International Travelers: Volume and Expenditure Patterns.

Year	*Arrivals (millions)*	*Per cent Increase*	*Expenditures (U.S. $ billions)*	*Percent Increase*
1950	25.3		2.1	
1960	69.3	173.9	6.9	229
1970	158.7	145.0	17.9	159
1980	204.8	29.0	102.4	472
1990	425.0	107.5	230.0	125
Source: World Tourism Organization Secretariat 1991				

Many countries and regions which have possessed the necessary resources for tourism development have chosen, either consciously or otherwise, the path of developing large scale tourism as a major national or regional activity. Tourism has become a major employer, taxpayer, and physical and political presence in many jurisdictions. As a result, tourism has often altered the very nature of social, political, and economic interaction that occurs in these places. Frequently, the transformation has been no less dramatic than the shifts that took place generations before, as agrarian ways were pushed out by industrialization.

Now, in industrialized countries, tourism is frequently pushing out (or more correctly, replacing) manufacturing, distribution, or extractive industry as the economic mainstay. In developing countries, the shift typically has been from an agrarian economic base to a touristic economic base, bypassing an industrial phase altogether.The reasons for this explosion of growth in tourism are many and interrelated. At one level, transportation systems, especially with respect to the automobile and commercial air travel, have opened new opportunities for potential tourists by making transport from home to destination less expensive (in real terms), more convenient, quicker, and safer.

Increases in real incomes since 1950, especially in the industrialized countries of Europe, North America, and Australasia, have expanded the numbers of potential long distance tourists from solely the upper classes to virtually all social strata.

Shortened work weeks, increased leisure time, earlier retirement age, and extended life expectancies have provided many more people with the discretionary time and opportunities to undertake frequent holidays, or "get-aways," or to pursue lengthy exploratory excursions.

Improved communications and information dissemination, ranging from travelogues on television, to movies filmed in exotic locations, to extensive word-of-mouth networking, have familiarized potential tourists with the far corners of the globe long before they consider visiting them.

The desire to see famous natural or man-made sites, to experience new or familiar adventures, different cultures, or one's own historic or ethnic roots, or just to change one's environment from the cold chill of winter to the warmth of sun-drenched beaches has been enhanced and stimulated by the marketing efforts of such various components of the tourism industry as airlines, destination resorts, and tourism authorities in their efforts to increase volumes of business or visitorship to specific locations.

On the supply side, various improvements have been made which have catered to the tastes and preferences of potential tourists. No longer is long distance air travel considered a major ordeal. With the combination of increasingly experienced travelers and customer sensitive airlines, trips that would have been considered extremely demanding only one or two generations ago are now taken in stride by all but the most fickle of travelers.

The uncertainty of the availability or quality of accommodations that may have prevailed in the past has been replaced by worldwide reservation services, hotel franchises that guarantee quality standards and potable water, and the familiarity and assurances generated by prior visits, visits by friends, or observations by travel writers.

However, tourist development has not progressed without controversy. Disillusionment with "mass" tourism and the many problems it has triggered has led many observers and researchers to criticize vociferously the past methods and directions of tourism development and to offer instead the hope of "alternative tourism," broadly defined as forms of tourism that are consistent with natural, social, and community values and which allow both hosts and guests to enjoy positive and worthwhile interaction and shared experiences.

To date, however, such reactions have been more notable for their harsh judgements against mass tourism than their positive contributions as to what "alternative tourism" means. As many of the articles in this volume point out, it is easier to grasp and speak against the negative results of mass tourism than it is to formulate a realistic and cohesive view of what "alternative tourism," however defined, can reasonably offer.

The flurry of research and publication concerning mainstream and alternative tourism in the past two decades can be placed in historical perspective. Most analysts recognize that tourism takes on forms appropriate to an era, and therefore historic styles develop consistent with population size, economic status, available modes of transport, and geographical habitats of home in comparison with destinations abroad.

Public participation creates mainstream tourism, usually in several variations at any given time; and the needed infrastructure develops accordingly. In addition, the existence of "alternatives" to mainstream tourism is not new.

Sigaux documents the history of tourism from the time of the early Greeks to the period after World War II, and this chronology clearly shows both mainstream and "alternative" tourism for more than two millennia. According to Casson, for example, during the Empire the seven hills of metropolitan Rome supported an estimated 1.5 million people, many of whom must have shared modern motivations for travel including the need for fresh air and a change of scene.

Wealthy Romans traveled to Naples, where their vacation homes were constructed on piers built over the water, providing a fine view of Mt. Vesuvius reflected in the Bay. A fragment of etched glass depicting this salubrious scene may well be the first known tourist souvenir. Around this cluster of superior accommodations, lesser folk rented lodging in small rooms on side streets.

The rich traveled by chariot from Rome to Naples and built private villas (*diversoria*) for their overnight stops along the highway. Even though used only three or four nights per year, these en route accommodations were elegantly furnished and maintained by a permanent staff of servants. Their gardens were filled with fruit and flowers, but water was so scarce in the hill country that it was necessary to "water" the plants with wine!

To house the commoners who also toured, farmers whose land fortuitously fronted the Roman highway built *tavernas* to provide lodging, meals, and stables and soon were in business as innkeepers.

Not all Romans could travel so far. Early in the Imperial era Tivoli (originally *Tibur*), only a few miles outside Rome, became a popular holiday centre noted for its gardens and waterfalls. "Second home" tourism also dates at least to Roman times in the many villas and spas constructed outside every major city of the Empire.

Near Rome, Hadrian's Villa, built between 125 and 135 AD, is still a much-visited attraction.

Tourism became a major industry in the nineteenth century. The *Dictionnaire universale du XIXe siécle* of 1876 (quoted by Sigaux 1966:7) defines tourists as "people who travel for the pleasure of traveling, out of curiosity and because they have nothing better to do" and "even for the joy of boasting about it afterwards."

Construction of railroads and the innovations of Thomas Cook and George Pullman created new forms of "mainstream" tourism such as group tours. In his first nine years in business (1857-1866), Thomas Cook alone handled more than a million customers, building an economic empire in mainstream tourism with his hotel vouchers, rail tickets, traveler's cheques, and a global travel agency network.

As Dennison Nash (1979b) details, European aristocracy (together with the gamblers, ne'er-do-wells, and voyeurs who followed them) created at Nice the first European winter resort where a cluster of palatial hotels with ballrooms and adjoining concert halls provided annual recreation for some 60,000 *hivernants* (winter visitors) amidst opulence, indoor toilets, and a discriminating hotel staff. And tiny adjacent Monaco attained its fame with the establishment of a resplendent casino to serve the so-called "international set."

But "alternative" forms of tourism also developed in Europe during this same period, as reported in the 1985 Special Issue: The Evolution of Tourism, of the *Annals of Tourism Research*. Noteworthy is the article on "tramping" by members of the British working classes for whom these "tramp trips appear to have become rites of passage to full male adulthood".

The similar French *Tour de France* and the German *Wanderpflicht* provided European journeymen with an opportunity to gain work experience away from home, and thereby served to "regulate competition by geographically dispersing workers and delaying entrance to master craftsman status" for as long as four to five years. *Compagnonnage* as a rite of passage into manhood is said to have been one of the most powerful working class institutions ever developed in France. For domestic tourism, Fichtner and Michna (1987) trace the rise of Europe's famous amusement parks, the forerunners of today's theme parks.

In the twentieth century, the first passenger jet service in 1958 is credited with inaugurating modern mass and charter tourism, with all its attendant problems of overcrowding and pollution. Thus mainstream tourism in subsequent decades has used airplanes for long-haul travel and autos on the local scene.

The railroad which reigned supreme during the nineteenth century fell quickly into decline, as Martinus Kosters documents in this volume. Mainstream tourism in this century has been primarily north-south because of climate and, as Hall observes (1984:540), "destination countries represent a much wider spread than originating countries, reflecting a spatial diffusion of tourists from the developed world across the globe, with fastest growth in the more remote regions of the Third World."

Rapid development of resort infrastructure to receive and accommodate airborne guests in favored spots was responsible for the Miami Beach/Waikiki atmosphere, advertising sun, sea, sand, and sex on beaches from Antigua to Zihuatanejo.

Alternately sun, ski, snow, and sex have become winter sports attractions in resorts from the Arlberg to Zermatt, with the attendant gridlock on mountain access roads. By the 1990s, there is a sense that the public has become "tired" of the crowds, weary of jet lag, awakened to the evidences of pollution, and in search of something "new."

Innovative but rapidly gaining in popularity as "alternative" vacations for this decade are walking tours (some of which are very costly because of the level of accommodations and cuisine provided), barge and canal tours (many of which are also deluxe and expensive), bicycle tours, home and farm stays (as discussed by Pearce in this volume), and, at least within the United States, an increase in domestic tourism.

Youth tourism has also taken many forms over time, most of which seem to have been a simple expression of youthful energy and curiosity about the world beyond their bounded society. Their travels were usually a form of "alternatives" to prevailing tourism. Historically, these have involved travels to medieval universities and such institutions as the "Grand Tour," with its year abroad for young scholars and their tutors.

In recent years, the youth hostel movement encouraged "hitchhikers" and the 1960s generated the "hippies," followed by what Riley now terms the "long term budget traveller". This last group is to be distinguished from the "drifters" first described by Cohen whose deviant, drug-related behaviour and counterculture still persist in some locales such as Thailand and Sri Lanka.

Thus, to seek "alternatives" to the tourist mainstream is a contemporary but by no means a novel theme. The history of tourism is replete with centuries of parallel examples.

ECONOMIC TRENDS AND BYPRODUCTS IN MAINSTREAM TOURISM

Because of the growing awareness of tourism as an activity, an industry, and a catalyst for economic growth and development, competition for the tourist and for tourism expenditures has been significant in recent decades. One result has been market segmentation and a considerable broadening of the perceived and actual opportunities available for potential tourists. Thus tourists can choose from "sun and sand" holidays, "adventure travel," "theater tours," "shopping sprees," summer or winter sports vacations, cultural immersion, historic re-enactments, and various other tourism experiences. An interesting illustration of product identification and market segmentation is offered by two of the fastest growing tourism destinations in the United States: Orlando, Florida and Las Vegas, Nevada.

Both of these tourist-dominated cities offer predominantly artificially created tourism experiences: Orlando with the presence of Disney World, Epcot Centre, and MGM and Universal Studio "Hollywood"-themed parks; and Las Vegas with its variety of themed "must see" casino-hotel resorts such as The Mirage, Caesars Palace, and Excalibur, along with high-technology showroom extravaganzas and unparalleled convention facilities, all framing a wide variety of gambling opportunities.

Both Orlando and Las Vegas offer escapism and fantasy in highly artificial environments and have been tremendously successful in doing so. It is no accident that Las Vegas is often referred to as providing an "adult Disneyland" for its visitors, whereas Orlando provides the "real" Disney experience. With the exception of the slot machines and gambling tables, there are strong similarities between these two rapidly growing tourism destination cities. Indeed, it may not be so farfetched to call Orlando, with all of its thrilling but non-etheless artificial attractions, an "adolescent's Las Vegas." It is worth noting that the economic success of both Las Vegas and Orlando has led to many recent attempts to emulate them; legalization or attempted legalization of casino-style gambling has been widespread in the United States, Canada, and Australia over the past fifteen years, and Mickey Mouse has gone abroad to France and Tokyo to found new Disney Worlds to conquer.

However, in spite of the many forms it has taken, not all tourism industries in the developed or the developing world have been beneficial. Success in attracting tourists and tourism-related investments has sometimes led to over-exploitation of tourism resources, which has deteriorated the tourism experience for visitors and hosts alike.

Conflicts have arisen between natural and constructed tourism resources as governments and entrepreneurs have cooperated in competition with those of other locations to attract the economic benefits and prestige that popular destination resorts could bring. Sheer numbers of tourists have altered the "pristine" or "natural" experience that some regions initially offered.

The development of high volume tourism facilities, such as high-rise hotels and tourist-oriented strip retail centers, with inadequate attention paid to traffic patterns, urban planning, infrastructure needs, or aesthetic considerations, has created more than a few "tourism disasters." It is clear in retrospect that, in many cases, the benefits linked to tourism development were quickly dissipated, either due to inadequate or inept planning or because of short-term, shortsighted exploitation.

Disillusionment with mainstream or mass tourism is reflected in the retrospective disappointment of many locals and tourists alike with the ultimate results of tourism developments. An interesting illustration is provided by the case study of Maui, Hawaii, written by Farrell in this volume. For the locals — the hosts — the concerns may be of promises unfulfilled, destruction of an older and simpler way of life, inadequacy of employment opportunities, or dissatisfaction with other economic changes which came with tourism development.

For tourists the view is often summarized with statements such as "This used to be a nice place, but now it is ruined" because of overcrowding, overcommercialization, or overdevelopment. The "mass tourism," the tackiness, and the variety of problems experienced in such places as Niagara Falls, Waikiki, Spain's Costa Brava, and Australia's Gold Coast have too often created eyesores alongside beautiful natural settings; herded large numbers of tourists as if they were so many cattle; disrupted traditional cultures and occupational patterns by creating a pervasive tourism industry characterized by low-paying service jobs and manipulative values; and ignored the needs of local citizens and the community values that were inconsistent with pragmatic economic requirements of the tourism industry.

The decade of the 1990s has been predicted to become the "Decade of Eco-Tourism," and the travel industry is becoming sensitized to mounting global concern about the social costs and environmental damage created by too much tourism. In the past, planners in the private and public sectors have relied heavily on short and intermediate term economic and investment criteria for decision making and for resource allocation considerations regarding tourism projects.

This has often led to problems of overdevelopment accompanied by rapid decline in a destination's general appeal to more upscale tourists. Select coastlines in Florida, Spain, and Mexico provide a variety of examples of this pattern of development.

One reason for this short-sightedness is that the market pricing mechanism and other economic processes do not always provide a full and complete accounting of all costs and benefits associated with tourist developments. In instances where important resources are held as the property of "all the people," or where individual property rights are poorly defined, externalities — defined as costs (or benefits) resulting from transactions undertaken between buyers and sellers but falling on otherwise uninvolved third parties — can and frequently do arise.

Pristine beaches and alpine settings, for example, are usually perceived as complementary resources for tourism development projects. Yet the attempt of too many projects to capture the common benefits from such shared resources can lead to congestion, pollution, and a general degradation of the value of such resources for tourism purposes.

Thus local residents at tourist destinations, as well as the general public, often bear the costs of overdevelopment through diminished aesthetic or use value of the resources; by paying for mitigation, abatement, or clean-up efforts through private endeavors or increased taxes; or with lower wealth through foregone opportunities, diminished incomes, or depressed property values.

There is also the socially destabilizing issue of redistribution of income and wealth that invariably follows rapid economic change. Tourism development creates "winners" and "losers" among the local residents, often without a common acceptance as to the equity of such redistribution.

Alternatively, many of the "winners" might be outsiders who are then viewed as exploiters of the native population and rapists of the land. Furthermore, the changes in income and wealth are often viewed in light of the long term depletion of an area's resource base; the ability of such destinations to capitalize fully on their tourist resources in the future may become permanently impaired because of rapid tourism development.

Good decision making procedures should take all such externalities and their costs fully into account in planning for tourism development and in directing the evolution of existing tourist industries. Private market forces by themselves cannot rectify such external costs and often ignore altogether — or treat amorally — the income and wealth redistribution issues. When such situations occur, policy makers should structure government intervention to stimulate more desirable outcomes. Regrettably, such enlightened planning is often not realized in practice.

Awareness of such resource and social conflicts, however, and their relationship to the health of a tourism industry is growing. Antonio Savignac, Secretary-General of the World Tourism Organization, was the keynote speaker at the International Travel Industry Expo 1990, held in Chicago. Among his comments delivered to some 3,000 travel agents and 400 industry suppliers were: "if the destination deteriorates, so do the profits."

This conference dealt with "green tourism," or tourism in the context of man's stewardship with nature, with the development of rural tourism, and with the need to develop responsible tourism policies. It was emphasized that industry and tourism planners need to establish criteria which would determine carrying capacities, both physical and social, for many tourist destinations.

Those criteria then require implementation to insure a more enjoyable and lasting experience for the guest and an economically and psychologically more rewarding environment for the hosts. This volume's article by Bryan Farrell provides discussion and a case study of the aspects and pitfalls of this process. In short, the direction of tourism planning in the 1990s should be toward enlightened self-interest and the value of preserving the quality and stability of both natural and human resources in tourism destinations.

CONCEPTUAL BASIS FOR MAINSTREAM AND ALTERNATIVE TOURISM

The concept of mainstream and alternative tourism needs to be reviewed in theoretical perspective. Although European guidebooks date to the fourteenth century and European scholars began to write about the phenomenon of tourism as early as 1899, serious interest in tourism as an institution spans only two decades.

Analyzing the literature to date, Jafar Jafari (1989a:20) has aggregated the individual opinions and writings about tourism into four groups, each with "a distinctive position or consolidated platform on tourism." The four platforms appeared in chronological order but are not mutually exclusive. One has not replaced the other, and all four platforms are still being individually used:

- The Advocacy Platform includes both private and public interests that "focus on tourism's importance to the economy" as a labour-intensive industry that generates foreign exchange, preserves environment, revives traditions of the past, and actively promotes cultural performances. This viewpoint became a strong voice in the 1960s as nationalism swept many countries into independence, heightening their need for funds, and is still prevalent. It was recently expressed as the route to success "with mass tourism as a ticket to development" *Economist.*

- The Cautionary Platform grew out of research and case studies largely undertaken in the 1970s by social scientists who questioned the validity of the benefit claims as contrasted to the realities of commoditization of culture and other negative impacts on a host society. An extensive literature supports the voiced concerns and challenges the Advocates.
- The Adaptancy Platform, benefiting from the arguments raised by its predecessors, seeks new strategies for tourism such as indigenous tourism, soft tourism, green tourism, sensitized tourism, responsible tourism, appropriate tourism, alternative tourism, cottage tourism, local level tourism. However, as Jafari has noted, "the Adaptancy Platform has emerged as a partial remedy, but strategies have not been fully developed to accommodate the mass tourism generated globally. Tourism's forms and practices can be influenced but its volume cannot be curtailed".
- *The Knowledge-Based Platform* is the most recent development and "aims at positioning itself on a scientific foundation which simultaneously maintains bridges with other platforms...the many studies are intended to contribute to a holistic study or treatment of tourism; not just its forms or consequences. The main goal is the formulation of a scientific body of knowledge on tourism."

As with many other aspects of modern life, tourism has brought with it benefits and costs, blessings and curses. Reflecting people's inherent curiosity, hedonism, desire for adventure and excitement, or just a need to change the pace and setting of everyday experiences, tourism has opened the door to many to seek out and fulfill their vacation needs. Furthermore, tourist industries have been the willing suppliers of the demanded services.

But all of this has not come without dissatisfaction. Perceived difficulties with mainstream tourism have encouraged planners, researchers, and social critics to rethink the logic of traditional tourist development, to examine the alternatives to mainstream or mass tourism, and to begin formulating better ways to integrate tourism into a broader range of values and social concerns that traditional tourism development has somehow put at risk.

Fully understanding the benefits and costs of tourist development in terms of their sources, possibilities for mitigation, and implications of "alternatives" will we hope play a major role in correcting the mistakes of the past.

Every body of scholars, working in a particular time span, develop an explanatory mode appropriate to their frame of reference. Just as Jafari has developed a typology of tourism literature (as discussed above), most of the members of the International Academy for the Study of Tourism have been involved in tourism research and/or as consultants to various facets of the travel or transportation industry.

As noted earlier, in the early 1960s the new self-rule of former colonies mandated an immediate search for new sources of foreign exchange and domestic employment. The World Bank and the United Nations recognized the potentials of tourism to meet those needs and negotiated loans and support for new resort developments, for modern airplanes, and for tax benefits for investors. The pace of this type of development has not yet slowed, both because of the development of new overseas destinations such as Boracay in the Philippines and because of the mounting interest in increased domestic tourism in virtually every country on the globe, including many Third World nations.

Of necessity, government planners and policy makers throughout the world are seeking direction for the management of their tourism industries. In many ways this book provides such direction.

The contributors to this volume and the members of the Academy are mindful, however, of the intellectual and ideological alternatives to a tourism management perspective: the emerging interest in eco-tourism, in local level and privatized development, and the concerns and implications suggested in dependency theory and in ecumenical edicts.

To a degree these issues are addressed here, but the body of data to test and verify theory in many of these areas is not yet at hand or is in need of refinement. Meanwhile, development goes forward, sometimes scarcely keeping pace with demand, and the need for direction and greater understanding by and for policy makers remains a most significant challenge. The pragmatic issue that can be useful to policy makers -understanding the broad implications of the various choices confronting them — constitutes the philosophical organizing core for many of the articles in this volume. It is hoped that this will serve as a major building block in the accumulation of knowledge of tourism and its various effects on societies.

2

Lessons from Development for Tourism

We don't want tourism. We don't want you. We don't want to be degraded as servants and dancers. That is cultural prostitution. I don't want to see a single one of you in Hawaii. There are no innocent tourists. A few years ago, in a short note published in *Annals of Tourism Research*, Georg Pfafflin approvingly quoted these sentiments of a native Hawaiian, expressed at a church-sponsored conference on tourism and the Third World.

In that note, Pfafflin not only repeated the view that the chances for genuine encounters between tourists and host populations are extremely poor, but also wrote that "the public" in Europe "now realizes that tourism to the Third World is always connected with such North-South problems as hunger, the debt crisis and its povertyproducing effects, and the destruction of the ecological system".

It is not obvious that Pfafflin is right about "the" public, nor is it easy to understand what mechanisms are involved in these very different connections. Yet however sweeping his view of the ill-effects of tourism and however much it ignores many years of patient work to distinguish different tourism situations from each other, this view nevertheless needs to be taken into account.

It is relevant to much that has been written about Alternative Tourism. The concept of Alternative Tourism has been used in so many ways as to make it meaningless. Even so, many of the approaches share an undertone of moral indignation, of rejection of normal, mass or "mainstream" tourism in which political hostility to transnational capitalism mingles with cultural and ecological unease over modern massconsumption society.

This undertone has also been present in the concept of "Alternative," or "Another," Development. However, it is not used in so bewildering a variety of ways as is Alternative Tourism. Alternative Development is a broader concept, which in some senses encompasses that of Alternative Tourism.

The parallels and contrasts between these two "alternative" concepts and the evolution in both cases from a predominantly "moralistic" or normative approach to one which is more concerned with analysis and understanding are the focus of the present analysis.

ALTERNATIVE DEVELOPMENT

There have always been a variety of approaches to development, and no one paradigm or theory has ever attained absolute dominance. Most discussions would recognize at least three contenders in the field: the neo-classical, the Marxist, and the structuralist "schools". During the 1980s, the recognition has spread that all three theories have failed to give satisfactory overall explanations of the process of development, or of its "absence"; and practitioners — decision makers, planners, advisers — in both market and state run economies have been clamoring for new guidelines.

Many have blamed the problems of development on the negative effects of a large scale direct role for the state in the economy, and a more or less hefty dose of neo-liberal ("Thatcherite") policies has been injected almost everywhere, even in many "socialist" economies.

This has resulted in a broad and widely shared development "mainstream," but we are, it seems, not far from yet another turning point, one likely to reincorporate the view that the untrammeled operation of the market does not provide the ultimate answer and itself creates new problems. We can expect to see a measure of rehabilitation of the state's role in forcefully regulating the market, though not perhaps in the direct production of goods and services.

The emergence into prominence, at least in Europe, of Green political parties (the political expression of one of the hitherto more remote "counterpoints" to that mainstream) is likely to push the issue of curbing the market higher up on the political agenda.

A few years ago, those with a "green" approach to our planet and development were seen as cranks, their organizations as marginal. Since then, partly as a result of the success of their efforts in putting their views across and partly because of the remarkable impact of the Brundtland Commission, itself a sign of the times, we have all been "greened" to a greater or lesser extent.

In recent years environment, ecology and even "sustainable development" have moved progressively closer to the centre of the stage of public concern and politics. It is no longer considered outlandish to speak of Alternative Development, or Sustainable Development.

There are many explicit and implicit definitions of Alternative Development. Their constituent elements have become rather more distinct over time, and some of the "evangelical" fervour has been lost. Concern with the environment has been there from the start.

Among the Greens there are still some extreme antagonists to mainstream development in "a vocal ecocentric wing (which) continues its rather shrill opposition to the destruction of almost anything", but the more moderate demand for "ecologically sound" development is now heard in wide circles of public and government opinion.

While environmental sensationalism and scientific amateurism still abound, there are also indications that among critics of mainstream development a more sobre assessment of global ecological problems is emerging, in which less reliance is placed on discredited doom-laden predictions from the 1970s and more allowance is made for technical change and the probability that it will modify the problems as well as their solutions.

In addition, the proponents of Alternative Development agree that scaling down the operations of production and government is both necessary and desirable. It is necessary if development is to become sustainable — defined by Brundtland as development that "meets the goals of the present without compromising the ability of future generations to meet their own needs".

It is desirable in order to achieve a development which is more "people-oriented," in contrast to the present style. Such development revolves around maintaining economic growth without concern for the effects of such growth in ecological and social ("who benefits?") terms, especially with regard to the "essential needs of the world's poor".

Such scaling down involves encouraging smaller enterprises at the local level — paying attention to what has been called the "informal economy" — as well as promoting devolution of power from central political systems to local, self-reliant communities.

The resemblance of the political prescriptions to those of the nineteenth-century anarchists is striking, and they can be criticized on similar grounds; some of the purer ideas on community production also smack of nineteenth-century utopianism.

It is no wonder that these now dominant Alternative Development views are attacked from a more radical "red" perspective for disregarding the structural causes of ecological and other problems and for being naive about the political action required to change these structures.

Yet the basic traits of Alternative Development are clear: ecological soundness, small-scale production, recognition of needs other than those of material consumption, equal consideration of the needs of all (including future generations), and political involvement from below. These are also, broadly, seen as the traits of development that is sustainable.

As a concept, Alternative Tourism lacks even the tentative Gestalt which can be recognized in Alternative Development. While Alternative Development always refers to the developing economy or society, Alternative Tourism can have as its prime reference the host economy or society, the tourist, or the national or transnational tourism industry.

In fact, Alternative Tourism means all things to all people: "nowadays all travellers who do not undertake a normal type of vacation are lumped together under the general heading of 'alternative tourism'". Some writers appear to suggest that anything other than mass tourism should be graced with the "alternative" label: the collection put together by the Ecumenical Coalition on Third World Tourism leaves such an impression.

Various recent studies, such as the article by Pearce in this volume, have attempted to put some order into this confusion, mainly by distinguishing the different people or situations to which the concept refers.

Nevertheless, there are a number of themes that recur in many discussions on Alternative Tourism which echo the central issues of Alternative Development. First, Alternative Tourism is applied to tourism which does not damage the environment, is ecologically sound, and avoids the negative impacts of many large-scale tourism developments undertaken in areas which have not previously been developed.

Second, Alternative Tourism is thought to consist of smaller developments, or attractions for tourists which are set in and organized by villages or communities. These are seen as having fewer negative effects, social or cultural, and a better chance of being acceptable to the local people than mass tourism.

Third, and following from this, there is the question of "who benefits." Certain kinds of tourism are called alternative because they are not "exploitative" of local people, because the benefits flow to local residents or in general to poorer communities. Conventional tourism demands large-scale organization and resources not usually available locally or even in the country; as a result its rewards flow away to distant townsfolk or abroad. Finally, a shared perspective with Alternative Development is an emphasis on cultural sustainability. Tourism which does not damage the culture of the host community is often called alternative; more than that, Alternative Tourism may actively try to encourage a respect for the cultural realities experienced by the tourists through education and organized "encounters."

These last two characteristics dominate in the approach of churchoriented groups active in the promotion of Alternative Tourism. Holden's definition fairly captures this:

Alternative Tourism is a process which promotes a just form of travel between members of different communities. It seeks to achieve mutual understanding, solidarity and equality amongst participants.

While the symmetry of this approach may seem attractive, it is not the line followed in this analysis. Here we shall focus predominantly on tourism as seen from the perspective of the host country and its inhabitants, rather than concern with the motivations, attitudes, or behaviour patterns of the tourists, let alone their ethos.

AUTHENTICITY IN TOURISM AND MEANING IN DEVELOPMENT

The idea of Alternative Tourism as centering on the search for authenticity would appear not to have an equivalent in Alternative Development.

Authenticity as a characteristic of Alternative Tourism is wholly focused on the tourist; it concerns his or her perceptions of the reality encountered in the tourist experience.

Cohen's recent paper deals with this issue brilliantly and in detail, his main point being that authenticity does not have an "objective quality," but is attributed by moderns to the world "out there" and thus is a socially constructed concept with a connotation that is not given but "negotiable".

In spite of all the nuances brought to the discussion, authenticity remains an issue of importance only to the tourists, or to the hosts insofar as they want to please the tourists; the questions it raises lie outside the realm where Alternative Development provides the pointers for comparison.

Nevertheless, there is an area of overlap, because authenticity deals with meaning, and meaning — for the subjects of development — is an important issue in Alternative Development also. As Dudley Seers noted more than twenty years ago, the question of meaning in development addresses the issue of values often disregarded in the development discourse.

"The starting-point is that we cannot avoid what the positivists disparagingly refer to as 'value judgements.'...Development is inevitably a normative concept, almost a synonym for improvement". And however crucial it remains to the poor to have greater access to material goods, this does not define exhaustively what people regard as "improvement" nor what meaning they can discover in development.

Mainstream development is a child of Western civilization. With the growth of science and technology over the past four centuries, the manipulation and mastering of nature has become the driving force of material "progress." "Development," as it is now understood in mainstream Western thinking, translates this instrumental rationalism into action, constantly "transforming" and "improving" the world. Beyond science and technology, economics dominates the social and human sciences. The mainstream theories of development focus mostly on the economic processes in that material transformation (economics as the science of the management of scarce resources) and devote less attention to the ecological, cultural, and sociopolitical context within which the economy operates.

This has contributed to the dominance of economic policies in the political arena, with governments often paying scant attention to the impact of such policies on culture or nature or to issues arising in these spheres in the first place. Innovation in production and the stimulation of an everchanging demand for the latest in consumption became the final hallmarks of Western "consumer society"; these have provided the meaning of development for "Westerners" and those influenced by them.

Nature, culture, and community have been at the forefront of people's concerns in many non-Western societies. It is clear that in modern society these have moved backstage; they no longer provide the prime motivations for people's actions.

Proponents of Alternative Development want to change that and thereby give a new meaning to development. For even when their language is that of analysis and interpretation, the underlying thrust is political, ideological, and moral. "People-centredness" or "humancentredness" implies small scale institutions, a relocation of decision making, and a rearrangement of the locus of power.

Yet Alternative Development enjoins people to relinquish the meaning they have given to everyday life through the products of the consumer society.

They are called to reorient their *Weltanschauung* to the fulfillment of basic human needs, not only for themselves — the simplest life — but for all their fellow human beings (distributive justice) and their posterity (intergenerational justice). Included therein is a concern to achieve harmony with nature and its creatures. This ideological or moral streak in Alternative Development — and Alternative Tourism — has been prominent.

THE SENSE OF OUTRAGE

There are three areas in which this ideological concern has focused in regard to both Alternative Tourism and Alternative Development: nature, materialism, and culture. As long ago as 1971 the Founex Report, prepared for the Stockholm Conference, characterized environmental problems as the "effluence of affluence" and the "pollution of poverty"; this evocative terminology encapsulated a battle cry for action.

From the same decade came the predictions of doom from the Club of Rome with *The Limits to Growth*. In spite of the torrent of scientific criticism unleashed, these are still being used in ecological arguments to portray economic growth as a cancer eating away at the earth's resources. Bandyopadhyay and Shiva accuse transnational companies, operating in the global market economy which has no built-in mechanisms to ensure ecological rehabilitation, of being in the forefront of this misuse of nature; once a mining company has exhausted the mine, or agribusiness has destroyed the grazing lands and forests, it will move elsewhere to maintain its profits.

They argue that mainstream development, in encouraging the use of hitherto unexploited resources, fails to take account of the ecological interrelatedness of the world and the way in which scarce natural resources have competing uses; often damage is done not only to nature as such and to the future productive base, but directly to people. Protests may occur against the disregard for these basic interests, as in India with the so-called ecological movements.

Movements by those directly affected are spreading in other countries, too, as are more generalized protest groups to highlight the costs of present day attitudes to the environment (Greenpeace, Friends of the Earth, *etc.*). The alleged disregard for the environment by conventional tourism development also yields expressions of outrage. Hong expresses that mood:

Having ruined their own environment, having either used up or destroyed all that is natural, people from the advanced consumer societies are compelled to look for natural wildlife, cleaner air, lush greenery and golden beaches elsewhere. In other words, they look for other environments to consume. Thus armed with their bags, tourists proceed to consume the environment in the countries of the Third World — that last "unspoiled corner of earth."

Protest movements also arise around tourism development, witnessed by the recent impassioned call for international support by the Federation of Ecological Societies of the Dominican Republic to deal with the "extremely delicate situation" that has arisen as a result of ecologically destructive tourism development, involving massive damage to such elements as forests, mangroves, marine life. Such protests have helped place these matters on the agenda of analysts and policy makers.

Materialism has also brought its own hegemony. The emergence of "modernity" and consumer society as the twin pillars of mainstream development has already been commented upon. Neo-liberals believe that the market should provide the basic organizing principles of economic activity and that the role of the state in this area should be drastically reduced.

The market as it operates in reality, however, is far from "perfect." On the one hand, small numbers of powerful producers can influence market choice in their favour; on the other, large numbers of consumers are left with decreasing areas of choice and often with insufficient resources to operate in the market to their advantage. Individual acquisitiveness is at a premium; intervention by the state, notably to promote distributive justice, is limited domestically and virtually absent internationally.

This kind of development is seen as being narrowly focused on economic growth and expansion of the market; it leads to the growth of consumerism and is founded on short term commercial criteria. Many have applied similar arguments to tourism. A recently published Swiss doctoral dissertation can speak for them all:

The thesis is put forward that the chief beneficiaries of tourism development in the Third World are foreign capitalists and, secondly, the local economic and political elite. Tourists from abroad benefit from comparatively low prices in Third World tourist destinations, while the local population is left with modest employment opportunities, the loss of economic and political decision-making, and predominantly negative socio-cultural effects from institutionalized tourism.

This, as Krippendorf puts it, is because in "industrial *society*, values of being have been crowded out by values of having; possession, property, wealth, consumption, egoism are ranked above community, tolerance, contentment, modesty, meaning, honesty." The economy dominates and "man and the environment are at the service of the economy".

Krippendorf and Bachmann also extend their censure to the sociocultural effects of tourism and the "loss of culture," and in this they echo the more general anguish about the effects of modernity and industrialism as cultural homogenizers. The keynote address of the Jordanian Crown Prince to a conference in Morocco picks up many of the doubts about development as modernization and Westernization.

"Progress" has come to be identified with improvement in quantitative indicators; these concern mainly economic processes, seldom social, hardly ever cultural — and if they do, then it is simply to "measure" such matters as the number of museums operating or books published. As Prince Hassan pointed out, however, culture is more: a system of values and norms which give order and meaning to a society. Planners, however, simply cannot deal with what people want out of "development" and even less with why they want it (the meaning of development, again). And as the planners treat "our peoples as simple numbers, they respond as numbers, multiply like numbers, increase their consumption like numbers" (author's translation). Others have examined this cultural impact of mainstream development on Less Developed Countries through the lens of dependency theory.

Erisman, for example, argues in a discussion of the West Indies that cultural dependency exists when those values, norms, and rules are conditioned by or reflect those in an external culture, leading to a relationship of domination and subordination between the cultural centre and the cultural periphery.

Cultural dependency results in the "incorporation of exogenous norms and values into a nation's socialization process, which can then be said to be penetrated," so that eventually the main stimuli for cultural development come from the outside and people lose their desire to maintain a cultural identity separate from that of the dominant nation.

In a more ideological and outraged vein Nyoni writes that ideas coming from outside the community are expressions of "imposed universalism" which "destroy local initiatives and self-reliance" through "self-colonization and elitism" of local elites, which "are heavily influenced and dominated by foreign and unworkable ideas".

Loss of culture is also explored with respect to the commoditization of relationships, when things and activities that were hitherto outside it are brought into the sphere of market transactions through exchange values. This is often said to be the result of tourism, but in fact it usually arises primarily out of those broader processes promoted by mainstream development.

The already mentioned debates over authenticity are also relevant. Though these have been pursued above all in relation to tourism development, those opposing mainstream development may also allude to these questions. Thus we read in an already quoted article in IFDA Dossier, one of the main outlets for *engagé* discussions of Alternative Development is that the market economy defines people as poor who do not participate very much in the market and do not consume the products of consumer society — that is, if they eat "self-grown nutritious millets" instead of junk food or if they wear "indigenously designed handmade garments of natural fibre" rather than clothes made of manmade fibres. "The culturally conceived poverty based on non-western modes of consumption is often mistaken to be misery".

This quote represents the polar opposite to the often thoughtless sense of social and cultural superiority of those who stand for mainstream development because in its anger with cultural domination it appears to play down the very real poverty of hundreds of millions in the Third World. These neither eat their insufficient diet of "selfgrown nutritious millets" nor own just one set of simple "indigenously designed [?!] handmade garments of natural fibre" out of their own volition, and they would gladly exchange these for basic needs of the modern variety if they were available. There are, however, signs that more balanced approaches are winning adherents both in the scientific community and in the political arena.

SUSTAINABILITY AS AN ORGANIZING CONCEPT FOR POLICY

We have already seen how the Brundtland Commission's report has helped to place the issue of sustainability closer to the centre of the political agenda. This has drawn renewed attention to three areas in which the approaches, and reproaches, of Alternative Development can help to modify analysis and action without a "revolution" in social and economic organization: resource use and renewability, the issue of scale, and the equitable distribution of benefits (including to future generations).

The following discussion also suggests that making sustainability the focus of Alternative Tourism may possibly be the most productive way forward. It would not, of course, address the more tourist-oriented and normative issues often raised, but it would narrow the discussion to some of the central issues for the host economy, society, and culture.

In policy terms, making tourism sustainable would involve not just encouraging the development of "an alternative to" conventional tourism (though this could be part of it), but above all would force conventional tourism development to take greater notice of the three areas mentioned above.

First, we turn to the issue of resource use and renewability. The notion of sustainable development has been promoted largely from the rich countries of the North. Reducing pollution, carbon dioxide emissions, or the destruction of forests for the sake of "Our Common Future" is all very well for those whose unsustainable actions over decades have underpinned their high standard of living. But what about the poor countries? Their need is continuing economic growth, for which they require many of the natural and environmental resources that are under stress. Where continued exploitation of these without concern for sustainability has occurred, as in Amazonia, it has brought out the Northern television crews and galvanized the North's politicians.

For Less Developed Countries, then, a crucial aspect of sustainability is the maintenance of the productivity of resources. One relatively easy means would be to seek a sustained increase in recovery and recycling.

The use and further development of new technologies, in which the materials of production or its polluting effects are decreased, can also help achieve this. Because the latter is an option that can be pursued without greatly affecting existing vested interests, it is attractive to some of the more advanced Less Developed Countries such as Brazil; this concept was also promoted by the Brundtland Commission.

More generally, environmental degradation can result from many small increases in environmental neglect, none of which is catastrophic in itself. Conversely, sustainability can be safeguarded by the avoidance of such cumulative negative threshold effects.

Tourism development again raises similar questions to development in general. Pigram sees Alternative Tourism as an exercise in sustainable resource management, where "safe minimum standards" would ensure that the threshold of irreversibility would not be crossed. Wilkinson (1989) discusses the possible negative environmental impacts of tourism development on small island environments.

Each such development raises different and specific issues, for example, the dangers of damaging coral reefs, beach sand loss, or the contamination of coastal waters. Sometimes, especially in self-contained and very small natural environments, it is clearly essential for the maintenance of the value of the "asset" to protect its ecological *raison d'être*, and so the enterprise itself has strong reasons to do so. But often these costs will not be "calculated" by the users unless an external authority forces them to do so, usually by means of taxation or other incentives and disincentives. What is clear, however, is that such issues are now being more widely discussed and that the analytical tools for moving in this direction are becoming available.

One such analytical tool is the concept of carrying capacity, which has been available to tourism planners for many years. Tourist carrying capacity is the number of tourists that can be accommodated without creating negative environmental effects. It links questions of resource use and renewability to the issue of scale, to which we now turn.

The proponents of Alternative Development, as has been discussed, are anxious to see a scaling down in virtually all areas of economic, social, and political activity — in production, distribution, consumption, government, and administration. Brundtland, who addresses United Nation agencies, governments, and multinationals rather than "the people" as such, says virtually nothing on this issue. In discussions of tourism development, however, the question of scale has been an issue for many years, and recent writings have kept it in the limelight.

Four issues may be mentioned. First, how to deal with tourist carrying capacity in general. While there are obvious ecological advantages to keeping the number of tourists down, attention is also being paid to measures that can both increase tourist carrying capacity and improve the capacity to protect the environment. Second, there is the matter of the promotion of tourism in less massive form.

This can involve, as has been done in Bhutan, concentrating tourism development efforts on facilities for a small number of rich tourists. This option, however, raises questions of the environmental impact (e.g., energy and water) generated by facilities for the wealthy: "luxury tourism tends to require more imports, to be more capital-intensive, to be more dependent on outside control of capital, to encourage more of a sense of conspicuous consumption, and to result in a greater sense of relative deprivation than more modest facilities".

Conversely, of course, smaller operations not aimed solely at wealthy outsiders may be more within the reach of the local middle classes -also for non-resident use.

Scale can also be dealt with by dispersion, fostering the development of tourism in a larger number of smaller places. While this will incorporate development areas hitherto unaffected by tourism, the effects can be more easily monitored and controlled, especially from an ecological point of view. An example is the plan of the Indian Government envisaging the creation of a number of regional travel circuits.

These were to cover a total of 441 small centers to cater for budget and low income tourists interested in traveling "off the beaten track". More spontaneous developments can also follow this lead. A notable example is that of farm tourism in Europe, to which Pearce refers with much insight elsewhere in this volume.

Third, there is the question of organizing for smaller scale operations. Multinationals are successful precisely because they reap economies of scale and "aggregation" through massive integrated operations, as discussed below. If scaling down is to be effective, new institutions and organizations will be required (also true in the wider areas of Alternative Development). In tourism development the questions relate especially to the setting up of cooperative arrangements between small scale enterprises and the strengthening of local planning and regulatory capacities; this also is discussed later.

Finally, a word should be said about socialist systems and the question of scale. Command economies, where investment decisions are made centrally and where all significant productive resources are owned by the state, typically promote large scale tourism development. Hotels, built by state building enterprises or foreign contractors, are large and relatively standardized and usually owned and run by the government tourism para-statal.

Moreover, in such economies the legal system prohibits capitalist accumulation and only permits the employment of a very small number of workers by private concerns. Prior to 1989, this was the pattern over most of Eastern Europe, and continues to be in Third World socialist states such as China, Cuba, and Mozambique.

Yet even before recent changes which have resulted from economic and political reforms, this was never the whole picture. The earliest of the "reformers," Yugoslavia, has shown the way in this respect at least over the last 25 years. While statistics are unlikely to be wholly accurate, in 1987 private establishments such as boarding houses and restaurants made up almost 60 per cent of all such establishments and employed, in addition to the owners, 10 per cent of the employees in this sector.

The private boarding houses provided 34 per cent of all beds available, which accounted for almost one-fifth of the bed-nights. These are impressive figures. Hungary and Poland are now also following this road.

The general point to note is that anti-capitalist provisions in economic legislation have often left room for limited family enterprise. As political and economic conditions became more favorable to the latter, or more unfavorable to the public sector, more workers or farmers became small scale entrepreneurs and ventured into the tourism sector.

Nevertheless, economic legislation has continued to constrain essential aspects of these enterprises, for example, the number of workers that may legally be employed. Consequently, growth occurred in breadth (the number of establishments) but not in depth (their size). The result was a large, or growing, sector of very small establishments side by side with the large hotels and restaurants run by the state, and very little in between.

Another ongoing area of concern is the equitable distribution of benefits. Alternative Development has always emphasized the necessity to focus on basic human needs, but its frame of reference has often been the advanced consumer societies. The implications of its nogrowth or low-growth prescriptions for the poor in Less Developed Countries have been given rather less attention. Most people in the Third World are still struggling to meet the minimum material conditions of a "decent" human existence. Distributive justice in many Less Developed Countries cannot be achieved by development policies which ignore that fact; if there is no cake, there is nothing to distribute.

The poor, wrenched out of their isolation by the transistor radio and the bicycle, do not want to be told to discard their aspirations as consumers — nor, incidentally, do the elites, who wish to emulate the life styles of their counterparts in the rich North. The Brundtland Commission, with strong representation from the South, has corrected that bias. Brundtland has been accused of not facing up to some of the conflicts its proposals are likely to engender and of having a rather "bland" view of sustainable development.

But the Commission has not fallen into the basic-needs-via-no-growth trap. "We see...the possibility for a new era of economic growth.... And we believe such growth to be absolutely essential to relieve the great poverty that is deepening in much of the developing world".

So the Commission takes a position that is "reformist" of the present productive, socioeconomic, political, and international systems; and it raises the issue of equity wherever this seems relevant. Distributive justice is thus deemed henceforth to include consideration of the needs of future generations.

In the critique of conventional tourism development, the issue of equity also plays a role. For example, in a recent overview article on the sociocultural impacts of tourism, Dogan argues that tourism has aggravated income inequalities.

He stresses the need to differentiate between various host population groups (notably between those who are better off, who get more out of tourism) and the poor, whose lifestyle and culture are less like those of tourists and who stand to gain fewer benefits from tourism. He also draws attention to another distinction, that between those who are younger, who tend to be more susceptible to modern consumerism and the older people, who are more traditional in their way of life.

The impacts of tourism development differ between such different groups, and policy makers have to take account of likely outcomes in this respect. The lessons of European farm tourism have some relevance to this issue, too, as Pearce notes in this volume.

MODIFYING THE ANALYTICAL TOOLS

The congruence of mainstream economic (development) theory and conventional economic development policies has been referred to a number of times. The emergence of Alternative Development has led to a critique of the standard tools used in (economic) analysis and the development of new concepts and approaches more appropriate to a policy concerned with sustainability.

This is also visible in tourism studies. Two aspects will be examined: the refinement of certain tools of conventional economic analysis, and the beginnings of the formulation of different methodologies and theories.

Cost-benefit analysis and associated methodologies are the main targets of those who would refashion the tools of economics rather than "start from scratch." Cost-benefit and cost-effectiveness analysis are micro-analytical tools which set out to give guidance on investment choices, often as between different types of (investment) projects.

These methods deal with what happens within projects, or productive units; outside positive or negative impacts, commonly referred to as externalities, are not considered. Projects or enterprises can "externalize" costs; this means "the shifting of costs to third parties, or onto society, future generations, and nature".

In general, the weakness of many economic and business calculations has been that they do not take ecological issues sufficiently into account, that there are neither enough built-in "signals" nor institutionalized incentives and disincentives to warn decision makers away from environmentally damaging courses of action.

The same is true of the distributive effects of economic activity, and when industry damages nature it often also damages the livelihoods of poor people who, especially in Less Developed Countries, are particularly dependent on nature.

Productive enterprises cannot be expected to take account of such externalities when they calculate their costs. On the contrary, normal business practice motivated by profit maximization will attempt to "externalize" the relevant costs, thereby, for example, causing pollution. Governments, however, can force them to internalize such externalities and can shift the costs back to the problem-causing economic units through regulation or taxation.

By that means the state alters the price and cost signals on waste prevention, energy conservation, and the like taken into account by firms in their costings. Changing the legal and cost balance (the principle that the polluter, or even better the likely polluter, pays) could also help bring about a shift from ex-post to ex-ante solutions, from emphasizing cure to emphasizing prevention.

Exactly the same considerations apply to the tourism industry. In tourism development, too, the cost of protecting the environment needs to be treated as an "internality," that is, as a cost of doing business. And, of course, the longer the time perspective of the developer, the easier it is to absorb such costs, as in the construction of a sewage treatment plant instead of using a sea outfall.

Government agencies themselves, however, can and should incorporate ecological effects in their broader cost-benefit calculations. They should modify the methodology itself so that it will take into account, as a matter of course, the costs and benefits of proposed actions for the environment.

Impact assessments do try to achieve this, at best also for other non-material (e.g., cultural) effects; and the Brundtland Commission discusses a whole array of institutional changes, as well as some new tools for analysis, that are relevant in this respect. This approach also needs to be followed by tourism planners.

Can changes in emphasis and perspective such as these direct us towards a new economics? The proponents of Alternative Development and Alternative

Tourism continue to devote most of their time and writing to policy issues and to the advocacy needed to place these at the centre of attention.

Yet more interest is now also being shown in the theoretical underpinning of sustainable policies, and hence in the reformulation of economics itself. It is argued that the "nature" component in sustainability is neglected by economics; environmental questions are not taken into account in models or measurement.

The question of measurement has considerable importance. This is graphically captured in a quote which Brookfield lifted from a paper written by Repetto for the World Bank's Sustainability Issues in Agricultural Development: "a country could exhaust its aquifers, cut down its forests, erode its soils, and hunt its wildlife and fisheries to extinction, but measured income would rise steadily as these assets disappeared".

Traditional economic accounting, which produces that standard international "comparator" of GNP, omits essential elements. National accounting is incomplete on flows (notably non-marketed, directly consumed environmental services), while stocks (such as the surface area under forests) are left out of the picture altogether.

So "measured GNP can increase as a new industry starts production, but if associated air and water pollution are serious, the total welfare derived...may actually decrease." The tools of economic measurement need to take account of the fact that sustainable development "is essentially an asset management problem".

The economics of enterprise, particularly under a capitalist system of production, is oriented to profitability and the expansion of markets; hence growth is a favored outcome, monitored in terms of measurable output, physical quantities, or money equivalents. In nature, however, growth is not the driving force. Rather, nature appears to strive for stability (equilibrium, homeostasis), and it can be argued that ecological stability is the main precondition for sustainability.

Economic policy would take account of this basic fact by moving from the simple maximization of flows (growth) to paying more attention to increasing efficiency and maintaining substance. This would require a redefinition of the concept of GNP by including ecological measures, so that account could be taken of the different effects (positive, neutral, or negative) on the environment of different components of growth as measured by output.

The incorporation of environmental measures in standard national accounting would not solve the problem of "valuing" irreplaceable resources, as in the case of a wilderness region lost because of a hydroelectric development. But at least it would draw attention to the issues and force those responsible to make their value judgements explicit.

That would also be relevant to weighing the immediate consumption needs of the poor in Less Developed Countries against the long term demands of future generations, which is itself an extremely difficult issue. Finally, there are those such as Bandyopadhyay and Shiva (1989) who would give economics an even more fundamental reorientation. Conventional economics deals, they argue, with market economics (or, one might add, command economies). Its models and theories, however, have no relevance to the operation of two quite separate and equally important "economies": the economy of survival, and the economy of natural processes (*i.e.*, what happens in nature) to which the economy of survival is linked.

The market economy and the dominant form of economics employed in its analysis have been concerned with the use of resources for commodity production and capital accumulation. The resource needs of the people outside the commodity economy, the subsistence farmers and pastoralists who make up the majority in so many of the poorer Less Developed Countries, are quite different. In their survival economy, satisfaction of basic needs is the organizing principle for natural resource use.

In such economies there are normally built-in checks on overexploitation unless crisis, such as has been seen in Sub-Saharan Africa over the last decade, sweeps traditional safeguards away, leading to deforestation and similar phenomena.

Herein lies the link to the economy of natural processes, the third type, the economics of which analyzes the processes by which resources are regenerated in nature, as in the production of humus by forests, the regeneration of water resources, or the evolution of genetic products.

Bandyopadhyay and Shiva deepen the basic Alternative Development charge laid at the door of conventional economics — that it externalizes costs. They point out that the market economy has neither substantive nor analytical links with the natural nor survival economies.

Therefore it is not perceived that resource-intensive development, seen as positive within the market economy based on profits and accumulation, actually damages both nature and poor people. Unfortunately, they neither tell us what the economics of nature and survival would look like nor what tools need to be developed.

One may suspect that professional economists would have many good reasons for being skeptical of their approach, and that the approach would be particularly vulnerable to the criticism of neither understanding nor taking sufficient account of the findings of science. Nevertheless, it does provide food for thought and a starting point for others, concerning both Alternative Development and the development of more sustainable forms of tourism.

Thus, we have attempted to document the emergence of more analytical approaches to Alternative Development and Alternative Tourism. To end this part of the discussion a few words will be said about related changes in the political discourse of Alternative Development:

The world view of Another Development is likely to remain that of a minority, in part because most of its adherents adopt an uncompromising all-or-nothing stand which tends to alienate even those who could afford to adopt its back-tonature lifestyle.... The ideas of Another Development are likely to remain on the fringe, crushed between its somewhat dogmatic puritanism and the wish or need of most people (especially the poor in the Third World) to partake of the "fleshpots of Egypt."

These lines written only a few years ago, would no longer be accurate. The rather cranky image of the "alternative movement" is slowly dissolving, and its approach is no longer based solely on moral indignation and utopic blueprints.

Moreover, Green political parties have begun to make an impact in Europe. Of course their programmes are not yet fully worked out and many differences of view persist in their ranks, notably between the "greener" and the "redder" Greens. The latter accuse the former of too much reliance on trying to change people's views.

As Marxists, they believe views change through action; they generally accuse the non-Marxist Greens of a lack of realism, particularly as to what would be needed to bring off their bold and essentially revolutionary challenge to the mainstream capitalist system. They hence argue for a "vigorous dialectic" between the new ideas and the creation of new economic and social structures "by practical — even revolutionary — collective political action".

Yet the Greens have had a major influence on the Brundtland Commission and have jolted many of the established political parties into paying at least lip service to the issues of the environment and sustainability.

In addition, as they can begin to aspire at least to participation in practical power, their self-image is no longer quite that of a group doomed to continue crying in the wilderness. Some serious thinking about realistic courses of action is being done by their political leaders as well as by intellectuals identified with them. Mats Friberg, for example, recognizes that the Greens will not be able to achieve their full set of goals and that some goals will have to be given up, especially those that would "threaten corporate actors."

But he does believe that a "counter-cultural strategy of building a new society from the bottom up" could be put into practice. This would take much time to have an effect. (Friberg has studied earlier social movements in Europe, and the "distance" gained from such historical work gives him a sense of perspective.) Given perhaps fifty years to grow, the result could be a dual economy with the continuation of large scale bureaucracy and industry on the one hand and the growth of self-governing local communities and informal sector enterprises on the other.

There is no way of knowing whether, or when, this prediction will come true. We do know two things, however. First, that the future never quite follows any predicted course. Second, that the road towards more sustainable development policies, globally or nationally, will not be easy or smooth. Because of the widespread ramifications of sustainable development policies there will be many obstacles to their implementation. But, as the next section attempts to show, there are opportunities, too.

WORRYING ABOUT POLICY IMPLEMENTATION -CONSTRAINTS

The difficulties of policy implementation are greatly underestimated. Too often policy is made, but the instruments for its management have not been put in place. If moves towards a more sustainable tourism development pattern are to be successful, attention will need to be paid to institution building in the spheres of policy management and implementation.

Various constraints and opportunities are discussed in some detail in the balance of this analysis, but attention should first be drawn to the fact that not all policies have identical implications for implementation. Certain policies that operate at the macro-level, even though they may encounter resistance before adoption, "can be accomplished with minimal development of new institutional capabilities to support implementation".

Examples include adjusting exchange rates, removing subsidies, raising interest rates, or freeing trade restrictions. In contrast, micro-policy reforms depend on complex institutional changes that are difficult to implement. While there may be much less initial opposition to the new ideas than with macro changes, implementation is very hard.

In a similar vein Harvey, who deals with problems of structural adjustment in Africa, notes the difficulties of "sacking civil servants and marketing board employees, removing the power and patronage of those who appointed them, and cutting the costs and raising the prices of other forms of parastatal".

Comparable considerations apply to policies for sustainability. For example, once accepted, an increase in the tax on fossil fuels to raise the cost of contributing to the greenhouse effect (internalizing the externalities) can be implemented relatively easily, while monitoring polluting emissions by industry or hotels is more difficult.

Creating viable organizations to help smaller national or local enterprises make an economic success of Alternative Tourism is a difficult task. Changing the ingrained habits of the consumer society's consumers on the one hand, and the "instincts" of any private enterprise to "get around" obstacles to the promotion of its particular products on the other, are likely to be very hard indeed.

The following paragraphs examine some of the specific difficulties likely to be encountered when attempting to implement policies for sustainability.

Those who benefit from existing arrangements prefer to see them continued; and social, political, and economic institutions reflect such "vested interests." Sociologists examine social classes, political scientists study interest groups and parties, and economists look at the strain towards monopoly (which is the concentration of control over resources, and decisions relating to them, in the hands of minorities).

Recent work has emphasized that the state itself can be the instrument of private interests. This is also the case in tourism, as James Elliott has shown for Thailand. While the balance of power between different parts of the state apparatus allows the private sector room to manoeuvre, as discussed below, Elliott also points to the importance and power of the bureaucracy: its permanence, stability, internal cohesion, and knowledge of the administrative system.

The bureaucracy does not take initiatives but uses its power negatively, defending the status quo. It protects its own position, the "main aim being self survival and departmental growth, including more jobs". As the Thai bureaucracy needs resources for survival, it has been opposed to the abolition of the high taxes on hotel (16.5per cent) and restaurant (8.25per cent) bills, a step considered desirable for the further promotion of tourism.

So it comes as something of a surprise to read Richter's early views of the policy process in tourism development. She may be right in her assertion that little conflict is apparent in the initial stages, but to suggest that in tourism policy there are "substantial rewards and few interests to placate or offend" is surely incorrect for most situations.

Those interests are especially apparent with respect to the transnational system, but a move to greater sustainability would also hurt many national and local established interests.

Tourism also responds to the demands of people for what Hirsch has called "positional goods," goods and services that give status because they are inherently scarce.

Ironically, long distance budget travelers (those paragons of Alternative Tourism) seek such exclusivity, which tends to be destroyed by its very success as wider groups learn of the new destinations and small scale local businesses expand or are displaced by conventional tourism enterprises. Where a tourism destination has become an exclusive status symbol for the very rich, recreating their favored environment at considerable cost, strong vested interests in the status quo within the industry are reinforced by those of their customers.

Among those organizations with vested interests in the status quo, transnational enterprises are particularly powerful. Their resources are often greater than those of the governments in the countries where they operate; they employ high-powered experts to advise them on the most profitable operating arrangements within existing legal and regulatory frameworks.

During the late 1960s and 1970s they were widely criticized for their role in the international economy; the scandals over the use of unsafe drugs, over the promotion of artificial baby milk, and over transfer pricing (subsidiaries charging their head office enormous prices for goods or services in order to repatriate profits) represented the low water mark.

More recently the controversies have died down. The political climate everywhere has moved back towards market forces and private enterprise; the worst practices of transnationals appear to have been eliminated, while Less Developed Countries' governments have become rather more adept at framing the necessary laws or regulations and at imposing relevant and collectable taxes.

Even so, forcing more sustainable policies onto transnational corporations will demand considerable skill as well as collaboration among governments of Less Developed Countries.

Many researchers have emphasized the power of transnationals in the tourism industry. Erisman, writing about mass tourism in the West Indies, shows how the industry there is primarily run by and serves the interests of American corporations and their customers, through marketing networks in the United States.

Already in the early 1980s, these networks were becoming increasingly vertically integrated, formally or informally, with the airlines standing at the centre. The three most lucrative components of tourism are handled by these networks: marketing and the procurement of customers; international transportation; and food and lodging.

More recently, Wilkinson has argued that micro-states which become involved in tourism find themselves enmeshed in a global system over which they cannot exercise control. They become the targets for "exogenous decision-making," as "many decisions governing their lives, even those dealing with local matters, are made elsewhere by other countries, multinational companies, or airlines". Richter draws virtually the same conclusion and writes that in Less Developed Countries with few material and human resources "almost the entire infrastructure for tourism will be built with foreign goods, controlled by foreigners, and used by foreigners and...all too often profits will not remain in the country".

The decisions of the large international airlines are particularly crucial for small states in the realm of conventional tourism. Only by being on a regular flight route can a destination's associated services, notably accommodation, be included in the computerized networks now virtually indispensable for bookings through travel agents and tour operators. So the effective start-up decision often rests with an airline, or with the foreign donor who helps finance the building of an international airport.

The importance of those computerized networks and the power they give to those at their centre has also recently been stressed by Auliana Poon. She notes that computerized reservation systems, run by the largest airlines or by consortia of a few of these, are now used by about 90 per cent of the travel agents in the United States and the United Kingdom. They constitute a total information system offering, in addition to hotel reservations, such services as car rentals, champagne and flowers, information about destinations, or bus and train connections. Experience in the Caribbean has shown that "without links to [these] international marketing and distribution networks, hotel bed-nights cannot be sold".

The momentum of this system is enormous, the interests involved truly global. As to the extent that Alternative Tourism is regarded as no more than the tourism of "alternative tourists," being bypassed by these systems may not matter so much. But this is not a tenable position if, in contrast, encouraging Alternative Tourism is seen as a wider move towards tourism with "sustainable characteristics."

It should be selfevident that any such policy must come to terms with the reality of transnational electronic power. The development of sophisticated electronic sub-networks that join together a limited number of smaller facilities may be a more viable proposition than attempting to "buck the trend."

Implementation is also confounded by fragmentation of government responsibilities. The idea of sustainable policies is likely to have a growing influence on international organizations and United Nations agencies, as well as on the declared policies of many Northern governments. Brundtland will be heard.

Yet as her Commission's Report emphasized, a few well-sounding declarations are but the first step on the road to sustainable development. Implementing the fine phrases demands enforcement. The responsibility for the different aspects of environmental and distributive policies is, however, dispersed throughout the government machine.

Sectoral organizations tend to pursue sectoral objectives and to treat their impacts on other sectors as side effects, taken into account only if compelled to do so. Hence impacts on forests rarely worry those involved in public policy or business activities in the fields of energy, industrial development, crop husbandry, or foreign trade.

Many of the environmental problems that confront us have their roots in this sectoral fragmentation of responsibility. Sustainable development requires that such fragmentation be overcome.

The complexity of modern government and administration, where authority must be delegated in order to be exercised effectively, is one cause of this problem. But there are others. Because those working in sectoral agencies, such as ministries and other official organizations, get few rewards for working with outsiders, intersectoral collaboration is at a discount.

In each sector one particular professional and disciplinary group tends to be dominant. Cooperation between such professional groups is limited because the different nature of their original training leads to different perceptions of what problems are important in the world. This is true even in contiguous sectors such as health, nutrition, and agriculture, where intersectoral collaboration has encountered many obstacles for such reasons.

This sectoral fragmentation in the public administration is reinforced by compartmentalized working links between civil servants and enterprises in the sectors their departments are supposed to regulate.

Ministries of agriculture deal with farmers, ministries of industry with industrialists, tourism departments with businesses in the tourism sector, and so on. Farmers, industrialists, and hoteliers soon form specialized lobbies; their viewpoints and interests come to influence the thinking of the bureaucrats in "their" sector. Sociocultural factors, such as "soft states," patron-client networks, clan politics, and "endemic corruption," may make this worse.

These sectoral dynamics of government and administration provide the backdrop to any effort at implementing more sustainable development and tourism development policies. While different from country to country and from culture to culture, they are deeply entrenched everywhere.

They are reinforced by the specialized multilateral agencies which usually have links with one ministry alone, such as the World Health Organization in the health sector, United Nations Industrial Development Organization for industry, FAO in agriculture.

Advice on tourism development comes from the World Tourism Organization, which is "concerned quite naturally with developing tourism and not with using tourism as a vehicle for development". Superministries, or highly centralized forms of government, may mitigate these problems but cannot overcome them completely. Constraints which need to be bypassed as much as possible are likely to remain.

ACHIEVING POLICY IMPLEMENTATION –OPPORTUNITIES

While it is compelling to recognize constraints for what they are, it is important not to exaggerate them and to be aware of opportunities and room for maneuvering. For example, certain aspects of the functioning of state and public administration have been revealed as obstacles to the achievement of more sustainable development policies. But in other respects it is only the state which can provide the conditions for movement towards greater sustainability.

In most countries tourism development will always centre on private enterprise. While current conventional wisdom stresses the benefits of the market, the pendulum shows signs of beginning to swing back from recent extreme positions.

As Butler argues in this volume, in the absence of control and external responsibility the free play of the market will almost inevitably lead to overreaching capacity limits, and hence a lack of sustainability. It is likely that in general more attention will again be paid to the imperfections of the market and to those specific interventions which can correct the tendencies to disequilibrium and monopoly power, both in the private and the state sectors.

Interventions by the state are also essential with regard to the problem of externalities discussed earlier. By disregarding the costs of negative effects they may have on others or on nature, productive units in and out of the tourist industry are better able to maximize their profits.

So the state, or rather development policy makers and planners, must force productive units to take account of such effects. They do this by building appropriate cost and price signals into the framework within which productive units operate, by creating incentives and disincentives, and by straightforward regulation. Insofar as maintaining ecological stability is essential to sustainability, this institutional framework also needs to safeguard the reproduction of natural resources.

In the sphere of tourism, governments have long exercised controls in a number of areas, most fundamentally, of course, in the conditions on which tourists are admitted to a country and on the rate at which their currencies will be exchanged.

Governments have leverage to influence the development of tourism in specific areas or particular ways: they set the conditions of investment and access, determine what concessions will be given to foreign enterprises, and they can legislate about access to land, such as, for example, by not allowing straight purchase, but only long term leases. In general, they can and do include tourism in their development plans, and they often play a major role in providing infrastructure for tourism development.

This general capacity can also be focused on creating the conditions for sustainability. It helps if sustainability, as a general issue, is high on the agenda of government policy as this can draw attention to sensitive issues such as restrictions on physical development or the effects on local populations. As they can for conventional tourism, governments can create an appropriate incentive structure for sustainable tourism.

Transnationals, if left to operate according to their own agendas, will prefer large scale developments and accommodations provided in mega-hotels; they will usually not be sensitive to ecological or local issues and will not be concerned that their projects yield benefits for the host country's development in general and for the poor in particular.

Such issues are more likely to be addressed by the state if tourism planning is integrated with development planning in general. This is, of course, more difficult in small countries with a slender government apparatus and a scarcity of professional staff.

Wilkinson also suggests that Alternative Tourism development, insofar as it comprises small scale facilities which are likely to be low rise, cottage style, and energy efficient, may require rather less government involvement than the conventional variety. Infrastructure demands should be less extensive, and with respect to regulation and incentive structures a more "passive" attitude towards this sort of development may be warranted.

However, Alternative Tourism development will require substantial institutional innovation (and hence certain kinds of state involvement) if it is to be successful. Some of this innovation may have to be aimed at methods of increasing participation and decentralization.

From the historical perspective which Mats Friberg brings to bear on his analysis of the emergence of Green political movements in Europe, he sees the next phase as a deepening of earlier achievements (citizenship, democracy, social justice, and equity) by means of a further transformation of the state and the extension of participation through civic organizations. Participation has, indeed, become one of the rallying cries of development ideology of the 1980s.

It is heard in sundry contexts, from discussions of the informal sector in production to generalized blueprints for better health services. Non-governmental organizations (NGOs) have benefited from this new interest, attracting government development grants for carrying out small scale projects together with people at the grass roots.

The role of NGOs in development has shot into prominence, and they are seen as possible agents of "empowerment" of local communities vis-à-vis those who do, or may in future, dominate.

Similar views are expressed with respect to tourism. Wilkinson's paper, which focuses on the factors influencing the chances of tourism development with "alternative" characteristics in micro-states, ends with a clarion call for community participation in the development of local tourism.

Earlier he quotes Murphy, who holds the view that tourism development can be positive if the needs of the local community are placed before the goals of the tourism industry. Tourism should be seen as a local resource, and its management "for the common good and future generations should become the goal and criterion by which the industry is judged".

Yet such calls for community participation gloss over the well-known tendency for local elites to "appropriate" the organs of participation for their own benefit. Many studies have demonstrated that those who are locally influential and wealthy, will become the spokespersons for communities unless specific measures are taken to counter this pattern; this is so whether one examines local political structures or such less formal arrangements as community organizations and NGO-sponsored associations. As regards participation in decision making on tourism development, there is a further problem. Communities have coped with problems in areas such as agriculture or health from time immemorial and, therefore, have a store of traditional experience and knowledge which can be the starting point of their participation in such areas.

But local experience with tourism is wholly lacking, and people are largely at the mercy of the opinions of those who are presented to them, or who present themselves, as "experts." As Richter points out in her discussion of tourism development in the United States, this places the "developers" at an advantage; yet their expertise may well be that of an interested party.

In Less Developed Countries, too, advice is often provided by the "wrong" people. Perhaps specialized tourism related NGOs from the North, or international NGOs involved in tourism such as the already mentioned Ecumenical Coalition on Third World Tourism, could help in this respect and fulfill the "monitoring" function suggested by Richter.

A similar situation of unfamiliarity with relevant issues prevails within the public administration, where awareness of tourism issues is limited, even in so highly developed a country as the United States. In view of the shortage of public servants knowledgeable on tourism issues, public administrations in the U.S. all too often turn to the hardly disinterested travel industry for advice.

Such problems are exacerbated by the fact that many decisions about tourism development are made at lower levels of government and administration, where the range of expertise is usually more limited and the competence of senior public servants less solid, especially with respect to the broader questions of ecological and social sustainability. Hence there is a need to consider seriously what institutional and organizational changes are required if policies for more sustainable tourism development are to be put into place.

Perhaps the most formidable task on the road to sustainable development, and tourism development, is that of building the institutions needed for policy implementation. Earlier we saw how the Brundtland Commission, too, regards this as the greatest challenge.

There are no quick fixes in this domain. Public administrations do not respond easily or quickly to new situations. And devising workable organizations that interface between the public and private sectors is also fraught with problems.

The variety of marketing, advisory, and support services available to European farm tourism enterprises, to which Pearce refers in this volume, emerged gradually over a fairly long period of "natural growth," itself helped by the large domestic markets for this kind of Alternative Tourism.

When these conditions do not prevail, devising such institutions is far from easy. We are then in the sphere of micro-policy; for this to be effectively implemented, knowledge of processes of learning and change is required and a real understanding of the interests involved is needed. This refers not only to those "vested interests" who might oppose the policy shift but also to those who are the potential beneficiaries of the changes, and hence potential allies in the process. Recent developments in the organization of industrial production provide some useful pointers to the kind of innovations that might help achieve institutional support for Alternative Development and Alternative Tourism. Much has been written on "flexible specialization," the system pioneered in Japan and made famous in Europe through the fashion business of Bennetton, which enables enterprises to respond with much greater agility to changes in the market. Poon refers to that literature in her interesting paper on the relevance of these new forms of organization to Caribbean tourism.

Some of the characteristics which have been identified in earlier sections as coherent with sustainable tourism development, notably that of smaller scale, also figure in the discussion of flexible specialization. If more tourists were to take their holidays in "sustainable tourism environments," their handling in smaller batches would become a major organizational issue.

Poon shows that smallness by itself would not promise success for tourism enterprises under these conditions, notably because of the inexorable march of computerization discussed above. She emphasizes, however, the very great importance of networks: "For small firms, networks and systems have become their fundamental survival route".

Best, Murray, and Pezzini have made the same point, showing how the small manufacturers of Italy innovating with flexible specialization, in clothing, furniture, and so on, have been successful thanks to the creation of networks of mutual support. Particularly important have been the cooperative organizations which provide services — in design, or marketing — for all, which no one enterprise could have afforded by itself.

Sometimes simple institutional innovations are worth exploring, such as producing a serious local "Good Food Guide," as in the United Kingdom where there is a highly respected and widely used guide produced by the Consumers' Association. This approach, which is also being tried in Cyprus, helps tourists find good traditional eating places — a bit of Alternative Tourism in the face of much standardized international catering — while at the same time strengthening the local economy.

Developments such as these have often also involved innovative interface organizations between local industry and local or regional government; this contains further lessons for institution building for sustainability.

We have come to the end of a long road. We have seen how the somewhat strident advocacy of Alternative Development and Alternative Tourism, by movements on the political fringe and more often based on moral indignation than on sound scientific arguments, has made way for a broader concern for sustainability underpinned by a growing body of scientific and analytical work. Of course, in many ways conventional and alternative development paths not only diverge but go in opposite directions. Yet this analysis has tried to demonstrate that in many respects it is better to regard those opposites as continua; policies can push countries along those continua in either direction. This suggests that policy makers can, indeed, promote sustainability by constantly striving to make the conventional more sustainable. This is also true for tourism. Most Less Developed Countries cannot hope to create acceptable living conditions for the majority of their people without continued economic growth and for many of them, especially the large number of smaller tropical mini- and micro-states, tourism represents one of the few apparently viable routes for such growth.

Policy makers can only proceed from what already exists in this respect, and that is a powerful and still growing, highly integrated, international tourism industry.

"Alternative" forms will presumably continue to evolve spontaneously, as Valene Smith notes in this volume, almost inevitably "riding piggy-back" on the more cost-effective forms of the conventional, integrated international tourism industry. How to coax that behemoth into less destructive behaviour is surely the main task ahead.

3

Selecting and Attracting the Right Customers

TASK OF CREATING AND DELIVERING SUPERIOR CUSTOMER VALUE

The task of creating and delivering superior customer value must be complemented with the selection of the appropriate customers and the effective management of relationships with those customers. The hospitality industry is a fascinating one from a CRM perspective, because of the quality and quantity of customer touchpoints. In the world of servicing guests, there are as many challenges as there are, well... challenging customers, but in the current age of "branding" one of the biggest ones is ensuring a consistent customer service experience.

Today's hotels offer a multitude of lucrative services, all of which need to be recorded immediately against the right customer's bill. Zonal can integrate any third party billing programme to ensure that all room-charged items can be cross-checked quickly and easily at the point-of-sale for matching name against a stated room number. Commonly, hotels have a number of different sales areas for patrons to drink, eat and enjoy services. Hotel management has the ability to define different products and prices for each of these sales areas, allowing them to apply premium price bands for exclusive areas.

This challenge is three-pronged: First, managers must be able to manage consistency in the face of interchanging slow and busy times and seasons. Second, consistency needs to be ensured across job titles, roles, and pay ranges. Third (or perhaps First, if you'd like), the marketing message must be in tune with a plan to set guest expectations according to the season and customer tier considerations. Customer retention leading to more custom and bigger profit is easier if you can keep your customers happy.

This can be achieved in your restaurants with minimal wait times for food orders and accurate service delivery - every time. The fully integrated kitchen management system communicates all food orders, with special instructions if necessary, automatically from the PoS in your sales areas directly to the kitchen to minimise customer wait times. Real-time awareness of current stock holding and usage gives you the power to manage supply and monitor profit margins more effectively.

The stock control system is one of the most powerful in the industry and gives you the flexibility to monitor movements of products of all divisions between the different zones in your site. Emergency transfers of champagne cases from the cocktail bar to the function room can now be recorded easily. As with any strategy, the goal is to help meet the corporate objectives, which often begin with defining the customer segments that can help move the enterprise in the right direction, and then approach them with the right marketing message, via the right marketing channels.

On the subject of job roles, while some job roles had specific training on interacting with customers, others did not, or worse, were trained in an inconsistent way. So the first order of things in this area is to establish a clear procedure for greeting, servicing, and addressing guest issues across various situations.

All employees which come in direct contact with guests need to be in tune with this common standard. A set of behaviour and service standards also provides clear guidelines which can empower employees to provide special, or "magical" moments to their guests. The guest servicing standards themselves should focus on not just consistent responses, but also should prevent consecutive negative experiences.

In other words, if a guest has experienced a negative event (*i.e.* complained that the room wasn't clean upon check in), this fact needs to be captured and made available to customer-facing employees so that they can put an extra effort into making sure that the remainder of the hotel stay or restaurant experience is as positive as possible. A further back-end benefit to capturing the negative event information is that it will enable analysis of customer experience shortcomings. This in turn allows for active methods for managing, monitoring, and predicting customer satisfaction, which can then lead to fine-tuning the marketing message, interaction standards, and employee training. Predictive analytics can be used to understand latent pain or dissatisfaction before it percolates and impacts customer loyalty.Managing customer relationships should be guided by an understanding of what the customer's equity is to the firm.

Customer equity, the value of customer to the firm, improves as superiority in customer value improves. Since customer equity is perhaps the firm's most valuable asset, the firm must continually seek to improve customer value for it best customers. A firm's potential return on customer equity should determine the investment it makes in customers. For its most valuable customers, the firm must guarantee superior service quality and customer service, with special attention to recovering from inevitable product failures when they occur. Maximizing long-term profitability comes from maximizing customer equity—

firms must maximize the lifetime value of the customer, including revenues, referrals as well as costs of serving the customer.

Customer acquisition and retention efforts must be guided by the worth of the customer to the firm. Maytag provides premium service to its premium customers—those who purchase the Neptune line of laundry machines. Neptune customers get a dedicated staff, a separate toll-free number and fast response on service calls. This is an example of the common business practice where firms allocate resources by the profitability and value of the customer. They utilize the opportunity in directly interacting with individual customers to determine customer profitability and allocate assets accordingly. And what are the benefits of the practice of differentiating among your customers?

Broadly referring to the practice as CRM can sometimes defeat its purpose by losing sight of the basic meaning of the term: managing customer relationships. Managing customer relationships would mean actively planning, organizing, directing, and controlling a firm's business relationships with its customers. The term might be "new" in its current usage, but the business practice of managing relationships with customers is certainly not new. What has prompted the increased attention to CRM is new technology: how well firms can practice CRM has been advanced by information technology in the new economy.

Technology brings with it the risk of missing the benefits of huge investment costs if used inappropriately, however. The benefits can seem so attractive that the costs are rationalized until the technology fails to deliver. The American Customer Satisfaction Index, a measure of customer attitudes towards about 200 companies from over 30 different industries, has actually shown a decline, while at the same time CRM technology investments had grown about five times.

When used with a fundamental understanding of CRM's purpose, the benefits of CRM technology enabling the business practice of managing customer relationships are clearly powerful. Siebel, Peoplesoft, Oracle, and other CRM technologies are really customer information management or customer knowledge management systems. These systems gather data and convert it to knowledge that will help firms in their customer relationship management activities. The most significant contribution of CRM technology to the practice of business is not the technology itself, of course.

It is in what the technology does to the practice of managing customer relationships. Because technology has now made it easy to do all the tasks of gathering and analyzing customer information, firms have been able to discover and realize the incredible benefits in proactively managing customer relationships. For example, Continental Airlines' customer information system allows its staff to mine data on passenger profitability and is also able to suggest remedies and perks for special requests or complaining customers. Customer benefits from relationships with firms have been conceptualized under three categories: social, psychological, and customization benefits, in a two-part study using interviews and surveys.

Financial services such as brokerage and banking are heavy users of CRM technology. Deregulation and information technology have effectively blurred the boundaries between those two once-different financial institutions. They have had a heavy reliance on information because these are primarily knowledge businesses. "Signature"-level customers at Charles Schwab wait no longer than fifteen seconds to reach a customer service person, whereas other customers can wait ten minutes or more. Some banks have coded their customers so that customer service reps can decide on rates and fees depending on the customer's profitability code.

Centura Banks rates its customers on a profitability scale of 1 to 5. The most profitable customers get service calls from staff and an annual call from the CEO. Attrition rate at the bank is down 50 per cent in four years, and—more interesting—the percentage of unprofitable customers has gone down from 27 per cent to 21 per cent. The hospitality industry was able to slash 50 per cent of its promotion programmes and increase response rates by 20 per cent with a good database of response behaviour from its mailing list.

CRM systems have provided firms with the data they need to determine the revenues and costs to serve at the individual customer level, allowing firms to prioritize their allocations of value-creating assets and resources to the more profitable customers. According to AMR research, the CRM market grew from $200 milllion to $1.1 billion between 1994 and 1997, and is expected to reach as much as $16 billion—an indication of how much firms want this technology to manage customer relationships. A firm's knowledge about its customers has allowed it to adjust customer value based on the profitability of the individual customer.

Just as with power, information technology has to be used judiciously. Discriminating against less profitable customers can seem unreasonable to all paying customers and could backfire with publicity. ATandT withdrew its minimum usage charges for its basic-plan customers who were unprofitable. GE Capital tried to charge credit-card users who were not accruing a minimum level of interest charges and ended up having to sell its credit card business. When used appropriately at the individual level, information technology can be very rewarding. Capital One's senior vice-president for domestic card operations, Marge Connelly, says, "We look at every single customer contact as an opportunity to make an unprofitable customer more profitable."

CRM systems are not just about profiling customers and loyalty programmes. To derive maximum benefits, one must broaden the thinking about CRM technology. The technology should be viewed as knowledge-based systems that seek to prioritize commitment of a firm's assets and resources to the more profitable customers while enhancing the relationships with ALL (right) customers. Pricing may not be the appropriate means to deal with the unprofitable customer. CRM systems give the firm access to information that may reveal other ways to manage the unprofitable customer. *Enabling* the managing of customer relationships is the goal of the CRM system.

Managing customer relationships is about selecting, acquiring, retaining, and enhancing relationships with customers by using an intimate knowledge of the customer's consumption domain to maximize the return on the firm's assets. With CRM systems, firms have the knowledge and the technological capability to identify, retain and enhance more desirable customer relationships.

This covers issues regarding which customers to acquire and retain for maximum sustainable profits. How do you assign value to customers and what is involved in that evaluation? Who is the right customer? Who should be in your customer portfolio? Firms look at customers as investments. How do you value these investments? Or, What is the equity of your customers?

GUESTS VALUE EXPERIENCE OVER LOCATION AND PRICE

Why do guests choose a particular hotel? Experience. You might guess location and price top the list. But assuming you're operating a hotel and not building one, there isn't much you can do about location. Price, likewise, has a lot of constraints. Rate cutting is not sustainable. It may goose business in the short term but it can set unreasonable expectations and restrict future price increases.

Experience, on the other hand, gives you a lot to work with. Creating great experiences for your guests is by far the best way to keep your best customers and attract others. Just look at the data to the right: Experience tops the list of things you can do to influence hotel selection. And with all the fuss nowadays about online reputation and reviews, it's interesting to see experience is four times more likely to influence hotel selection. Yes, a large portion of travellers do consult online reviews (and let's be clear here, they are extremely important) before making a booking. But it appears that online reviews are more often used to gather information rather than as the primary reason for selecting a hotel.

EXPERIENCE DRIVES LOYALTY AND REFERRALS

What's really powerful about experience is that it is the key to future bookings. Experience is what builds loyalty, drives referrals and creates positive word-of-mouth and online reviews.

Experience has always been among the top things travellers consider when choosing a hotel. But in recent years it has grown in significance. The importance of past experience in hotel selection has climbed over the past few years while the emphasis given to location and price has remained constant.

Why? There are numerous explanations. Hotel experiences have gotten better and guests are taking notice. Customer satisfaction scores have increased for six years in a row. Emotion scores (ratings about how guests feel during their stay), the biggest drivers of loyalty, have also increased. Improved customer satisfaction has also pushed loyalty scores higher, increasing eight points in the past five years. Guests are more likely to be loyal because of a positive experience rather than a hotel's location or its prices.

Social media has also added visibility and attention to the customer experience, which has compelled hotels to pay more attention. Hotel companies, wanting to avoid the impact of negative reviews, are listening to guest feedback, improving service recovery and incentivizing their hotels to improve the guest stay. Meeting planners and corporate travel managers are also paying more attention to feedback and are giving more consideration to the overall guest experience rather than just seeking the lowest price. As a result, guest priorities have shifted; positive experiences now driving hotel selection more frequently. This is especially true at the upper end of the market where past experience plays a bigger role.

CREATING WINNING EXPERIENCES

Every company can create unique experience for its customers. But aligning products, services and the guest's emotional experience with a target market and goals of the company is a big challenge. Companies focusing on improving their customer experience typically follow a simple model of continuous guest feedback and learning. This process often includes collecting reliable guest feedback, empowering and incentivizing employees to act on results, investing to improve weaknesses and celebrating success.

All over, hotel companies are focusing on the guest experience. They are redirecting their resources on the guest experience as they discover its link to loyalty and overall business results. It's no longer enough to offer a good product or service, you have to wow the customer in order to win his advocacy and keep him from trying someone else next time.

MARKETS CONSIST OF CUSTOMERS

Markets consist of customers with diverse needs and differences in customer profitability. When serving multiple groups of customers, the goal must be to maximize the profitability of the combination of segments.

When different segments are targeted, the firm essentially has a portfolio of customer segments—just as investors have an investment portfolio that maximizes returns at a certain level of risk, firms manage customer portfolios for maximum profits. As standard, hotels are fitted with an integral magnetic stripe reader for credit and debit cards and our EFT system is approved by all the major banks and clearing houses. However, in an age when credit card fraud is on the increase, hotels can protect you and your customers from fraud with the addition of Chip and PIN devices. Chip and PIN solution can be integrated to operate with your Hotel billing system's configurable client credit limit. In other words, this is the selection of customers at any point in time, compared to other segments, from which the firm can generate maximum profits.

Firms must attract these most profitable customers and then must establish systems and procedures to retain them. Most firms serve different segments depending on how the definition of segment is aggregated. The "segment-of-one" used in common business parlance to refer to customization at the individual level is really a maximum disaggregation of a market segment.

As we saw, most firms facing fluctuating demand and experiencing peak, shoulder and low periods of demand find it inevitable that, at different times, different segments must be served. Of course, each of these segments must have a compatible fit with the overall corporate image as well as a compatible fit with the products, services, employees and other customers. The question is, are they selected based on their combined long term value to the firm?

Most firms forecast the volume and revenues from various segments at certain price points at different times in the purchase cycle. In the typical firm, sales and communications efforts follow these underlying assumptions in pricing and in messages targeting sales prospects. The typical firm then attempts to formalize advertising campaigns to reach as many people as possible in the case of packaged goods. In the case of business-to-business services, the salespeople focus on making a sale. Most firms then struggle to orchestrate all these messages for acquisition of the customer in a coordinated fashion.

Much less attention is paid to the retention of the customer. Barring the well-run operation, common business practice for many firms is short-term oriented. On the contrary, a customer-focused firm begins by approaching sales as acquiring the right customer. The customer-focused firm also approaches the acquisition of customers as only the first step in managing the relationships with its customers. Once acquired, the customer must be retained. But, not always retained at any cost—a necessary condition is that the benefits outweigh the costs of acquiring *and* retaining that customer. Customer-focused firms align all their activities and processes in acquiring and retaining the right customer. They see their value-creating assets as most profitably leveraged by focusing on the most valuable customers. In principle, the value of the customer is determined by contribution to the firm's objectives over the lifetime of the customer. The right customer is that customer whose inclusion in the firm's target market helps maximize returns on the firm's assets.

CUSTOMER EQUITY

Ask a manager, "What is your firm's most valuable asset?" Chances are that you will not get the response, "my customers." You will find even fewer firms that actually make an assessment of this value in any real sense. The valuation of the customer is implicit in sales figures—essentially, the revenues generated by customers of the firm. What is the flaw in using sales as a proxy in valuing a firm's customers? Consider this.

Two customers with the same cash value of purchases may not be of the same value to the firm. There may be differences in the cost of serving these two customers. The true value of the customer to the firm, or the equity that the firm has in that customer, must include all revenues and also all costs related to that customer, as in financial investments. A recent framework by a team of researchers defines customer equity as the "total of the discounted lifetime value of all the firm's customers."

DRIVERS OF CUSTOMER EQUITY

They articulate three drivers of customer equity: value equity, brand equity, and relationship equity. They define value equity as the objective assessment of the utility of the brand, and value equity is driven by quality, price, and convenience; brand equity as the subjective assessment of the brand above and beyond the perceived value, and brand equity is driven by brand awareness, attitude towards the brand, and corporate ethics; and relationship equity as the tendency of the customer to stick with the brand, and relationship equity is driven by loyalty programmes, special recognition and treatment, affinity programmes, community-building programmes, and knowledge-building programmes.

Their framework—the customer equity diagnostic—is offered as a way to determine which customers to acquire as well as what will enable their retention. If we define customer value as the value of the firm or a product as perceived by the customer, customer equity is the converse and refers to the value of the customer to the firm. If the objective is to maximize the returns from your investments—the customer portfolio—you must maximize customer equity. This makes sense because you can maximize sustainable return on assets by maximizing customer equity for the long term.

To maximize customer equity, we must be able to measure it. If customer equity is simply the value of a customer to the firm, we can articulate that value in the same way that customers articulate our value to them. Just as customer value is the difference between benefits and costs to the customer, conversely, customer equity is the difference between the benefits and costs to the firm in serving a customer.

One team of researchers describes their method of measuring customer equity as follows: "[we] first measure each customer's expected contributions towards offsetting the company's fixed costs over the expected life of that customer. Then we discount the expected contributions to a net present value at the company's target rate of return for marketing investments. Finally, we add together the discounted expected contributions of all current customers."

Evident in their metric are the following important points about customer equity:

- It is the sum of the equity of all of a firm's customers.
- It summates the gross contribution of each customer, taking into account benefits as well as costs of serving a customer.
- It includes consideration of future revenues and variable costs from each customer.
- It is a time-discounted present value of future benefits to the firm.

It becomes evident that the customer equity concept when disaggregated to the individual customer level allows us to look at the revenues and costs of serving an individual customer. It helps answer the question, which customer should we serve? The ideal customer to the firm is the one that gives it the maximum long-term customer equity, which theoretically you want as a brand-loyal customer. However, as we will see in the next section, the converse is not true, because not all brandloyal customers provide maximum customer equity.

CONCEPT OF BRAND LOYALTY

WHO IS THE RIGHT CUSTOMER

The concept of brand loyalty is a well-researched topic. The notion of a customer having a lifetime value and the prominence of database systems in managing customers have spawned a renewed interest in relationship marketing. Just making repurchases doesn't make a customer brand loyal. There must be some commitment by the customer to the firm for relational continuity reflecting a positive patronage bias.

Not all brand-loyal customers have a positive disposition to the provider—some relationships may be forced because of a lack of choice. Brand loyalty reflects a financial, social, or structural bonding with the customer. Relationship marketing seeks to enhance the mutual benefits from the relationship with the right customer—seeking brand loyalty from the right customer. To determine who the right customer is, we need to understand what benefits the firm expects from an ideal customer. Management system is designed with you in mind. Knowing the needs of modern hotels, simplifies the communication between the waiting and kitchen staff.

Customer's orders are communicated automatically to the kitchen for display on a kitchen management system or for printing on a kitchen printer. This minimises wait times and eradicates ordering mistakes that can irritate customers and cost your restaurant unearned revenue. When combined with handheld terminals, orders can be taken directly from tables, speeding up the ordering experience further.

At the outset, it is clear that the stream of purchases from the brandloyal customer is the primary benefit. In truth, the value of a brand-loyal customer to the firm must go beyond the purchases made over the lifetime of the relationship with that customer. As shown, revenues can be direct and indirect. Direct revenues are all of the customer's purchases, and indirect revenues are the cash value of all of the other benefits the customer accrues to the firm, in the form of direct revenues from referred customers. Costs to serve are drastically reduced, as brand-loyal customers are generally easier to serve. The argument is that as customers get familiar with the firm, its processes and products, customers will require less costly assistance from the firm in purchasing and using the product.

Loyal customers may even be able to open up ways in which to reduce the costs of serving the customer. Other benefits of brand loyalty would include product improvement contributions, new product opportunities, ideal sources for market information, and favourable word of mouth. At an overall level, all these benefits add up to a degree of stability and potential growth for the firms. Those brand-loyal customers who are committed in their patronage recognize their benefits from the firm and show commitment in the provider firm.

To select the right customer, the firm must be able to measure the value of the loyal customer from all these benefits as well as the costs of acquiring and retaining that customer. It is not easy to quantify all of these benefits. But it is possible to calculate the direct and indirect revenues from each customer. It is also possible to calculate the acquisition costs and relationship maintenance costs. Information technology has allowed us to obtain that data and made it easy to calculate the lifetime value of a customer.

LIFETIME REVENUES

Lifetime revenues are the sum of all purchases that the customer will make. An assessment of the progression of purchases over the lifecycle of the customer is a key point to be made here. For instance, consider what a college student's financial lifecycle would mean to a bank. First, it is a savings or checking account with a debit card and perhaps even a credit card. The college student may also be a good candidate for an education loan. Once graduated, this ex-student is now in the market for a car loan, and quite soon a home mortgage.

Once other life events such as marriage and children occur, there are more car loans, mortgages, home equity loans, trusts, custody accounts, education loans for children, and associated financial products that a typical family would need. USAA, the life insurance and financial services company, follows marriages, births, and other life events so that it can advise customers on changing needs. Every firm should attempt to develop such a long-term consumption profile for the typical customer in each segment, charting their potential purchases over a lifetime to take into account the life events of the customer—a customer lifecycle analysis. A similar case may be made for business customers based on an assessment of growth potential, so that any B2B firm has to project the growth of its customers and factor that into a lifetime value calculation.

Not all customers become brand loyal. We have seen that superior customer value is a prerequisite for brand loyalty. What percentages of new customers find the firm's customer value to be superior? The lifetime value of a customer must also factor the probability of the acquired customer becoming brand loyal. Thus, the lifetime value of a customer is the first purchase, plus the probability of repeat purchases for the duration of the relationship with the firm. The probability consideration takes into account that a customer may not be a good fit, that a competitor may have been able to provide a better fit, or that the need situation changed for the customer, such as in the case of relocation of the consuming unit.

LIFETIME COSTS

An activity-based costing approach allows a firm to account for direct costs that the firm incurs in the relationship with a specific customer. Once again, with information technology it is possible, where it makes sense, to attribute marketing and operating costs to individual customers. To obtain the full benefit from CRM investments, it is important to track costs at the individual customer level as well. Costs include acquiring and remarketing to the customer over the lifetime of the customer.

Costs also include value creation and delivery costs of serving the customer. Thus, the costs after acquisition include not only the costs of serving the customer, but also relationship maintenance and development costs such as the costs of cross-selling or upselling, called remarketing costs. Once again, the costs related to the first purchase are separated from that of lifetime purchases so that the probability of repeat purchase is taken into account when calculating lifetime costs.

THE CALCULUS OF LIFETIME VALUE

A commonly used practice inherited from the direct marketing industry experience is called RFM (referring to "recency, frequency, and monetary data")—a method to determine whom to send promotions from among your customers. It takes into account the value of a customer's purchases, how recent they were, and how often they were purchased. As with the danger of any one approach, RFM has been used without much consideration for other important dimensions of the most valuable customer, such as how profitable the customer really is. RFM is therefore not a proxy measure for the lifetime value of a customer.

Indeed, if the costs of serving different customers show a variance, then the RFM method could attract the wrong customer. As, there are three main factors in calculating the lifetime value of a customer. It is not just a simple product of the value of each purchase and the number of times the customer will purchase the product over that customer's lifetime. The lifetime value of a customer should also include referral value. And, it should include the lifetime costs as well. CRM technology has made it possible to do this, but, how many firms actually use this understanding in how they design and implement their CRM solutions?

REFERRAL VALUE

The indirect revenue of referrals from a loyal customer is an often overlooked aspect of customer equity. The typical CRM solution and database marketing approaches ignore the referral power of a customer in calculating the lifetime value of a customer. Most firms do not even capture this data, partly because it is difficult to obtain information when knowledge systems in a firm are not configured to obtain it. The other reason may be that firms are not proactively looking for referrals from their loyal customers in any systematic way.

How is the value of referrals from a customer calculated? To answer this question requires looking at the process and mechanics of how referrals work. Who provides a referral? Customers who are satisfied and who have a certain degree of loyalty are the ones who are likely to convey favourable messages about a firm and its products and services.

A key piece of information needed here is what level of satisfaction a brand-loyal customer needs to have before being likely to refer a customer. The next obvious question is, who receives the referral? Customers are likely to convey this information to family, friends, and colleagues.

However, not all who receive the referrals are appropriate customers for the firm. What proportion of the customers who received the referral are good candidates for the firm? Out of the ones that are appropriate for the firm, not all are likely to be suitably influenced by the referral to make the first purchase.

Finally, if a purchase is actually made, what proportion of referred customers makes repeat purchases? Those that are moved to try the product may not all turn into loyal customers, but if they do, then their lifetime purchases add to the value of the customer making the initial referral.

THE COLLECTIVE LIFETIME VALUE OF ITS CUSTOMERS

MAXIMIZING LIFETIME VALUE

Maximizing the collective lifetime value of its customers should be the goal in managing customer relations. Head office Managers can analyse the performance of the business via the extensive reporting options on all aspects of your business and make product and price decisions for the whole organisation. Head office can either assume complete control of all matters (suitable for new sites or sites with inexperienced managers) or devolve varying amounts of control to site managers.

At the furthest end of the spectrum you can reduce head office to a merely supervisory role where you only view global reports and produce financial audits. By increasing the number of customers *and* by increasing the lifetime value of each customer, firms can maximize their long-term profitability. To maximize the lifetime value of customers, you need to:

MAXIMIZING LIFETIME REFERRAL VALUE

Referral customers have very low acquisition costs, since your brandloyal customers did the marketing for you. Following the mechanics of the process of word of mouth, maximizing lifetime referral value requires maximizing the number of referrals from each customer and maximizing the lifetime value of each referred customer. To maximize the number of referrals, one must maximize the drivers of referrals from a customer. In other words, firms must attempt to increase the probability of a customer making a referral of profitable customers. Firms must move loyal customers to become advocates of the firm.

When word of mouth is seen as a powerful customer acquisition tool, firms will find a way to stimulate referrals. Many firms are not proactive in stimulating referrals, assuming simply that "good word of mouth will happen if we do a good job." What must firms do to increase the value from referrals?

First, firms must identify the current and potential advocates of the firm. Firms must proactively look for individuals and organizations that are likely sources of referrals and stimulate and reward them for the right kind of referrals. Satisfied and loyal customers are not the only ones who can stimulate positive word of mouth. There are opinion leaders: such individuals and organizations as consumer reports, firms such as Gartner and Forrester, who might be considered experts in the field, and most important, the general and trade media.

Other ambassadors for the firm include players in often overlooked sources such as suppliers, resellers, employees, and other stakeholders such as investors. Community chat rooms on the Web are rich sources of information for the firm about what word of mouth is transpiring among its stakeholders.

Second, firms must attempt to stimulate referrals. Any new customer acquisition activity should record information on how the customer was moved to deal with the firm. When the firm obtains and records this information in the consumption profile of any customer, it is able to use it to calculate the average number of customer referrals made by each current customer of the firm. Customers and advocates with similar profiles need to be approached about playing a referral role. Since some customers may be amenable and others not, firms must explore what it would take to move suitable customers to play an advocate role. Finally, from Equation C it is also clear that the better the fit between the referred customer and the firm's products, the greater the lifetime referral value. Research has also shown that the customers referred to by satisfied customers tend to be a particularly good fit with the firm and its products and services. The fit is better than with those customers attracted and acquired through marketing messages such as advertisements and coupon mailers. Brand-loyal advocates bring in like-minded customers. To get referrals to actually make a purchase or try the firm's offerings, it is necessary to get some incentives into the hands of the referred customers.

MINIMIZING LIFETIME COSTS

Reducing the costs of acquisition, costs of serving, and the cost of remarketing per customer can increase the lifetime value of a customer. Reducing costs to serve means that you need to be more efficient in the yield from your value-creating assets. We are drawn back to the yield management. Costs to serve per customer are reduced when you increase the cost efficiency or the capacity utilization efficiency. To reduce costs of acquisition and remarketing you need to be more effective in your marketing, both to new and to current customers. CRM technology can be used to continually learn from experience and utilize knowledge to reduce operating and marketing costs at the individual level.

MAXIMIZING LIFETIME REVENUES

Potential customers in a target market are by definition not yet customers. They may or may not be aware of or inclined to purchase from the firm. Firms have to nurture customers' dispositions to the firm through a number of stages before they can benefit from the loyalty of those customers. The acquisition process of customers could begin at any of the different stages on the road to loyalty. Customers may or not be aware or have an understanding of the features and benefits of the product. If the knowledge of the product is favourable, customers may have a liking or preference for the product.

Some customers may even have purchased the product but may not be repeat purchasers, may not be loyal to the product, or may have switched to a competitor. The right customers from any stage need to be moved towards a state of loyalty to the firm and its products. Can CRM technology be configured to capture information about the customer's stage in this process?

Once the appropriate customers are acquired, firms must look for increased usage and frequency, cross-selling opportunities, and trading up to premium versions. Retaining customers requires proactive customer management. If not, customers are likely to be indifferent to the firm, and a heavy user may become impatient and switch to the competition. Proactive customer management seeks to increase interest in the light user and treat the heavy user with appreciation and respect. Thus, the goal of maximizing lifetime revenues is achieved by maximizing the average purchase per year as well as the duration of the customer's relationship with the firm.

MAXIMIZE THE TOTAL LIFETIME VALUE OF THEIR CUSTOMERS

REMARKETING TO THE RIGHT CUSTOMERS

With remarketing, you can reach customers who have shown an interest in your product or service by visiting your site, and show them relevant ads across the Google Display Network.

It's a powerful way to match the right people with the right message:

- Reach the majority of the users on your remarketing lists with the vast scale of our network. Reach them multiple times in a month, week, or even in a single day.
- Easily create custom list combinations to reach exactly the right customer.
- Combine with contextual targeting, frequency capping, and other proprietary technology to target with the utmost precision.

To maximize the total lifetime value of their customers, firms must proactively manage customer relationships. As, proactive customer relationship management should seek customer appreciation from the heavy user and attract more interest from light users with better value bundles if they can contribute more in their lifetime value to the firm.

This is in contrast to the firm that may have good customer service, for example, but in its reactive mode will leave the light user relatively indifferent to the firm and the heavy user susceptible to a competitor. Most loyalty programmes involve some kind of reward for the continued patronage of their customers.

Referred to as frequency marketing, continuity programmes, awards or points programmes, or simply loyalty a programme, the goal of these programmes is to market and manage relationships with customers. First instituted by American Airlines in the 1970s to get around government regulation that prevented price competition, now many firms' programmes attempt to solidify their relationships with its customers. The rewards or awards, as they are called, may come in the form of free products and services at the firm, or sometimes even free products from other firms.

The smart firms impose restrictions on the use of these rewards, so that they are used to increase demand when and where needed. For example, the hospitality industry blocks out certain dates so that the promotions are targeted at different segments to entice customer utilization at low demand periods. The problem is that many of these programmes are misguided in design and implementation. One obvious omission is evident when the lifetime calculus is compared to the criteria for the rewards. The rewards focus on revenues for the most part. That costs are taken into account is not clear at all.

A recent *Harvard Business Review* article offers data that would be a surprise for managers who have not considered costs of serving the customer. Brand-loyal customers are not necessarily profitable customers. In their knowledge of their own value and indispensability to the firm, the brand-loyal customer could make costly demands of the firm.

The firm, in doling out the goodies along with the product and other business favours, may actually be spending more than it recognizes as costs of serving that customer. The only criterion for these (brand) loyalty programmes should be that they should maximize the customer equity for each customer, based on the calculus of lifetime value that we have discussed. To be meaningful and powerful in managing relationships with the right customers, these customer acquisition and loyalty programmes must specify the following:

- Objectives of the programme
- Market and customer scope of the programme
- Value for customer scope of the programme
- Impact scope (costs, timing, impact on people, process, physical assets, other customers, publicity opportunities, *etc.*)

The objectives of the programme need to be stated in the context of customer relationship management. What is the expected value of the programme to the firm? What specifically must the programme accomplish? Perhaps it is to shift demand from peak to low periods, to attract new segments, to get light users to become heavy users, to promote a new product offering, or some other specific objective. Without a known objective, no programme can be assessed on merit.

The next specific decision for customer relationship programmes is to specify the customer that the programme is intended for. Often, frequency programmes are so loosely formulated that the rewards are earned by the wrong customer. Consider this example of the unfortunate consequence of a poorly guided programme. One Mr. Phillips logged 1.25 million frequent flier miles—about $25,000 worth of airline travel—with an investment of 50 hours of his time and $3,140. Mr. Phillips took advantage of an offer he found on the package of a Healthy Choice frozen entrée: 500 American Airlines miles for every 10 UPCs, with early birds receiving a double count of miles! A Mr. Fisher participated in the same programme and got 12,000 Northwest Airlines Miles.

Even if the airlines got an awfully good financial deal with Healthy Choice, one must ask who the loyalty programme attracts—whether the airlines are in the grocery business or in the airline business. How do their returns from this investment compare with the returns that they would have achieved with programmes that targeted the frequent flier instead of the frequent grocery shopper? The objectives of the programme should determine the appropriate segment or customer for the programme.

The problem with most programmes is that they don't take into account the profitability of the customer. Who should be the target of the programme? Not every customer is right for the firm, as we have seen, nor is every customer right for every programme. The best programme is one that tailors the award to the target customer. Thus, giant supermarket retailer UK-based Tesco mails 100,000 variations of promotions to its loyal customers.

Further, some customers may be more costly to retain, while others may be increasing their profitability to the firm. As, it is evident that firms need to look at the acquisition costs and retention costs of its customer base when determining the focus of their retention efforts. The calculus of the lifetime value of a customer is clear in its indication of what needs to be factored into deciding to which customer to target the promotion. Low acquisition costs and low retention costs are realized from your most profitable customers.

At the other end are your customers who were costly to acquire and cost you a lot to serve. Given the acquisition costs, the firm must keep a close eye on the customer's cost of retention. If the firm misjudged a customer's lifetime value or committed more resources to the acquisition of the customer than the revenue stream would justify, the firm has to either reduce retention costs or stop serving the customer if possible.

For the chosen customers, the firm needs to decide what they would do to motivate the customer to act. Customer knowledge should indicate what the customer is sensitive to, so that the value of the promotion can be appropriate for the specific customer or segment. The value of the promotion may be in the form of additional product, a complementary service, a straightforward price-break, or a discount for future purchases or a gift, among other things. Software firms are able to use lead customers in beta-tests and other benefits about new and innovative offerings before the rest of the market will find out, giving these B2B customers early mover advantage in their value chains in their industry. Of course, a projected cost/benefit analysis is a must—what additional revenues have been realized and at what cost?

For service firms, and where the programme is about service components, it is imperative that the promotion take into account what it would do to the demand patterns of customers. The last thing you want is for customers to strain your operation if your programme ends up drawing more customers during peak times when you are already at optimum levels of served customers. Any programme must consider the impact on other customers, on the staff, physical assets, and the delivery system or process.

For example, a shortage of airline seats infuriates frequent fliers who, as brand-loyal customers, having diligently set aside miles for use on family vacations, find they are not able to use the miles because use of awards is limited to a certain proportion of the volume on each flight and are restricted to certain times and dates. Estimates are that about 10 per cent of all miles flown on a carrier can be from people cashing in on these rewards.

Does it make sense for frequent flier awards to range from personal digital assistants to designer watches? Are the costs and impact of these awards assessed? Another less obvious criterion is the potential for publicity in a promotion. A promotion that is newsworthy could attract the attention of a large number of potential customers and other stakeholders.

Firms must prioritize the management of customer relationships as a firm-wide imperative. Dell Computer, for example, has a "customer experience council" consisting of senior executives from each division or business line and major function that reports to a corporate vice chairman, no less. The council oversees measurement of several aspects of customer behaviour, including the effectiveness of its loyalty programmes.

Dell even measures all the costs its customers incur in purchasing and using their products, including such things as shopping, ordering, installing, operating, servicing, and disposing of products. The real value of tracking these revenues and costs over the lifetime value of the customer is that it allows firms to understand their brandloyal customers and anticipate their future needs. Such management practices will be able to deliver benefits to the heavy user to maximize their lifetime value. The lifetime value of the customer must be calculated for each customer—an assessment of revenues and costs over the lifetime of the customer's relationship with the firm. The investment in acquiring and retaining a customer must be made based on the customer's lifetime value to the firm.

A continuous monitoring of up-sell and cross-sell opportu-nities could increase the lifetime value of the customer. The potential customer equity from each segment or customer should determine the extent of value-creating adjustments to be made in terms of delivery process or product outcome customization in terms of value or other benefits to the customer or in terms of adjusting the price and other costs to the customer.

These changes in promotion offerings to acquire a new customer or remarket to a current or inactive customer will impact both costs and revenues and their effect on the lifetime value of the customer will determine subsequent investments in acquiring and retaining customers.

GUARANTEEING CUSTOMER VALUE

Maximizing customer equity requires maximizing customer satisfaction by providing superior customer value. Ensuring product quality as the key driver of customer satisfaction requires checking the links between the firm's assessment of customer expectations and its ability to translate that assessment into product concept, operations design, and execution. The doorman greeted the guest as the taxi pulled up to the Windsor Court Hotel, a 324-room hotel in downtown New Orleans, one of 120 independent luxury hotels of Preferred Hotels and Resorts Worldwide. Later, the waiter at the restaurant in the hotel accommodated off-the-menu orders—but the waiters did not make eye-contact with the diners. The guest room did not have the current edition of the Yellow Pages. This guest was one of Richey International's hotel spies, who had just conducted the Preferred test for the hotel. He has determined based on his experience as a customer that this hotel had met 88.5 per cent of the Preferred standards, passing the 80 per cent minimum. Firms such as Preferred want an unbiased assessment of the quality of their product and hire independent quality assessment firms such as Richey International to do the benchmarking of its hotels.

Firms also want to hear from you directly if you are a heavy user of their product. For instance, if you have over 1 million miles on your Sky Miles frequent flier account, or you fly 100,000 miles, or 100 trip segments, or 20 transoceanic segments in a year, you are a most-valued "platinum member" of Delta Air Lines and may be called to dinner in a private dining room in a luxurious setting. Delta wants to know what you think about the quality of their service.

Customers, especially the most profitable and valuable ones, are being called on for their perceptions of quality of the product received. Deliver a quality product and you are likely to have satisfied and loyal customers. The logic is pretty straightforward, and yet most firms struggle with at least some of the links in the chain: What is quality from the customer's perspective and how can the firm ensure the design and delivery of that quality?

Beginning in the late 1980s and continuing into the early 1990s, there was a groundswell of attention and interest in quality, primarily as a result of falling competitiveness of U.S. firms in the wake of Japan's advances. Quality gurus like Deming, Juran, and Crosby preached the gospel of quality. The Total Quality Management (TQM) movement's cornerstone, the prestigious Baldrige award programme administered by the National Institute of Standards and Technology, was a coveted prize for a great deal of effort by companies large and small. *Business Week* ran a number of articles profiling such winners as L.L. Bean, FedEx, Xerox, Motorola, Disney, and others.

As established and emphasized throughout this book, an understanding of customer value is a fundamental element of customer focus and service orientation. This provides a model for delivering customer value by focusing on the quality of the product, as judged according to how it meets customer expectations. To maximize profitability, the firm must maximize the lifetime value of the customer. A key driver of this goal is customer loyalty, which is dependent on customer satisfaction. To achieve customer loyalty, it is imperative that firms create and deliver a quality product—as defined by the customer. What does the customer evaluate in determining the quality of a product? And, what actions of the firm can be linked to that customer perception of quality?

Perhaps the most significant research on perceived quality in services was conducted by Parasuraman, Zeithaml, and Berry and sponsored by the Marketing Science Institute in Cambridge, Massachusetts. Their contribution was timely and thorough, and revealed a number of important facets of customer perceptions of service quality. These researchers defined service quality as the difference or gap between customer expectations and customer perceptions of service. Their systematic study of customer evaluations across a variety of services revealed that customers evaluate services along certain key dimensions grouped under the acronym RATER: the R eliability of the firm's products, the A ssurance customers feel that their needs and expectations will be met, the T angibles associated with the service, the E mpathy displayed by the firm, and the R esponsiveness of the firm to their specific and individual needs.

Further, they found that there were four principal factors that contributed to the difference between what customers expect and what the firm delivers:

- How accurate is the firm's understanding and interpretation of customer expectations?
- Is this understanding of customer expectations effectively translated into product design?
- What is the gap between what is envisioned and what is delivered?
- How good is the match between what is delivered and what is advertised?

Quality translates customer experience with the product to customer value. Quality of customer experience is framed with the costs of access to and use of the product. Customer value is what customers ultimately evaluate in making the decision on future patronage. Their loyalty to a solutions provider depends on their comparison of actual customer value with expected customer value. What determines how well a firm meets a customer's expected value?

DRIVES THE RELATIONSHIP WITH THE CUSTOMER

THE MECHANICS AND MANAGEMENT

The model presented here is based on Parasuraman, Zeithaml, and Berry's work on service quality. It uses the same logic to incorporate more directly the notion of costs to the customer. *Quality* may not fully convey the point that it is customer value that drives the relationship with the customer. Analysis of quality without the associated costs will not completely capture the customer's frame of reference.

The crux of the model is that there are an ideal and an actual for both the customer and the firm:

- The customer's ideal—expected customer value
- The customer's actual—experienced customer value
- The firm's ideal—product concept
- The firm's actual—operations design

The ideal and the actual of the customer's expectations and perceptions and the firm's product concept and operations design are placed in the context of the competition, the technology, the economy, and the legal and social environment within which they operate. For example, competitive forces and the social environment can shape customer expectations and affect their comparative evaluation of customer value.

The firm's ability to hire the appropriate personnel to deliver the product as conceived and designed can also be affected. Firms design a product concept based on their understanding of the customer's expectations, and then configure their value-creating assets accordingly in an operations design, which for the most part determines what they actually deliver as customer experience.

Thus, customer expectations, product concept, operations design, and customer experience are all linked. Customer value is dependent on this *expectations* link, the *design* link, and the *execution* link. The product concept needs to be closely aligned with customer expectations—the expectations link into the firm. The firm interprets and converts the customer's ideal—expected customer value—into what becomes the firm's ideal—product concept. The firm's actual—the operations design—is the firm's implementation of the firm's ideal—the product concept. The design link is how well the firm has been able to implement the firm's concept of customer expectations with its productive assets.

The design or configuration of a firm's assets executes the product concept, which is what the customer experiences. The execution link reflects how well the customer's actual experience is aligned to the intent of the operations design. Thus, firms must align the customer's ideal expectations to the product concept with a strong expectations link, which in turn is linked to the operations design by a strong design link, followed by an execution link, which determines the customer's experience.

Customer expectations management, studied with a sample of about 100 managers at the leading service firms in the U.K., was found to be composed of three key dimensions: keeping promises, marketing orientation, and employee skills. Another study in a small electric utility company in the United States found that frontline employees had a good understanding of customer expectations. If we assume that customer's expectations were perfectly understood, reflected in the product concept and translated into operations design and therefore customer experience, we should find that customer value is high. However, in practice this is an invalid assumption. Customer expectations play a very critical role in shaping customers' perceptions of quality. When customer expectations are met, we find perceived quality is high, and when not met, we find perceived quality is low.

A closer look at the model will reveal that it is a good vehicle to frame all that can be done to improve customer value by increasing benefits and decreasing costs to the customer. It is a safe assumption to make that improving quality will improve customer value. Creators of the University of Michigan's American Customer Satisfaction Index have shown that customer expectations are linked to perceived value and customer satisfaction over time. Improving quality relative to costs to the customer requires strengthening all the links in the model. Tracking the logic from expectations to product concept, to operations design, to customer experience are a number of management actions that must be taken to ensure the desired customer value.

As, firms can make several check to ensure that the customer-focus and service orientation helps keep the value created and delivered closely aligned with customer expectations. Firms devote most of their attention to the value creation and delivery that affect the perceptions of the customer. However, if service quality is defined as the comparison between expectations and perceptions, shouldn't firms be focusing attention on shaping customer expectations as well?

MANAGING THE EXPECTATIONS LINK

How closely the firm's conception of the product resembles the customer's expectations is a key conceptual link. This link is a function of how well the firm understands customer expectations and how well that understanding is translated into product concept and design. Evaluating the quality of products, especially that of services and service components of products, is difficult for the customer.

To understand the implications of this difficulty, think of services as being dependent on search, experience, and credence dimensions. Some services are higher in search qualities that can be evaluated before the purchase.

Experience qualities are those that can only be assessed during or after consumption, whereas credence qualities are hard to evaluate even after the service. Similarly, customer expectations are just as complicated as customer evaluations. Research has shown that there is a zone of tolerance in customer expectations.

The zone of tolerance is the range of expectations on any of the attributes that are important to the customer. The low end of the range is the minimum level of service that determines what is adequate. The high end of the range is the maximum level of service, referred to as what is desired. Customers will accept anything below the desired, as long it is above the adequate level.

To be able to manage expectations, firms need to understand how customer expectations are shaped. Firms need not only to understand customer expectations but to help shape them so that they are realistic. Customers form expectations from their own past experience with the firm's product as well as with similar products from competitors. In the absence of such experience, customers draw from their experience with the firm's other products or from similar products in general. The firm's own communications, both explicit and implicit, shape customer expectations.

Explicit communications come from all overt marketing messages. Implicitly, all visible actions and evidence of the firm—its prices, its location, its culture reflected in the way it conducts business—could communicate something about the firm. Customers are also influenced by others regarding consumption need situations and the solutions appropriate for those needs. This product-related information can come from messages they receive from the media, family, and friends. Firms are generally focused on their own overt communications and ignore the effect that other sources have on customers and their expectations.

It should become clear now that customer knowledge management is a critical starting point for any firm. The firm's effective use of CRM technology can enable the firm to have a more thorough understanding of customer expectations. Based on customer knowledge, we can see that a failure in this regard could be the result of ineffective use of available sources of information on the market segment and individual customer information. Are all the touch-points set up to capture and record customer information? Is there a process for sharing customer information across the firm?

For example, is there bottom-up communication from frontline employees to managers who participate in product design? Recognizing that customer expectations are dynamic, market research and customer research should be a continuous exercise. Instruments used to gather customer information should be evaluated for validity and reliability and should be easy to use. Inappropriate or inaccurate market research could result in management designing the product concept based on poor information from the marketplace about expected customer value.

An effective customer information system is critical in designing a product concept that would deliver the expected customer value. Management could perceive market needs and customer expectations inaccurately or make poor use of information in defining the service concept. How good is the information on the customer? How complete is it? How well has the information been analyzed, interpreted, and assessed by the product designers? Information regarding the market needs to be disseminated and shared among individuals who are responsible for the service design. Is the information current, and is there adequate indication of how these expectations are likely to change in the near and long-term future? Corresponding changes in product design should be prompt and responsive. Linking the product concept to the needs/ expectations of the customer is dependent on how well information has been obtained on customer expectations and how well they have been utilized in the product concept.

The irony is that sometimes the information is about the wrong customer! The value and validity of the information for product design depends on whose expectations are obtained and used in developing the product concept. The heaviest users or, more precisely, the ones with the most lifetime value should be the priority. In other words, the weight given to the information should be prioritized by the lifetime value of the customer. There is also the possibility that the customer not being the right customer could simply be a result of poor segmentation methods or targeting the inappropriate segment(s) or customer(s).

As we have seen, it is important that the right customer be drawn to the firm. Marketing communications could be attracting customers who are not intended for the service. This might be manifested in poor media or message strategy, setting up inappropriate customer expectations for the product concept. The question here, of course, is whose expectations were obtained and who is actually using the product.

Thus, if the firm has not attracted the customer whose needs it can best satisfy at sustainable profits, then at the outset, the firm is at a disadvantage. Customer expectations are hard to measure. As we saw on customer knowledge management, firms may not have good information on the critical aspects of what customers expect. Research can be flawed and the data not valid, or the means of ascertaining the information is not reliable. Frequently the information is stale and customer expectations, being dynamic, have changed. If you have an inappropriate or inaccurate account of customer expectations, the product concept is not going to be aligned with what customers actually expect.

THE EXECUTION LINK

If the product concept is not supported by the appropriate corporate culture, frontline employees are at a disadvantage in executing the product concept. Backroom employees should see frontline employees as internal customers and the entire corporate culture focused on customer satisfaction. A number of things must happen for the firm to ensure that the product concept can be delivered. All productive factors must execute the design to deliver the product as conceived.

Employees need to be selected, hired, trained, and motivated to execute the design. They need to be empowered so that they have the ability and the inclination to provide the service as designed. Employees need to be allowed the discretion to accommodate and customize to each customer as far as possible. With the right kind of training, frontline employees in services other than just professional services can also make the right decisions.

What was actually delivered and the customer's perception of the product experience need to be continually monitored by the firm, so that the firm understands whether customer expectations were met. Perhaps, during customer interactions, the provider was ineffective in obtaining customer-specific information or in interpreting and using it in customizing the experience for each customer. In many services, customization is a key determinant in how well each customer is satisfied with the product experience.

For example, customers use tangibles (service provider's smile and other non-verbal cues) differently. Some customers need more assurance regarding the product than others. Some customers' information needs are different from others, and their evaluation of the service provider's responsiveness depends on how well the service provider is able to accommodate them. The service provider's ability to empathize with the customer reflects the ability of the service provider to understand the individual customer so that the actual delivery is closer to the individual customer.

Customer perceptions are just as critical as customer expectations. Customer experience may in reality be different from the intial concept. One way firms reduce the disparity between perceptions and reality is to encourage or require managers to work in the front line. By the same token, an argument can be made for allowing the frontline to work backstage, so that they are knowledgeable about how the backstage works to support the frontline.

Another way is to empower the frontline employees so that they have the flexibility and authority to accommodate specific customer preferences that standard operating procedures preclude.

This is an effective customer relationship management practice as long as the front line is also appropriately trained to make informed judgements as to when and where such accommodations are reasonable and beneficial to the firm. Such a policy is especially useful to handle disgruntled customers following a product failure.

THE DESIGN LINK

The link in the chain between what is conceived and what is designed into the firm and its value-creating processes depends on how effectively the firm's resources (people, raw materials, supplies, and systems) have been configured to create and deliver the product as per the product concept. The link could be broken with inaccurate configuration of a firm's resources, for instance, in poor selection of employees. In other words, the fit between job description (responsibility and tasks) and employee profile (skills, education, experience, and personality) represents a significant factor in how well the design is linked with the concept.

Poor empowerment of the frontline employee could fail the product concept in design. This could result from inadequate technical and customer service training, information systems, backroom efficiency, and other support structures. To be able to deliver the product as conceived or designed, internal marketing should be effective. For example, lack of clear communication of such things as the product concept, customer expectations, the marketing strategy, *etc.*, to the frontline employee reflects poor internal marketing—and similarly in reverse, when the product concept decisions have not incorporated the frontline employee, the product is not conceived and operations not designed with that valuable input from the frontline.

In any firm, there is an inevitable disconnect between what the customers expect and what the frontline perceives that the customer wants or what the managers think that the customer wants. For the frontline personnel to be empowered, they require the knowledge and the tools as well as the authority and motivation to use them. If not, the firm will find a disconnect between product concept and execution.

PROMISE ONLY WHAT YOU CAN GUARANTEE

Whatever resides in the minds of the managers as product concept is what is promised in advertising messages from the firm to the customer. And whatever resides in the minds of the frontline or sales people as product concept is promised during direct interactions with the customer. These promises are conceptual manifestations of the product. A useful diagnostic exercise is to check the customer experience as articulated in customer surveys and other methods of customer feedback against the product as imagined by managers and all customer contact personnel.

Similarly, the design of the operation in terms of the configuration of the productive factors can be checked agaisnt whatever resides in the minds of the customers as customer expectations. Is the firm's operation set up to deliver on those customer expectations? Customer expectations and the firm's promises must be delivered. Customer-focused firms should be able to guarantee what can be delivered. That which cannot be delivered must not be promised. Promise what can be delivered and deliver what is promised.

This means providing product performance such that customer perceptions are that expectations will be met. As we have also seen, every customer feels a certain amount of risk prior to purchase and during consumption. Even loyal customers know there is a risk of non-performance and simply place confidence in the provider and are comfortable with taking that risk with that provider.

Helping with risk perception is a task of managing customers. Service guarantees are a powerful mechanism to manage customer's perceived risk in having their expectations met. A service guarantee is simply a promise to compensate the customer if service delivery fails established standards.

EXPECTATIONS AND PERCEPTIONS

For all the reasons inherent in the characteristics of services, intangibles in a product are bound to fail. There is no opportunity to "recall" a service, as is possible with the physical component of the value bundle. Therefore, guarantees are a meaningful and powerful technique to reduce the customer's perceived risk. The most important precondition is of course to ensure that the firm is able to deliver as promised, or in other words ensuring that you can deliver what you guarantee.

For example, Amtrak recently scrapped its service guarantee because it couldn't meet the goal of unconditional customer satisfaction or a complete refund of fare. They found the refunds were getting too expensive because of their frequency, about 4 per 1,000 passengers, which was four times what they had hoped for. In designing service guarantees, firms must consider the scope of the guarantee, the specific risks that the guarantees are aimed to alleviate, the ease of invoking a guarantee, *etc.*

To make these decisions in a customer-focused manner requires an analysis of the customer's context. What is it that needs to be guaranteed and from what? To get at this, one needs to understand the key customer concerns and what the perceived risk levers are. It is useful to examine this along the RATER dimensions since by definition these are the dimensions that customers use to evaluate quality. With this analysis, it is possible to determine what the scope of the guarantee should be. It is useful to think of the consumption activity cycle and the process blueprint to help with deciding the scope of what should be guaranteed.

Xerox and others in the copier business, for example, provide a guaranteed response time for service calls, or an "up-time" guarantee to relieve the risk of failure. Once the scope of the guarantee is decided, it now makes sense to think about under what conditions the guarantee is offered. This is a litmus test of sorts; if you cannot deliver something that you are guaranteeing, you tend to start putting conditions on the guarantee. The problem then is that the guarantee becomes meaningless. Conditional guarantees violate the spirit of a guarantee.

The fear of abuse of guarantees prompts firms to render guarantees worthless with numerous disclaimers and other conditions. The reality is that customer abuse of guarantees is minimal compared to the incremental benefits accrued by the firm from a guarantee. Customers who invoked guarantees cost Embassy Suites $3.94 million in 1996, while the hotel gained $23.14 million in incremental revenue from guests who said they stayed at the hotel only because of its guarantee.

At Hampton Inn it was $3.98 million in costs offset by $31.7 in incremental revenue. Following a significant loss of market share from poor quality, in the early 1980s Holiday Inn improved its standards and launched its successful satisfaction guaranteed programme: "Your room will be right when you check in and if not we will make it right or your stay is free." The conscientious firm will ensure that the quality is in place before promises are made in guarantees.

The benefits of service guarantees to the customer are obvious. The interesting thing about service guarantees is that there are benefits to employees as well. Team Xerox found that the employees knew what they were working towards and the service guarantees put the internal goals in perspective. The firm won its Malcolm Baldrige award because it was able to engage the whole firm in its quest for improving customer satisfaction by focusing on what customers were telling them about their firm and everything they did.

CUSTOMER SATISFACTION MEASURES AND THE DATA

CUSTOMER SATISFACTION DATA

One of the most frustrating issues in practice is that most customer satisfaction measures and the data obtained are inept at guiding improvement efforts. A frequent reason for this is a basic flaw in the measures themselves. There is no way the firm can determine what a "courtesy rating" of 3 out of 5 means in terms of where and how improvement needs to be made. The way to get direction for product remedial and improvement actions from customer satisfaction data is to ask the question specifically so that you can trace customer perceptions to specific processes that pertain to customer experiences. Take a look at surveys of customer satisfaction and ask yourself, does this information give me enough guidance on what I must do to improve customer satisfaction—or will I end up saying, "I know I have to improve frontline courtesy, but I don't know which touch-point the customer is referring to?"

For actionable data from customers, it is imperative to align the customer feedback to specific actions or experiences that the customer has had with the firm. A useful vehicle to sketch the customer experience and also a useful frame of reference for customer feedback on the quality of their experiences with the firm is a service blueprint.

Ensuring that the customer survey questions are directed at specific points in the purchase and consumption experience requires aligning them to the blueprint, so that customers are relating their feedback to a specific point in any number of interactions they may have had with the firm, its products, its processes, or its people. The Xerox story about how it improved its processes to deliver quality is a case in point. Xerox focused its whole organization around the goal of customer satisfaction and service quality. It instituted the customer relations group at headquarters, regional, and district levels.

It instituted the Customer Complaint Management System for improvements in technical services, information systems, and telephone system. Xerox developed tools to continuously measure, manage, and improve customer satisfaction.

Two major sets of data were developed and utilized:

1. *External customer feedback data* included a series of customer satisfaction surveys as well as the Customer Complaint Management System. Four sets of surveys were used:
   - Periodic survey of a random sample of Xerox customers,
   - Post-installation survey of all Xerox Customers,
   - New product postinstallation survey of a random sample of customers,
2. Blind survey of Xerox and competitor's customers to establish benchmark levels.
3. *Internal quality and quantity measures of Xerox* included work processes and outputs that delivered products and services. Xerox processes that affected each area of customer interaction were identified and systems were put in place to measure and monitor these internal processes. The main objective was to provide leading indicators of Xerox performance and improvement opportunities.

Xerox mapped its customer feedback onto its (internal) value-creating and delivery process. This helped locate the necessary improvement effort on those processes that were responsible for customer comments.

The content in customer satisfaction surveys need to cover the RATER dimensions and to be mapped with the source attributable to each customer response on the survey. As standard, terminals are fitted with an integral magnetic stripe reader for credit and debit cards and system is approved by all the major banks and clearing houses. However, in an age when credit card fraud is on the increase, protect you and your customers from fraud with the addition of Chip and PIN devices.

Since the firm needs to prioritize allocation of its resources in any improvement to its value creation and delivery process, it would behoove the firm to understand what its most important customers say by cross-referencing the customer satisfaction data with the lifetime value of the customer. Ensuring that the value created is as close as possible to customer expectations is a daunting task—and perhaps the most important task for any firm.

Customer-focused firms will use feedback from customers and from the front line regarding customer experiences along the RATER dimensions. This customer information, when mapped onto the blueprint of the value-creating process, can identify the failpoints in the process. The processes at the failpoints need to be reviewed, redesigned, and monitored using customer and frontline feedback to ensure that customer value was improved.

The expectations link, the design link, and the execution link in the chain of intellectual and operational translations of customer expectations to customer experience will need to be closely examined to reveal where the links have been severed, causing customer value to be subpar. In an estate of hotels can have a varying level of control over operations. From full integration into your reservation system, through to company credit accounts, ledger accounts and room service, got it covered.

Chains of older hotels may offer a differing range of facilities, restaurant menus, price bands and wine lists, while modern chains are often custom built offering identical services at every outlet. Solution for hotels is flexible enough to meet the requirements of any estate of hotels. Working with Hotel industry can offer a complete end-to-end solution making complete hotel operation seamless.

In the hectic environment of a busy hotel, one of the main concerns for a hotel manager is that all the facilities, meals and drinks enjoyed by your customers are charged to the correct account and paid for before the customer leaves the hotel. Whereas previously customers might have checked out before the breakfast charge had made it onto the system at your front desk, that information is transferred in real-time. Whenever a customer charges a service to their room, system can interrogate the database to double-check the details of that occupant.

4

Third World Critique of Tourism

Third World tourism continues to expand apace. The tourism industry's promotional materials are replete with images of a "frontier" industry, new vistas of "paradise," "virgin" beaches, and "untouched", landscapes. Indeed, the imagery is that of exploration, conquest, and domination. For the people of the Third World, whose natural, human, and cultural resources provide the raw material for this industry, this is no imagery, it is reality.

The challenge of tourism to Third World people is not merely that of ecological degradation, economic exploitation or even cultural spoliation. While the expansion of Third World tourism pits the forces of modernity against those of the pre-modern, it is, in a much more fundamental way, a challenge to respond to a new political force. It is a challenge to locate, define, and articulate a livable space in changing world fragile borders, whose contours are still being mapped.

The ambitious plan of the governments of Cambodia, Laos and Thailand to build a huge golf resort in a pristine forest area where the three countries meet has elicited a heated debate about the way tourism is being developed in the region. The proposed 27-hole golf course will have nine holes in each of the three countries. Thai environmentalists strongly oppose the so-called Emerald Triangle Development Project as the Thai portion is located in a first-class watershed area in Ubon Ratchathani's Phu Chong Na Yoi National Park.

Ironically, the area is also rife with landmines, planted in the 1980s when it served as a battleground between the now defunct Khmer Rouge and the Vietnamese-backed Hun Sen government. To make the project site safe for tourists, costly and protracted mine-clearing operations will be necessary. Yet, governmental officials argue the project is "needed at any price" because it will bring in a large amount of tourism revenue.

In response to environmental concerns, the head of Thailand's National Park Division, Vichit Pattanagosai, has said the golf resort could be defined as an "ecotourism" project and as such would co-exist well with the surrounding protected forest as golfers could watch wildlife while playing on the fairways.

This example illustrates some of the problems associated with contemporary tourism development in the Mekong River Basin area, a watershed that includes Burma, Cambodia, Laos, Thailand, Vietnam and the Yunnan province of Southern China. Thailand, with its free-market economy, had been until recently the only country in the region to have systematically developed a tourism industry, designed to boost foreign exchange earnings, investment and job creation. With the collapse of the state socialist block in the late 1980s, however, all Mekong nations decided to reform their economies and promote tourism as an engine for growth.

Since the beginning of the 1990s, Mekong countries have increasingly participated in regional economic co-operation programmes. One such programme is the Greater Mekong Subregion (GM S) initiative, led by the Asian Development Bank (ADB). Established in 1992, the GMS initiative has become the prime mover of Mekong tourism. Through the ADB, the initiative has financed or co-financed over 100 infrastructure projects—including road, railway, water and air transport, electricity generation and telecommunication—aimed at developing regional tourism and trade.

The GMS tourism working group—known as the Agency for Coordinating Mekong Tourism Activities—is based at the headquarters of the Tourism Authority of Thailand, in Bangkok. It has garnered support from governments, international aid agencies, large industry associations and corporations to promote the Mekong River Basin area as a single tourism market and to remove physical, economic, organizational and legal barriers to travel that are still hampering the visitor industry in the region.

Apart from the ADB, representatives of the six Mekong countries' national tourism organizations, international tourism associations such as the World Tourism Organization, the Pacific Asia Travel Association, the Association of Southeast Asian Nations' Travel Association, as well as the UN Economic and Social Commission for Asia and the Pacffic have been involved in the programme.

In its policy documents, the GMS tourism initiative emphasizes "sustainable tourism" and "ecotourism" as worthy goals. The Concept Plan for Tourism Development in the GreaterMekong Subregion 1999-2018, which outlines the GMS strategy for the next 20 years, forecasts that the Mekong will be "one of the world's most important ecotourism and cultural tourism destinations" by 2018. However, the list of proposed priority projects reflects a heavy emphasis on establishing large-scale transportation systems and tourism complexes.

The plan is to attract 2 to 2.5 million new international tourists per year to the Mekong area by the end of 2006 (over the current level of 14.1 million visitors in 2000). And even higher growth rates are expected in the following years after the ADB infrastructure programme is completed.

The massive GMS programme appears to be incompatible with the concept of ecotourism, which is supposed to nurture small-scale, environmentally and socially sound development. For instance, the GMS initiative envisions the creation of several "economic corridors" linking various parts of the region with advanced transportation facilities, some of which are already underway. The rapid construction of highways, ports and airports, along with hotels, resorts, casinos and other facilities, has already damaged ecosystems, disrupted community life and made local people vulnerable to exploitation by tourism and other industries.

A NEGATIVE MODEL

Thailand receives about 70 per cent of the tourists coming to the GMS and has seen the number of visitors soar over the last 20 years from one million to almost ten million annually. The country's tourism industry has often been described by academics and the local and international media as a negative model. There are countless media reports, academic studies and NGO statements on how reckless development has resulted in the environmental degradation of many places, exacerbated economic inequalities and contributed to undesirable social changes, such as the proliferation of the sex industry, AIDS, drug abuse, gambling, crime and cultural erosion.

Official and industry leaders framing Mekong tourism insist that with improved planning and management, past mistakes can be avoided in new destinations. But in reality, uncontrolled and outright destructive tourism activities have spread throughout the region over the last decade. Even officials and tourism entrepreneurs have expressed worries about the deterioration of unique cultural and natural attractions.

These include UNESCO World Heritage Sites such as Angkor Watin Cambodia, Luang Prabang in Laos, Pagan in Burma, Halong Bay in Vietnam and Lixiang in Yunnan.

Since the late 1980s, the aggressive promotion of golf tourism, first in Thailand and then in other Mekong countries, has also posed immense pressure on local communities and ecosystems. The construction of golf courses—often involving other large-scale developments such as hotels, residential houses, shopping centres, entertainment facilities, power plants, access roads and even airports—has come under heavy attack for consuming large stretches of land, replacing biodiversity-rich wilderness areas, fertile agricultural land and farming communities.

Critics have also pointed out the enormous waste of water resources and the excessive application of chemical fertilizers and pesticides for the maintenance of the courses.

More often than not, local communities have not been properly informed about the projects and the impacts they may have, such as deforestation, contamination, disruption of community life and even forceful eviction of villagers. In Thailand, several golf course developers have been accused of illegally grabbing land and encroaching on protected areas, and it is an open secret that politicians and military officers have financial stakes in the projects. The controversial Emerald Triangle Development Project mentioned above shows that the Thai government openly supports the building of a golf resort in a pristine watershed area, even though the National Park Act prohibits such activities.

Unfortunately, Thailand has longstanding experiences with the mismanagement of forests, beaches, marine areas and other natural assets. For many years, environmentalists have campaigned to stop the Tourism Authority of Thailand and the Royal Forestry Department (RFD) from opening national parks to private tourism businesses.

Under the pretext of "ecotourism", the RFD has in recent years implemented large-scale infrastructure projects in many national parks, with funding from the World Bank and Japanese Bank for International Cooperation. These projects have involved the clearance of many park areas for the construction of roads, parking lots, visitor centres, bungalows, campsites and other facilities, despite growing public criticism and local citizens' protests.

TOP-DOWN APPROACH

A hard look at tourism development in the Mekong subregion leads to the conclusion that the policies pursued by national tourism authorities and supranational bodies such as the Agency for Coordinating Mekong Tourism Activities have been those most suitable for promoting the industry rather than for the protection of the environment and the well-being of local communities. National and regional tourism agencies have done little to develop effective mechanisms to monitor and control developments aimed at curbing environmental, social and cultural problems resulting from rapid tourism expansion. Management plans, if there are any, are often sidelined, and environmental, zoning and construction laws are not being properly enforced. Many critical tourism-related issues—such as corruption, social vices, encroachment of public lands and diversion of natural resources, displacement of local and indigenous communities, and political suppression and human rights abuses—have been typically neglected by tourism policy-makers and project managers.

Whereas the concept of "sustainable tourism" implies a high degree of public participation in the development process, Mekong tourism remains a "top-down" affair. Despite the fact that governments and international institutions have in recent years vowed to work with civil society organizations to involve all stakeholders in development initiatives, critics remain highly skeptical.

As for the ADB, for example, Walden Bello, a sociology professor from the Philippines, notes, "The ADB prides itself with being the first multilateral lending agency to have a board-approved policy statement on good governance, which it defines as governance marked by 'accountability, participation, predictability, and transparency.'" Many ADB staff members are, however, very cynical about the new policy. Says one senior person, "It's a question of practicing what you preach. There's a lot of discontent inside the Bank, precisely because it is one of the most non-accountable, non-participatory, and non-transparent institutions around."

Indeed, there is so far little, if any, evidence that civil society now has more say in shaping tourism policies at the national and regional levels. In Thailand, people can at least advance their interests to some extent through a well-established NGO community and a relatively free press. But in other Mekong countries, particularly Burma, China, Laos and Vietnam, ordinary citizens barely have an opportunity to make their voices heard due to the lack of democratic institutions.

As a result, there is no adequate public discussion on these crucial questions relating to tourism development: who owns the land and natural resources earmarked for tourism; where and how tourism-related facilities and infrastructure should be built; how to handle the anticipated mass influx of visitors in the region; and how exactly to minimize tourism's impacts and conflicts of interests between government, industry and ordinary citizens?

The old question of who actually benefits from tourism also needs to be raised anew, particularly in the face of globalization and liberalization. As with Third World tourism in general, Mekong tourism is largely driven by foreign corporate interests, and the economic gains are often greatly overestimated. A 2001 UNCTAD study found that the economic viability of tourism in less-developed countries is threatened by levels of external financial "leakages" that can easily reach 75 per cent.

That means a high proportion of tourism revenue never reaches destination countries, or leaves as profits to foreign tourism companies or in exchange for goods and services imported to meet the demand from the tourism sector. The pressure on governments to open their travel and tourism industries is being augmented by the structural adjustment programmes imposed by the International Monetary Fund in response to the 1997 Asian financial crisis—despite increasing recognition of the risks.

For instance, most of today's foreign direct investment in tourism in the region is not devoted to new job-creating projects but primarily to mergers and acquisitions. Transnational corporations are rapidly buying up domestic tourism-related companies, which results in a massive transfer of wealth to foreign corporate hands.

This situation is compounded by ongoing efforts to deregulate the travel and tourism sector under the World Trade Organization/General Agreement on Trade in Services system. There are grave concerns that progressive liberalization of the service sector further undermines the economic viability of local enterprises and countries' ability to allocate necessary resources for the preservation of natural and cultural assets and sustainable community development. In addition to the political, social and ethnic turmoil that characterizes many parts of the Mekong River Basin area, events such as the Gulf crisis in 1991, the Asian economic crisis in 1997 and the September 11 attacks in the United States have shown the highly volatile nature of the global tourism industry.

Countries that rely heavily on tourism income are most vulnerable to unexpected setbacks, with millions of people directly and indirectly involved in the industry immediately facing greater economic and social insecurity. A recent report by the United Nations' Economic Commission for Asia and the Pacific, confirms that job losses resulting from September 11 has led to "new poverty" in Asian nations with a high dependence on tourism and exports.

Given the many political and economic uncertainties in the post-September 11 era, which emphasize the issue of unpredictable demand, it is of utmost importance that Mekong countries and regional intergovernmental agencies fundamentally rethink their tourism policies. They should recognize that inflated tourism promotion and development is an unsustainable route for any country and region. Governments should seek to reduce dependency on tourism and think about alternative development strategies to bring about greater stability of national economies, secure livelihoods for local people, and social and environmental sustainability.

Rather than opening up more and more areas in the name of "ecotourism", decision makers need to be persuaded to develop and implement proper rehabilitation programmes for areas already affected by inequitable and damaging tourism. Instead of relinquishing control over land and natural and cultural resources to outside tourism investors and forces of commercialization, the top priority should be to strengthen local residents' rights to self-determined development.

New and bold strategies are needed to help people in tourist areas create a new identity and rebuild livable communities—in social, economic, cultural and environmental terms.

The uneven and unequal nature of development was emphasised and it was argued that an effective analysis of tourism must acknowledge the importance of relationships of power. In this chapter we begin to consider the way in which power is reflected through tourism in more detail. We start with a consideration of concepts of power and how these can assist a critical comprehension of tourism development; ideology, discourse and hegemony will be discussed in turn. The chapter then reviews the most systematic attempt to explain the unequal nature of tourism development - the political economy of Third World tourism that seeks to emphasise the dominance and control of tourism from the First World.

The discussion moves on to trace other ways in which power has been implicated in the analysis of Third World tourism, particularly through the use of imperialism and colonialism. It is argued that these relationships of dominance have also emerged in new forms of tourism with the citation of 'neo-colonialism' and 'eco-colonialism'. This chapter also provides a review of the importance of 'authenticity' to the study of tourism. It is argued that a consideration of authenticity is a further way in which relationships of power can be traced.

While the political economy of Third World tourism is of considerable interest and applicability (and indeed remains an important framework for understanding unequal development, especially of mass tourism) it is argued that it does not provide such a penetrating critique of new forms of tourism in the Third World. Indeed, political economy approaches suggest that the dominance of the First World over the Third World can be overcome, in part, by the creation of new 'alternative' forms of tourism. We challenge this suggestion.

The final section of the chapter suggests an alternative critique through four key characteristics of much new tourism. The first emphasises that all forms of tourism are tied into the growth and expansion of capitalist relations of production. We call this characteristic 'intervention and commodification'. It builds upon the economic aspects of globalisation from the previous chapter and stresses the way in which holiday destinations are either drawn into a global system of interdependency, or are by-passed by it.

Given the context of global inequality and unevenness of development, the second characteristic stresses the 'subservience' that critics have argued characterises much tourism in the Third World, regardless of the form it takes. The final two characteristics seek to provide a more nuanced critique of new forms of tourism, referred to as 'fetishism' and 'aestheticisation', which seek to demonstrate the way in which the reality of the Third World is either hidden or is used to create a special aura of travelling in Third World regions.

Although we invariably associate tourism with pleasure and a certain playfulness, Indian academic, Nina Rao, reminds us that 'Tourism takes place in the context of great inequality of wealth and power', and power relations are central to our discussions in this book - we have already indicated in the previous chapter that power is crucial to a critical understanding of development. In pursuing this argument, we are seeking to address an identifiable weakness in much work on tourism.

On the one hand, much tourism analysis has played down relationships of power, which remain either implicit or are absent. Such studies have largely consisted of identifying structural and deterministic models of tourism. These are examined more appropriately. On the other hand, where power is invoked in a discussion of tourism it has tended to be in passing; references to ideology, discourse, colonialism, imperialism and so on, appear in a rather unstructured, even anecdotal, fashion. Although such analysis is commendable in signalling the importance of power in the study of tourism, the treatment of power needs to be approached more thoughtfully. As Crick (1989) concludes from a wide-ranging review of social science literature, there is an inadequate representation of the complexities of tourism.

Initially, it is necessary to consider concepts of power that may assist a critical understanding of contemporary tourism and the themes we introduced in the previous chapter (globalisation, sustainability and development). In addition, the discussion suggests how relationships of power are embodied in the 'project' of sustainability. In short, we are arguing that we require what Massey (1995b) refers to as a 'geography of power' to make sense of Third World tourism development.

IDEOLOGY

While ideology is a complex term, one profound trait stands out: namely, its concern with the 'bases and validity of our most fundamental ideas'. In using the term ideology, we will be referring not only to the sustaining of relationships of domination in the interest of a dominant political power (the USA as the only global superpower, for example) or social thought (the supposed significance of religion to 'civilization', for example), but also to interests that are opposed to dominant power (the anti-nuclear movement, environmentalists, feminists and so on) that are themselves capable of forming ideologies in the pursuit of power.

Although, as Eagleton (1991) notes, this may signal a degree of contradiction in the meaning of ideology, it is nevertheless fundamental to the notion that ideology is about the way relationships of power are inexorably interwoven in the production and representation of meaning which serves the interests of a particular social group.

As Dobson concludes, ideologies 'map the world in different ways' (1995:7), and it is the intention of this book to map the way in which different interests are implicated in the uneven and unequal development of tourism.

Sustainability is ideological in the sense that it is largely from the First World that the consciousness and mobilisation around global environmental issues have been generated and in the sense that sustainability serves the interests of the First World. Adams (1990), for instance, refers to the ideology of sustainable development, and in the context of tourism in southern Mexico, Daltabuit and Pi-Sunyer (1990) refer to the 'ideology of environmentalism'. The power implicated through First World environmentalism has led increasingly to the 'charge' of eco-imperialism and eco-colonialism.

Implicit in these criticisms is the idea that sustainability is ostensibly ethnocentric. Reconsider for a moment the quote from Robins where he talks about the export of western values and priorities. Such observations can also be applied to the current debate on sustainability. For the most part, it is a discussion framed in the West and imposed on the 'Rest', and hence the acrimonious debates between First and Third World countries at the Rio Summit, Seattle trade talks and the G8 Summit in Genoa to name just a few.

DISCOURSE

The second key concept, discourse, is closely related to ideology. Ideology is perhaps best thought of as a discriminator between power struggles which are central to a 'whole form of social life' (socialism, feminism, ecologism perhaps) and those which are, for whatever reason, relatively less holistic. Prioritising the most important forms of struggle may be an exercise of power itself, but it is important to signal which struggles are ideological and which are not.

Discourse can be considered as complementary to ideology. Indeed ideology is a matter of 'discourse', a 'question of who is saying what to whom for what purposes'. But discourse can also be non-ideological; in other words, it is not reducible to ideology.

The French philosopher, Michel Foucault (1980) suggests that discourse expresses how 'facts' can be conveyed in different ways and how the language used to convey these facts can interfere with our ability to decide what is true and what is false. Discourse, Foucault argues, is so much more than 'mere' words; words are not 'wind, an external whisper, a beating of wings that one has difficulty in hearing in the serious matter of history'; words as a discourse provide the conditions, practice, rules and regulations on thought.

As such, 'development' and 'sustainability' are powerful discourses as our earlier discussion suggested. For example, the term 'carrying capacity' (an important tool in the study of sustainability) can be subdivided into different types: ecological, social, economic, physical, real, effective, aesthetic; and all of these can be interpreted and measured in different ways by different people at different times and in different circumstances. But carrying capacity is often treated as if it were a 'neutral' ecological term. Zaba and Scoones challenge this neutrality: 'most of us have no problems with the notion of the carrying capacity of Botswana (pop. 1.3 m, area 567,000 sq km), but would be incredulous at the idea of calculating the carrying capacity of Birmingham (pop. 1.1 m, area 300 sq km)' (1994:197).

Not only does the notion of ecological sustainability bring some kind of scientific validity with it, but it also suggests that some places (in this case Third World environments) are more suited to its application than others. In this way, carrying capacity as discourse transmits and translates power.

There is no agreement over the exact nature, content and meaning of sustainability. It is a contested concept in all senses of the word. Different interests - supranational and transnational organisations, INGOs, socio-environmental organisations, social classes and so on - have adopted and defend their own language (discourse) of sustainability. The new socio-environmental organisations mobilised around issues of environment, for example, are not in power, and yet their ability to influence the meaning of sustainability for our everyday lives has been marked.

Similarly, consider the power to interpret and represent the Third World through travel books and brochures. On the one hand, we have the highbrow, intellectual accounts of best-selling travel writers such as Paul Theroux and Eric Newby, authors noted for the 'authoritativeness of their vision', and the serious travel pages of broadsheet newspapers.

On the other hand, we have glossy high street tourist brochures selling destinations from the Caribbean to Thailand, and which are the subject of much highbrow, intellectual criticism. These are simply different ways of outsiders representing and interpreting the Third World to their audience, each claiming authenticity and truth, albeit in very different ways.

Foucault's ideas may lead to the conclusion that knowledge in tourism is produced by competing discourses. Discourse, therefore, is a useful concept in emphasising how a certain subject or topic is talked and thought about and how it is represented to others. Most importantly, discourses are 'part of the way power circulates and is contested' (Hall, 1992b: 295).

HEGEMONY

Discourse is also an essential property of hegemony, our last concept, in the power jigsaw. Hegemony was a concept developed by the Italian marxist, Antonio Gramsci, to emphasise the ability of dominant classes to convince the majority of subordinate classes to adopt certain political, cultural or moral values; a more efficient strategy than coercing subordinate social groups into conformity.

Hegemony, therefore, is essentially about the power of persuasion and is immediately differentiated from ideology, which by contrast may be imposed forcibly (Eagleton, 1991), as in the former apartheid system in South Africa or through the imposition of IMF structural adjustment policies. The best way to conceive of hegemony is as a 'broader category than ideology' which '*includes* ideology, but is not reducible to it'.

The real innovativeness of Gramsci's thinking is the conclusion that hegemony is never fully realised in capitalist societies - that it is continually contested. As Williams concludes, hegemony must be 'renewed, recreated, defended, and modified' and is 'inseparable from overtones of struggle'; a relationship that does not necessarily hold true for ideology.

The concepts of the Third World, development, sustainability and tourism are examples of hegemony in practice. Tourism, as we shall see in later chapters, is replete with examples of hegemonic strategies ranging from tourism codes of conduct to the advocacy of more responsible, appropriate or sustainable forms of tourism.

It is also evident in the way in which tourism is contested between different social groups (traveller versus tourist, for example) and between different places (Thailand versus Chile, for example). Hegemony is especially useful for its dynamism and practical usage encompassing and focusing attention on a wide range of practical strategies that are adopted by a variety of interests.

Such characteristics place notions of struggle and contest at the centre of the enquiry. A useful example is provided by Hutnyk's critique of travellers-cum-volunteers in Kolkata (India). Considering questions of cultural hegemony, Hutnyk argues that travellers' ability to engage in and promote the complexities of Kolkata are compromised by:

- The insularity of traveller culture and traveller style;
- The cultural and class background of western travellers;
- The hegemony of western versions of Calcutta in "traveller lore"; and
- The hegemonic effects of the traveller "gaze"' (1996:44).

The advocacy by environmentalists of the need to act globally, for example, is an interesting aspect of the persuasiveness of sustainability and how it ties in both the global and local dimensions and stresses the interdependency of places. Residents of distant places are asked to 'consider' other places; in the dictum of Friends of the Earth, 'think globally, act locally'. Conservation measures in southern Africa and rainforest preservation in Central America can be lobbied for and financed from the First World; and a degree of control and influence over Third World affairs is exercised through First World conscience-prodding. Sachs refers to this as the 'hegemony of globalism':

Until the 1980s, environmentalists were usually concerned with the local or national space ... But in subsequent years, they began to look at things from a much more elevated vantage point: they adopted the astronaut's view, taking in the entire globe at one glance. Today's ecology is in the business of saving nothing less than the planet. Testimony to the hegemonic properties of sustainability, perhaps, is the rapidity with which the word has entered public usage on a seemingly global level since its use by Brundtland in 1987 (World Commission on Environment and Development, 1987), along with the large number of texts that are devoted to dissecting, interpreting, defending or reclaiming the idea of sustainability. For some it is a means of sustaining much more than just environment. It is about 'sustainable development' and incorporates indicators such as income, employment, health, housing, human welfare indicators that are concerned with a 'more rounded policy goal than "economic growth"'.

For others sustainability is to be reclaimed within a far more radical agenda of political ecology where ecological issues and questions of social justice are paramount. Characteristic of hegemonic positions, sustainability is contested within a continuum of viewpoints ranging from 'reformism' (often referred to as light green, conservationist or environmentalist) to 'radicalism' (referred to variously as dark green, deep ecology or, in Dobson's (1995) phraseology, ecologism).

Similarly, sustainability and its application to tourism should not be considered a once-and-for-all position - a neutral, scientific term to which techniques can be applied and upon which policies and programmes can be implemented and evaluated and blueprints, ideal types and models catalogued and advocated.

Rather, it constantly changes as the broader influences and interests change, reflecting a dynamic situation and concept. In the next section we turn to the most concentrated analysis of power in tourism: that offered by the approach known as political economy which is derivative of the neo-Marxist dependency theory discussed in the previous chapter.

THE POLITICAL ECONOMY OF THIRD WORLD TOURISM

By the early to mid-1970s it was already acknowledged that tourism did not necessarily offer a panacea to Third World countries struggling for economic growth. A number of highly critical studies focusing, in particular, on the fate of the small island economies in the Caribbean began to highlight the unequal economic and social impacts associated with tourism. Of special importance was the observation that Third World economies drawn to tourism as a way of earning foreign exchange witnessed the leaking of much of the money made, straight back out of their national economies. This leakage, as it is now commonly known, was seen to arise primarily as a result of the First World ownership and control of the tourism industry in the Third World: from hotels to tour operators and airlines.

These early studies also began to hint at the relationship between tourism and 'underdevelopment'. It was not until Stephen Britton's analysis of Fiji, however, that a more thorough attempt was made in applying dependency theory to the study of tourism. The importance of Britton's analysis is that he stresses the need 'to place tourism firmly within the dialogue on development' (1982:332) and investigate why tourism so often perpetuates uneven and unequal relationships between the First and Third Worlds.

The theory of dependency is best understood as a riposte to the *laissez-faire* (free market economics) approach to economic development and international trade. The global expansion of capitalism has drawn the Third World into increasingly tight economic relationships with the First World, and tourism, now the largest global industry, has been a significant component in this process. Dependency theory has sought to demonstrate how and why these tightening relationships are highly unequal. Dependency theory argues that western capitalist countries have grown as a result of the expropriation of surpluses from the Third World, especially because of the reliance of Third World countries on export-oriented industries (coffee, bananas, bauxite and so on) which are notoriously precarious in terms of world market prices. The theory uses the notion of centre-periphery (or core-periphery) relationships to highlight this unequal relationship, where the core is the locus of economic power within a global economy.

The most widely cited of the dependency theorists, André Gunder Frank, takes matters one step further in his notion of the 'development of underdevelopment' which stresses that it is the underdevelopment of the structures in Third World countries created by First World capitalist development that creates dependency.

Above all else, theories of dependency are in general agreement that the interdependence resulting from global economic expansion and the inability for autonomous growth results in unequal and uneven development. Britton applies this body of theory to tourism.

Centrally, he argues, dependency involves the 'subordination of national economic autonomy' (1982:334) as a direct result of the unequal relationships inherent in the world economy and that within the present structure of international tourism, Third World countries can assume only a passive role (1981a). Britton summarises his approach as follows:

Underdeveloped countries promote tourism as a means of generating foreign exchange, increasing employment opportunities, attracting development capital, and enhancing economic independence.

The structural characteristics of Third World economies, however, can detract from achieving several of these goals. But equally problematic is the organisation of the international tourist industry itself. But Britton's research and narrative are very much part of the analysis of the mainstream - mass - tourism industry.

As such, he argues that tourism in Third World economics is best conceptualised as an enclave industry as the 'golden ghettos' and by Krippendorf (1987) as 'holidays in the ghetto') where tourists only occasionally venture beyond the bounds of their hotel compounds (referred to as an 'environmental bubble'). While Britton's critique is widely cited and provides valuable insights into the unequal structure of Third World tourism, we must ask how useful his analysis is for a critical understanding of new forms of Third World tourism that seek to escape the 'ghettos'. We return to this consideration a little later.

TOURISM AS DOMINATION

Given the arguments advanced by an increasing number of tourism commentators that the Third World is structurally dependent on the First World, there is little surprise in finding a wide range of references to the principal forms of global domination: colonialism and imperialism. While these terms are often used loosely and interchangeably, colonialism is best conceived as a special form of imperialism (that is, the imposition of power by one state over another) involving the occupation of territories. The following sections begin to build up a picture of how these relationships of power are reflected in the analysis of tourism.

The significance of colonialism and imperialism to theories of underdevelopment and dependency has a special appeal to writers on tourism. Both the characteristic First World ownership of much Third World tourism infrastructure and the origin of tourists from the First World have for many become an irresistible analogy of colonial and imperial domination.

Indeed, the distinction drawn in dependency theory between a First World core and Third World periphery is part of a more general theory of imperialism. Nash argues that tourism only exists in so much as the metropolitan core generates the demand for tourism and the tourists themselves. He concludes 'it is this power over touristic and related developments abroad that makes a metropolitan centre imperialistic and tourism a form of imperialism' (1989:35).

Similarly, van den Abbeele (1980) laments tourism as doubly imperialistic both in turning Third World cultures into a commodity and providing hedonistic practices for wealthy First World tourists.

Clearly, this is more than just an academic concern or critique. Take, for example, Box 3.1 which provides the background to Survival's campaign on tourism and tribal peoples.

For Third World critics in particular, as Gonsalves observes, it is the very presence of tourists that leads to the 'view that modern tourism is an extension of colonialism (with all the attributes of a master-servant relationship)' (1993:11). It is an increasingly widely shared opinion within the Third World.

Chung Hyung Kyung's observations are illustrative of the passion and conviction with which these are expressed: 'Colonialism has many faces. Third World tourism, an advanced form of "post-colonialism", is a disease which destroys people's bodies and souls ... Third World tourism carries a major symptom of colonialism: "Domination and Subjugation"'.

It is this notion that tourism is implicated in the maintenance of neo-colonial states that is so important here. Perez (1974), for example, argues that 'Travel from metropolitan centres to the West Indies has served historically to underwrite colonialism in the Caribbean' (1974:473). And Bruner insists that, however much we attempt to deny or evade the relationship, 'colonialism ... and tourism ... were born together and are relatives' (1989:439).

They are, Bruner contends, driven by the same social processes involving the occupying of space (by tourist infrastructure and ultimately by tourists) opened through the expansion of power.

It is not just academics that are drawing parallels between tourism and colonialism. Srisang, a former Executive of the Ecumenical Coalition on Third World Tourism (ECTWT), the world's largest NGO on tourism, suggests that:

tourism, especially Third World tourism, as it is practised today, does not benefit the majority of people. Instead it exploits them, pollutes the environment, destroys the ecosystem, bastardises the culture, robs people of their traditional values and ways of life and subjugates women and children in the abject slavery of prostitution. In other words, tourism epitomises the present unjust world economic order where the few who control wealth and power dictate the terms. As such, tourism is little different from colonialism.

The ECTWT itself is equally outspoken, referring to the majority of Third World tourism as 'an expression of neo-colonialism contributing to racism, erosion of moral values, economic impoverishment and cultural degradation' (ECTWT leaflet, undated).

For other writers, however, the relationship between colonialism and tourism to which they allude amounts to little more than a casual or anecdotal observation, often on the tourists themselves.

Hence, the analogies between the affluent middle classes and 'scavengers', the 'easy-going tourist' and the 'conqueror and colonialist', the suggestion that 'for many tourists, aggressive - almost colonialist - behaviour becomes a norm while on holiday', and the charge that tourists are the 'terrorists of cultural expansion'. As Krippendorf concludes, in the absence of changes, tourism will remain for the host 'a special form of subservience'.

While such observations are understandable, even justified in the way in which tourism seems to reawaken memories of a colonial past, they represent a reaction to tourism based more upon an emotional response. In this vein, as Allen and Hamnett conclude, it 'can be argued ... just as some "Third World" countries have thrown off the yoke of colonialism, they have taken up the yoke of tourism'.

Two observations arise from this review. First, is the rather ambiguous fashion in which the charge of imperialism and colonialism is often made. Because tourism is a conduit for relationships of power, it has been easy for authors to use terms for these forms of domination to describe a vast array of relationships involved; from multinational hotel chains to a waiter-diner exchange.

It has, therefore, become an attractive comparison to make, with the words imperialism and colonialism immediately invoking certain images and responses in our minds. Second, as we observed with Britton, a good deal of the critique arises from observations of the mainstream mass tourism industry. It is somewhat blunt or crude in dealing with new forms of tourism whose claim is to escape these very relationships of domination. In the section 'Alternative critiques for alternative tourism?', therefore, we attempt to analyse (or disaggregate) these forms of power. This provides a clearer picture of how relationships of domination are manifest and suggests how these observations might be applied to new forms of tourism.

One way in which the discussion can be reframed, is through the reference to 'neocolonialism'. As Thomas argues, although colonialism as a pervasive moment in history has all but gone, 'the persistence of neo-colonial domination in international and inter-ethnic relations is undeniable' (1994:1). In the context of tourism, the charge of neo-colonialism has already emerged as a principal way of describing the retention of former colonies in a state of perpetual subordination to the First World, in spite of formal political independence, a view reflected in de Rivero's analysis of non-viable national economies (2001).

Hence, Britton (1981c) refers to Fiji as a neo-colonial economy and seeks to demonstrate why tourism reinforces the pattern of spatial organisation which evolved during colonialism. The tourist industry he argues is a 'neo-colonial extension of economic forms present in pre-independent Fiji'. Similarly, Shivji argues of Tanzania, 'Since the success of tourism depends primarily on our being accepted in the metropolitan countries, it is one of those appendage industries which give rise to a neo-colonialist relationship and cause underdevelopment'.

While such analysis is clearly significant in constructing a broader critique of Third World tourism, the discussion has too often been restricted to a consideration of economic impacts. So, for example, the complexities of class and race have been largely neglected and the spectre of neo-colonialism engendering a subtle, but pervasive racism, has remained largely unexplored.

Again, we will return to such considerations below. Most notably then, a discussion of neo-colonialism allows us to think in terms of the existence of discourses of 'colonialisms' (Thomas, 1994), and explore the many different ways in which power is spatially and socially expressed in a so-called post-colonial world.

One way in which we can immediately see the relevance of thinking in terms of different forms of neo-colonialism is its application to sustainability and environmentalism, and ultimately to development. On the one hand, there are emerging critiques of environmental organisations themselves, not far removed from the critical attacks launched on other supranational agencies such as the World Bank and IMF. Phillipson, an internal auditor of the WWF, for example, accuses them of 'egocentricity and neo-colonialism'.

Central to these criticisms is the way in which organisations seek to impose policies and programmes on Third World countries. On the other hand, a more thorough critique of environmentalism and ecologism as a movement has begun to emerge. Such criticisms have tended to focus on the morality vested in the 'environment' (an entity that must be protected and saved) and the crusade-like fashion with which environmental issues are pursued.

To advance the analogy, there is a sense in which an army of eco-missionaries, or as some would argue, eco-fundamentalists, have fanned out across the Third World to green the Earth's poor.

As noted earlier, the moral basis for environmentalists' claims has emanated from the symbol of interdependence and 'oneness' of the Earth which is founded upon the notion of a global ecosystem. Wolfgang Sachs neatly draws out the relationships of power and domination from this 'systems language' that is committed to 'regulation and control' (1992a: 22), arguing the 'terms "ecosystem" or "global system" cannot shake off the legacy of engineering', and the 'concept ecosystem that gave to the ecology movement a quasi-spiritual dimension and scientific credibility at the same time' (1992b: 31).

Sachs concludes that for many environmentalists 'ecology seems to reveal the moral order of being ... it suggests not only the truth, but also a moral imperative and ... aesthetic perfection' (1992b: 32). Central to Sachs's concern is the way in which the universalistic discourses on development, or the 'hegemony of globalism' as he refers to it, have imposed a system of global resource management that undermines nature and undercuts local autonomy, difference and diversity. Sachs concludes:

In the face of the overriding imperative to 'secure the survival of the planet', autonomy easily becomes an anti-social value, and diversity turns into an obstacle to collective action. Can one imagine a more powerful motive for forcing the world into line than that of saving the planet? Eco-colonialism constitutes a new danger for the tapestry of cultures on the globe.

From Sachs's (and others') writings, we are quickly led to question the intention and outcome of much environmentalism and the way it is advanced through notions of sustainability. As the environmental critic, Vandana Shiva, asks rhetorically: 'Global environment or green imperialism?' The importance, once again, is the way in which such discussion reflects back on the global changes considered. Globalisation drives us towards the logical conclusion that there is only one world: a global economy, a global culture, a global environment. It is the violent imposition of this idea from the First World, an imposition clearly reflected in the Rio Summit, which creates the 'moral base for green imperialism'.

These critiques of environment and ecology have clear and wide-ranging ramifications for the study of tourism too. It is the power invested in the concepts such as sustainable tourism and environmental tourism that have been central to critical responses. Reflecting the discussion of discourse, Herman argues 'sustainable tourism is rooted in much "double-speak"'.

This double-speak needs to be recognised as 'The misuse of words by implicit re-definition, selective application of ... words, and other forms of verbal manipulation'. Similarly, writing of tourism development in Quintana Roo, southern Mexico, Daltabuit and Pi-Sunyer refer to environmentalism as a 'powerful rhetoric' (1990:10).

A CALL TO SOLIDARITY

The debate on tourism, in the Third World, now nearly three decades old, was long dominated by voices from First World sending countries. However, during the past decade an indigenous Third World critique has been articulated, initially by and through the Ecumenical Coalition on Third World Tourism and its, global networks, and more recently, by NGOs, church's, tourism activists, evironmentalists and women, in destination areas, who have chosen to react directly to the issue, as well as indirectly through the communications media.

Acting on behalf of the "host" community, Third World tourism activists (particularly those in Asia) have souity with concerned people in sending nations. They have successfully conducted campaigns against five-star tourism (especially hotels and resorts set up by multinational corporations) with active collaboration of network partners in the West.

The action of the Goa-based Jagrut Goenkaranchi Fauz (JGF) against the Kempinski hotel conglomerate, in tandem with German-speaking members of Tourismus mit Einsicht (TmE), is perhaps the best known example of international solidarity on Third World tourism. Of late, the campaign to End Child Prostitution in Asian Tourism (ECPAT) has sought to create its own model of global collaboration on one very, specific tourism-related issue, child prostitution. Although the primary focus of tourism activists in the Third World is on building up local awareness and resistance, worldwide solidarity is an important aspect of the struggle against an industry that has a web of international links. For Third World tourism activists, the solidarity they seek is interms of a response to their local struggles. No less, no more.

TOURISM AND THE NEW DEVELOPMENT DEBATE

The ideological roots of Third World tourism activism lie in the post-World War II decolonization process and the resulting debates on socio-economic strategies to be followed in the "developing world." Central to the development debate were issues of class and state formation in these countries, as well as the nature and extent of capitalist development that had already taken place.

In the terms of this discourse, the tourism industry was once characterized by Frantz Fanon as a "European hedonocracy," where "the national middle class [in the host country] will have nothing better to do than to take on the role of manager for western enterprise and... will in practice set up its country as the brothel of Europe."

Three decades later, another war has ended, and the debate on nation-states and national identity has started afresh. While most visible in the former Eastern bloc (and countries such as unified Germany), its current is sweeping through much of the Third World as well.

No longer underscored by the economic and military might of the erstwhile Soviet Union, socialist countries such as Vietnam and Cuba are forced to embrace the gospel of global capitalism, in a desperate bid for survival. Even India and Brazil, with more resilient economies, have begun to restructure along lines suggested by multinational capital and its lending agencies, the World Bank and the International Monetary Fund (IMF).

Inevitably, the Third World development critique has come under pressure. It is being asked to re-examine its fundamental premise that the world is an unequal one, and to accept that, since development strategies followed so farhave "failed," a renewed attempt should be made to "uplift" the impoverished masses, with fresh doses of bilateral aid and private capital.

A decade into the struggle, tourism activists are being told that tourism is here to stay, and therefore, action towards a new form of tourism—humane, acceptable, eco-friendly—could win them new friends and influence more people They are being asked to participate' in tourism decision-making, in spite of the fact that they have already made a decision against' tourism.

RADICALISM OR ALTERNATIVE ACTION

In order to establish the kind of alternative tourism we would want to establish we would need a high degree of independerice from existing structures. Tourism activist Peter Holden notes that "this probably means we would need to own and operate out own airline, control vast amounts of capital, and operate a giant bureaucracy. Perhaps it's just as well that this is beyond our immediate grasp," Holden says, "and we are free of some of its pitfalls."

The idea (or hope, for some) that tourism activists would participate, in shaping tourism policy has been around for quite a while. As long ago as 1977, Harry Matthew was saying, "Whether or not future tourism policies...reflect constructively the radical critique will depend immensely upon the ability of the radical critics to put their point across to political leaders. How much political clout do critics of tourism have? In developing countries where tourism has not yet become a pervading sector of the economy, there may yet be time for radicals (who will no longer be radicals) to help shape tourism policy."

For the Third World activist, involvement in "alternative tourism" meant something quite different, however. Chayant Pholpoke, an early practitioner, described his work thus in 1984: "Alternative tourism, as I perceive it, can play a supportive role in building solidarity among people all over the world who want to build a more just society."

At about the same time, German churches, who were supportive of tourism concerns, evolved a set of "criteria for the promotion of study tours into countries of the Third World and for their reverse programmes (return visits)." The aims clearly stated such study tours "must be in line with the ecumenical principles of development which means that they have to be part of processes that strengthen liberating and just structures."

The message that Pholpoke and others were tying to convey was one that was picked up quickly, too quickly perhaps. While they saw their efforts as having an essential political basis, their "followers" saw a market for a new tourism. Literature aimed at the "concerned" tourist flooded Europe, the German-language *Sympathie* magazines setting a trend of sorts. Ludmilla Tuting and Kunda Dixit's *Bikas-Binas:Development-Destruction*, a collection of material on environmental issues in Nepal and the Himalaya, is a "handbook" that was published in 1986 for the new breed of "eco-tourists."

Commercial publications such as the Rough Guides and Lonely Planet handbooks reach out to the individual traveller rather than the mass (charter/ package) tourism market. Alternative tourism, in the wake of the Vietnam War, became a collage of red and green, reflecting the pro-left and (early) ecological agendas of the peace movement.

Uncomfortable with this rendition of alternative tourism, Chayant Pholpoke, wrote in 1985: "Our friends in the West still do not get the message we are trying to get across. And it seems that the word 'alternative' has confused them more than enlightening them on the negative aspect of mass conventional tourism. Indeed, the word 'alternative' has many alternative meanings. We may not have that many alternatives left but to build up more awareness."

Peter Holden joined the debate in 1988, writing: "I hope that: the 'red herring' of alternativelourism can be seen for what it is....I do not believe that alternative tourism is the agenda of the Third World, but rather the agenda of some elite people in the 'First World' who want to travel in an alternative way....Our business is to change the shape of tourism."

The view that modern tourism is an extension of colonialism (with all the attributes's of a "master-servant' relationship) is widely held by Third World' critics of tourism. It is hardly surprising, therefore, that the critique 'opposes any form of its expansion, and refuses to be drawn into a discussion of so-called "alternative," "responsible," or "acceptable" tourism. To a Third World critic, such proposals would resemble those on "acceptable" colonialism or "acceptable" nuclear power.

The following exchange between a Third World radical and a Western industry specialist illustrates the width of the divide that separates the two sides in debates about native participation in tourism promotion.

First, from activist Haunani Kay-Trask: "I don't agree with the fact that we have to accept tourism. I don't want tourists....I'm tired of people saying, 'Well, you know, you need tourism.' We don't need tourism. We lived for 2,000 years without tourism. There is no such thing as an innocent tourist. Everyone is culpable, and the violence that has been done against us and my people, against my culture and my sacred land, will be returned in kind."

In response to Haunani Kay-Trask's statement at the 1985 Bad Boll meeting on Third World People and Tourism, industry specialist Leo Theuns writes: "The church multinational (World Council of Churches) moves in strange company opposing multinationals in the travel industry. Not only in the sense that 'anti-imperialist forces' were brought together at the Bad Boll meeting under church aegis but, more than that, a revolutionary was given an opportunity to bring her message about the inevitable violence that she hopes will soon occur on the island of Hawaii."

Whether or not tourism is here to stay, many of its critics in the Third World will continue to oppose it, on the grounds that the tourism industry is a means of the continued expansion of Western domination in socio-cultural, economic and political terms. That tourism has the support of many Third World governments and national leaders does little to allay the doubts of critics.

As Satinath Sarangi says: "To demand 'people's participation' in planning such schemes is particularly illogical. It implies that a development process which goes fundamentally against the interests of the people can become acceptable if people participate in it."

THIRD WORLD POLITICAL ECONOMY OF TOURISM

Many—if not all—of the underlying factors that motivated Third World people in the first place to act on tourism (and a variety of other related issues) continue to exist and grow, and the development gap is widening. It is imperative to take stock, not just of the issues of tourism, but also of the perspectives Third World people have, particularly on the political and economic agendas of tourism.

This is not to say that a clear Third World political economy. of tourism exists. In the past decade, we have listened to a variety of Third World voices and arguments against tourism. These have ranged across a wide spectrum of philosophical and ideological lines: anarchist, nationalist, conservative, liberal, progovernment, feminist, nostalgic conservationist, radical ecologist, Marxist, religious, atheist, and just plain moralist.

The response of concerned people elsewhere has been largely to the issues raised (the text), with little attention paid to the varied ideological underpinnings (sub-text). As a result, we have failed in the effort to articulate and incorporate a comprehensive Third World critique of tourism. What dominates is a critique of tourism developed and articulated from a Northern, sending-country perspective.

A similar fragmentation exists in academic discussions on tourism and for much the same reasons. To quote Nina Rao: "Is there a forum for Third World narratives in international tourism discourse? Can Indian narratives like exploitation of gender, class, caste, poverty, [or] terrorism ever enter the tourism discourse? Can one really describe the encounter between the tourist Self and the Other in the so-called voluntary relation of guest and host? Such:

a relation is again dictated by the tourism discourse which seeks to sweep away the basic commercial nature of the encounter. What causes concern in the Third World narrative (the subversive narrative) is the effect on the Other."

Conflicting perspectives and expectations within the international networks concerned with Third World tourism have inevitably led to doubts, on the part of several Third World activists, regarding the reliability and motivation of their Western partners, on whom they depend for solidarity action. First raised by the JGF at the 1991 global meeting of tourism activists at Cyprus, these doubts have been more comprehensively expressed in Anita Pleumarom's paper "Understanding the Crisis in the Third World Tourism Debate."

Third World activists have a point. A sea-change is needed in the kind of solidarity that we have today, one that is shaped by contemporary realities. But we must realise, at the same time, that part of the responsibility for shaping the critique of tourism lies within the Third World itself. Too often we have depicted a romantic past that has been defiled by tourism and other evils of "modernity." Rarely do we acknowledge that our own histories are tainted, and not just by former colonial powers. As Sophie Dick writes:

This longing for what [E.] San Juan [Jr.] calls an "antediluvian paradisical origin before the Fall," which neatly tucks sexual politics into nationalism, makes it possible to replay every invasion of the Philippines in the rape of every Filipino child...minimizing continuities, ignoring moments of cultural change, and missing questions about family structure and sexual politics that have been monopolized by the right. As Michael Tan says, "a fascist solution is to repress sexual attitudes without solving the problem of poverty which nurtures sex tourism.

What the fascists want is to drive the women back to the kitchen and the bedroom, and not to display themselves 'indecently' in bars. So long as some nationalists also subscribe to a belief in mythical 'good old days' when women didn't have to be exploited in bars and brothels and never mind if they got beaten up at home, pushed into the funeral pyre, we (the nationalists) may well become willing accomplices to the fascists."

WESTERN SOLIDARITY

Recessions and economic slowdowns in the North have prompted many industries to relocate their manufacturing facilities in Southern nations in a search for cheap labour. Other "favorable' conditions offered by host countries in the South include less stringent quality standards, legal loopholes that permit companies to operate in ways that would not be possible in their own countries, a lack of environmental safeguards, corrupt bureaucrats and politicians, and so on.Northern economic agendas have also dominated discussions about intellectual property rights, GATT, and international aid issues. These discussions ensure that multinational investments are not merely protected, but are guaranteed artificial profitability, all in the name of "fair" trade and the "free movement of capital."Third World tourism figures prominently in these debates. It is not by chance that a recent annual theme of the World Tourism Organization promoted the "free movement of tourists." The plain fact is that tourism in the Third World is far cheaper than a holiday at home. Everybody profits from it: the industry, the tourists and the economies of the countries they come from. There is laughter all the way to the bank.

Solidarity on Third World tourism issues needs a clear recognition of this reality. The Third World is not a cesspool for the poverty of the West. International networks concerned with Third World tourism have failed to capitalize on opportunities to influence mainstream development debates at forums such as the Earth Sumniit and the World Human Rights Conference We must take better advantage of the opportunities that will certainly arise in the future.

The choicess are clear: either we find new ways of understanding our communicating our concerns, and thereby polilticizing the debate in the widest international arenas or we will remain at our present levels of functioning and interaction. If we choose the first, we must also be willing to accept and work with the consequences of radical change.

5

State-Civil Society Relations and Tourism

At the height of the outbreak of the Severe Acute Respiratory Syndrome (SARS) in Singapore in 2003, Singapore Airlines (SIA) pilots belonging to the Air Line Pilots Association of Singapore (Alpa-S) criticized their union's leaders for giving in too easily to management on wage cuts and lay-offs. When the leaders were eventually ousted, then Deputy Prime Minister Lee Hsien Loong (current Prime Minister), stated his support for the ousted Alpa-S leaders and issued this challenge: "the [new] leaders of this group have to think very carefully, do they really want to take on the Government?" ("Govt Will Not Let Pilots 'Do Singapore In': DPM", 29 November 2003).

He echoed what his father—the then Prime Minister (now Minister Mentor) Lee Kuan Yew—said in a similar dispute in 1980: "I don't want to do you in, but I won't let anybody do Singapore in" (ibid.). Lee Hsien Loong's support for the ousted union leaders reflected government concerns that industrial unrest would threaten Singapore's position as an international air hub.

The government warned that it would not tolerate a rebellious pilots' union ("Govt: We Cannot Afford Such Acrimony", 1 December 2003), and subsequently changed legislations to make it unnecessary for union leaders to seek approval from members on agreements ("SIA Pilots: Law to Be Tightened", 1 December 2003). The industrial dispute was resolved amicably between the new union leaders and the senior Lee ("SIA Pilots Pledge Amicable Solution", 24 February 2004). Minister Mentor Lee Kuan Yew said the fact that the pilots agreed to lower wages shows that the country could do what many other countries could not because Singaporeans understand "we got here because we work on special rules" ("Staying Ahead: It's All in Teamwork, Says MM", 14 October 2004).

This example is important because it points to the central role that tourism plays in the Singapore economy. The SARS outbreak and the SIA pilot's dispute threatened the tourism industry. The actions by the Singapore government clearly demonstrate its willingness to intervene for the sake of the industry. Despite the significance of these events and the central importance of tourism in Singapore's economy, tourism is under-examined in research on state-civil society relations in Singapore.

To address this gap, this chapter explores state—civil society relationships in Singapore, paying careful attention to three recent issues that have affected the tourism industry—the re-branding of Singapore, the casino debate, and the introduction of health and medical tourism. In the business of governing Singapore, the People's Action Party (PAP) government has been able to close, absorb, re-define, and open up civil spaces, as a result of which the line separating state and civil society in Singapore is blurred.

Tourism has opened up important civil and social spaces that were once closed. At the same time, the tourism industry has played a central role in shaping Singaporeans' own understanding of their national and ethnic identities.

This chapter is divided into two sections. In the first section I briefly review the body of knowledge on state-civil society relations and tourism.

The short review provides a framework for understanding the situation in Singapore. In the second section, three examples—the re-branding of Singapore, the casino debate, and the introduction of health and medical tourism—illustrate how state-sponsored tourism development and civil society in Singapore are intertwined. The role of the Singapore Tourism Board (STB) in the Singapore society will also be discussed.

TOURISM AND POLITICS

To many people, tourism is about having fun. For many governments, however, it is an important source of foreign revenue. It provides employment in restaurants, airlines, airports, hotels, and tourism attractions. In addition to their economic impact, tourists can also influence the host country's cultural and social environment.

The tourism industry impacts on civil society in a number of ways: it can lead to social and political activism seeking to balance the positive and negative impacts of tourism; local residents and foreign tourists may be politically socialized through tourism, and that process inevitably re-defines local identities and civil spaces; and the influx of tourists can lend support to the political regime in the destination country, such that tourists may eventually be treated by the government as if they are part of its constituency. These issues are explored in further detail below.

MANAGING THE IMPACT OF TOURISM

Besides the economic benefits of tourism, there are other ways that the industry affects the host society. Problems related to traffic and parking, pollution, wear-and-tear of heritage sites and price inflation may irritate and infuriate the local population. Aspects of the host society may also be commodified and touristified; mass trinketization, for instance, debases the value of local handicrafts. The social impact of tourism, however, is not necessarily negative. Attempts to create a balance between the positive and negative impacts are often underpinned by ideological and political considerations. While tourism businesses and researchers agree that a balanced approach is needed, there is still no specific agreement as to what constitutes a balanced strategy.

Attempts to balance these impacts emerge from negotiations amongst tourism stakeholders—residents, industry, cultural institutions, tourism attractions, tourists, politicians, and others—resulting in different destinations coming up with their own version of "balanced" tourism development. Civil society may emerge to challenge state-sponsored tourism plans and be engaged in the negotiation process but the amount of space that civil society has differs across host societies.

POLITICAL SOCIALIZATION AND RESPONSES FROM CIVIL SOCIETY

Tourism offers avenues and resources for the authorities to politically socialize local residents and foreign tourists through a process of "branding". Such exercises reify particular identities for locals to imagine themselves and their identities. In this process, tourism also becomes a vehicle for destinations to selectively market their crafts, their own philosophies, and their cultural identities.

Routing and zoning provides a framework for reorganizing space, while events and revising history in tourism settings transform the cultural and historical life of communities. State authorities may package and redefine customs and cultures, and reframe relationships between cultural groups in society through tourism.

While local residents may internalize officially promoted versions of political reality, the engineered reality may lead to the emergence of civil society organized along social cultural lines that the authorities have fashioned. The relationships between state and civil society are always open and responsive; this too can be observed in tourism.

POLITICAL SUPPORT

Tourist consumption of local politics is often implicit, rather than explicit. Tourists, despite their relatively short trips, are subjected to many of the same conditions as local inhabitants. Countries perceived as unstable and unsafe do not receive many tourists. Their governments are often portrayed as being out of control, corrupt, or incompetent. Therefore, when countries draw tourists, it implies that the tourists trust the host environment and system enough to come. And in effect, tourists indirectly give a vote of confidence to the political regimes in the places they choose to visit. Some governments justify political control of their own citizenry through reference to its tourism policy. For instance, the former Marcos government of the Philippines used tourism to endorse martial law. Under martial law, the imposed stability was said to have allayed the security concerns of tourists, leading to more tourists visiting the country. Therefore, tourism is important not only for economic development, but also for governments when they want to claim international support for their policies. While foreign tourists cannot vote for politicians, tourists' interests are often taken into account by the state.

Tourists may not organize themselves like voters in local civil society but they are able to act through their economic might. (The influence of external force on the Singapore civil society landscape is examined separately by others in this volume, namely, James Gomez ["International NGOs"], Kersty Hobson ["Considering 'Green' Practices"], and Lenore Lyons ["Transient Workers Count Too?"]). To gain political mileage, politicians and the state often address the interests of tourists, similar to them championing and appropriating interests of local civil groups. Tourists in effect have become a political constituency in the host country.

STATE-SOCIETY RELATIONS AND TOURISM IN SINGAPORE

This short discussion of various streams of research on tourism and state-civil society relationship helps frame the case of Singapore. As other papers in this special collection demonstrate, the line demarcating the state and civil society in Singapore is unclear. By focusing on three aspects of tourism development policy in Singapore I show how the Singapore government is able to absorb civil spaces, redefine cultural spaces and identities, and in some instances, let social spaces open up for reasons of tourism. These three examples deal with different aspects of tourism and their impact on the Singapore society. The re-branding of Singapore is the STB's conceptuatization of Singapore and how that imagination is distributed to and then embedded in the local psyche.

The decision on the casino raises moral issues and the decision was highly controversial, requiring the government to assert leadership and appease various civil groups. Education and medical tourism deals with professional services, and we shall see how this new form of tourism can affect the home economy. All three examples point to various strategies used by the PAP government to manage both the tourism industry and the Singapore society. To appreciate the impact of these strategies on Singapore, it is important to understand the role of the STB.

THE STB AND TOURISM IN SINGAPORE

Tourism development requires the cooperation of various agencies. Tourism authorities, local government, land control authorities, cultural management agencies, civil groups, and others have to cooperate to develop the industry. How the various agencies and political institutions within a country organize themselves to promote, plan, and develop itself as a tourist destination affects the speed, scope, and effectiveness in realizing its tourism development plan. Each agency has its own interests and agendas.

Official tourism promotion authorities often need to mobilize resources and take on a leadership role in the industry, and harness cooperation amongst various agencies through coercion and persuasion.

The STB is a statutory board it is a public body financially supported by the government, including through the 1 per cent cess collected from customers in restaurants and hotels in Singapore. The STB has the task of promoting the tourism industry in the island-state. It has cultivated close relationships with the private tourism sector, other state agencies, and local society. In 2004, Singapore attracted 8.3 million visitors and generated S$9.6 million in tourism receipts (STB 20 January 2005). The industry is estimated to be contributing 5 per cent of Singapore's GDP, and the STB has a target to triple tourism receipt to S$30 billion, increase visitor numbers to 17 million, and generate another 100,000 jobs by the year 2015 (STB 20 January 2005). The STB receives strong financial support; the government has allocated S$2 billion to achieve the 2015 goals (STB 11 January 2005). The STB plays not only a central financial role but also a social and cultural one; it is at the centre of the web of relationships in the tourism industry.

The STB works closely with other state agencies such as the National Heritage Board, Urban Renewal Authority, Ministry of Defence, the National Arts Council, and other agencies. For instance, in 1995 the STB and the Ministry of Information and the Arts (MITA) released a blueprint to make Singapore a "Global City for the Arts". According to the blueprint, there will be three national museums—the Asian Civilizations Museum, the Singapore Art Museum, and the Singapore History Museum. As in the plan, these museums help the tourism industry assert the city-state's unique Asian heritage and identity.

Just as importantly, the museums work with various state agencies to send out certain (social engineering) messages. For instance, the Singapore History Museum exhibits complement the Ministry of Education's history curriculum in the schools. In addition, the STB uses a carrot-and-stick approach to incorporate private tourism businesses into its vision.

The STB issues licences to tour guides and travel agencies, thus giving the authorities control over the products and messages that guides and travel agencies send out (STB 1998). The STB subsidizes the printing of promotional materials by travel agents if they support the STB's marketing and product policies. It engages consultants and actively helps in-bound travel agents to develop new products. For the new "Uniquely Singapore" branding campaign, the STB has, for instance, created new tour packages for tour agencies (STB

12 May 2004). Other private businesses in Singapore are also encouraged to take the initiative to promote tourism activities. For example, the STB has initiated and continued to support various business groupings such as the Orchard Road Business Association, which has not only assumed the responsibility to light up Singapore's main shopping street for Christmas, but has also taken the initiative to organize the Singapore Street Festival.

The STB also attempts to shape local life, as the re-branding of Singapore will show. The STB is the central coordinating body for the Singapore tourism industry, endowed with the financial and political resources to make itself relevant and important in the sector. The details follow.

RE-BRANDING SINGAPORE: FORGING SINGAPOREAN IDENTITIES

In March 2004 the STB began to use the phrase "Uniquely Singapore" in its promotional material. This slogan replaces the former tag line "New Asia" (Ooi 2004a). New programmes have been launched to generate a sense of brand ownership in the local tourism industry and among local residents. Uniquely Singapore products are being created and Singaporeans are encouraged to search for things that make their country special.

Uniquely Singapore—Unique is the word that best captures Singapore, a dynamic city rich in contrast and colour where you'll find a harmonious blend of culture, cuisine, arts and architecture. A bridge between the East and the West for centuries, Singapore, located in the heart of fascinating Southeast Asia, continues to embrace tradition and modernity today. Brimming with unbridled energy and bursting with exciting events, the city offers countless unique, memorable experiences waiting to be discovered.

As in the previous branding, "Uniquely Singapore" is a response to the manifestation of modernity and Westernization in Singapore. "Uniquely Singapore" self-orientalizes Singapore and accentuates the Asianness in the country by pointing out Asian practices, such as modern buildings arranged according to Chinese geomancy and Western dishes cooked with Asian spices and flavours. For instance, in creating a world-class museum to showcase the glorious ancient material cultures of Asia in the Asian Civilizations Museum, the story of Asia is presented within the framework of Singapore's Chinese, Malay, Indian, and Other (CMIO) ethnic model. All Singaporeans are ethnically classified into these categories despite diverse differences within these communities.

The Asianness that the STB is promoting is built along the state's ethnic engineering framework. "Uniquely Singapore" messages and stories are also sent out to local residents. Some Singaporeans have internalized these messages. For example, schoolteacher Miss Anjali Raguraman took her pupils to visit the STB. After the trip, she wrote a letter to the Straits Times ("Know What Singapore Has to Offer and Be Its Envoy", 28 April 2005). She cited the example that I have heard frequently from my respondents in the STB: Singapore is unique. Let me illustrate with an example that the speaker, Mr Dominic Raymond Chew cited. Think of the void decks underneath the blocks of flats all over Singapore. The phrase "void deck" is an oxymoron! But in that one place, we see a funeral taking place one day, and a wedding the next. There is beauty and uniqueness in that itself. (Ibid.)

As a voice from the "grassroots", Miss Raguraman further suggested "that the STB organize such talks for ordinary Singaporeans to make us that much more competent in promoting our motherland". The STB used to be involved only in the marketing of Singapore. In the 1980s, however, it became actively involved in product development and the shaping of local life. As Mrs Pamelia Lee, who headed tourism product development in the STB then, lamented:

Like other developing nations, we also watched the charm of our old city disappear and diminish, bit by bit.... In recent years, we have often been described as a city without a soul; modern, efficient and hygienic, but lacking in grace, refinement and charm.

With this realization, the STB "started to enhance areas in Singapore that did not come under the STB's purview. The festive light up of Chinatown, Little India and Kampong Glam were introduced". Essentially, private celebrations of these festivals in Singapore have become public spectacles, so that tourists can also celebrate with Singaporeans. As many of the streets of newly refurbished conservation sites became lifeless, Mrs Pamelia Lee pointed out that "through software organized by the STB and the stakeholders, we can bring back life so that tourists are not disappointed and to give market forces more time to settle".

This is a proud claim of not only how the STB has shaped the physical landscape but also how it is deliberately shaping human activities in Singapore. Effectively and rather pragmatically, the Singaporean government has married the interests of their social engineering programmes and tourism. The tourism authorities have claimed, asserted, and established a symbiotic relationship between local and tourist needs.

It is believed that attractions that are meant for tourists are also appreciated by local residents (National Tourism Promotion Committees 1996). Not only is that, messages meant for locals packaged for tourists and vice versa. In a pragmatic manner, tourism products are consumed and messages are sent out simultaneously to both residents and tourists. In the process, both groups are jointly engineered towards the PAP's vision of Singapore.

THE CASINO DEBATE

In 2009, Singapore will have two Las Vegas style "integrated resorts", hosting hotels, restaurants, theatres, museums, amusement centres, and casinos. The issue on the two casinos in Singapore was highly controversial.

The cabinet itself was not unanimous on the decision, and it generated one of the most heated public discussions in Singapore ever.

There had been occasional proposals for a casino in Singapore since the 1970s ("Timeline", 16 April 2005). But the suggestions were never taken up because of moral and social issues. However, in March 2004, the then Minister for Trade and Industry, George Yeo, mooted the idea again. Many religious groups voiced strong objections to having a casino in the city-state. Civil groups against any casino in Singapore emerged. For instance, a conservative Christian group started "Families Against the Casino Threat in Singapore" or "FACTS".

FACTS was created to rally all Singaporeans against Singapore hosting any casino; as reported on its web site, it managed to collect close to 20,000 signatures through an Internet petition, which was eventually sent to the Singapore President. The casino discussion was a lively money-versus-values debate.

An STB officer, voicing his own view, was exasperated and complained to me about those members of the public who were against the casino. Not only has a tourism project become a focal point for criticism; he was alarmed that naysayers like FACTS are ignoring the reality that Singapore is losing foreign exchange—Singaporeans have been travelling overseas and taking cruises just to gamble.

At one stage, the minister leading the decision-making process, Dr Vivian Balakrishnan, framed the discussion into a freedom of choice debate. He said in parliament:

So I want to set this debate in perspective. I think the real question which we need to confront is what type of society we are or, to be more accurate, are we now a more mature society than, say, decades ago, meaning can we trust the vast majority of Singaporeans to act responsibly, to exercise common sense and to make their own choices as to how they wish to spend their disposable income, how they wish to entertain themselves? ("Casino Here Is Not a Matter of Money versus Values", 17 November 2004)

Effectively, the minister invoked the argument that Singaporeans should have the freedom of choice. It is an indirect reference to whether Singapore should continue as a nanny state or a more open society.

Prime Minister Lee Hsien Loong reminded religious groups that his government takes a secular and pragmatic approach, based on the long-term interests of the country: "the government cannot enforce the choices of one group on others, or make these private choices the basis of national policy" ("Casino: Not Fruitful to Keep Arguing, Says PM", 27 April 2005).

While Singaporean civil society became active during the casino decision-making process, civil groups against the casinos were ironically campaigning against giving choices to Singaporeans. Even after the decision was taken in April 2005, members of parliament and the public continued to criticize the decision. Prime Minister Lee responded at the "Glassroots Club": Beyond a point, this [debate] can be counter-productive because the risk is we may harden views for and against, and polarize our multiracial, multi-religious society. And that is something which I think we should avoid at all costs. (Ibid.)

As part of the process to shape public opinion and appease civil society, the Ministry of Information, Communications and the Arts (MICA) issued a brochure—Why Integrated Resorts?—to convince the general public of the decision (MICA 2005).

The decision was basically presented as a pragmatic one—Singapore tourism, while still healthy, is losing market share; Singapore is facing strong tourism competition in the region; the casinos will give a S$1.5 billion boost to the economy and create 35,000 jobs.

Religious parties who are opposed to the casinos were reported to have expressed a willingness to help the government control the social problems that may arise from the casinos ("They Are Anti-Casino, but Ready to Help", 22 April 2005). The Straits Times reported that some Singaporeans felt that the whole discussion was merely a public relations exercise, through which pragmatism again rules. Others felt that it was an important consultation process ("Worthwhile Debate or Not? It's a Toss Up", 23 April 2005). Regardless, through tourism, the PAP government has invoked a freedom of choice argument. And civil groups have been roped in to handle future social problems that would arise from the casinos.

NEW TOURISM SPACES

Singapore has established itself as a modern destination with world-class services. Singapore is not only attracting tourists to spend time and money in a safe and secure destination but also drawing foreigners to use the country's educational and medical services. The STB has taken on the responsibility to market these services to the world. Visitors' stays can be relatively short (a few hours) to a few years. While it is debatable whether visitors staying in Singapore for a few months or even years can still be considered "tourists", what is remarkable is that the STB has assumed responsibility for wooing them to the city-state to spend money.

As part of the promotion of Singapore's educational services, the STB, together with the Economic Development Board (EDB), is promoting basic and tertiary education programmes, as well as professional and enrichment courses to the world.

Education tourism was first promoted in 1993 when the authorities found that many Thai students visited Singapore to learn English. And in August 2003, "Singapore Education" was launched. Under this scheme, the authorities aim to attract 200,000 full-fee paying students to Singapore for tertiary and professional education by 2012. Most of the educational services consumed by tourists are provided by commercial schools, which are less regulated than the public education sector. There has been an increasing number of complaints against private schools, including complaints from those foreigners whom the STB wants to attract. In normal circumstances, active groups within a civil society can intensify public scrutiny of the actions of businesses.

Such an option of getting organized, however, is not available to tourists on short stays. The complaints against private schools in Singapore threaten the Singapore Education brand. To maintain the integrity of its brand, the EDB has announced schemes to preserve Singapore as a reputable education hub. Instead of allowing the industry to regulate, the EDB has intervened to improve consumer protection and academic standards. The swift action taken by the authorities to protect the interests of "education tourists" indicate not only the efficiency and effectiveness of the PAP government but also the willingness of the government to act as de facto activists for education tourists. This intervention is not unique; the Singaporean government has shown its ability to absorb and appropriate the interests of emerging civil spaces, so as to neutralize political activism.

The EDB managing director said, "When we add to this the high standard in student protection and welfare, organization practices and academic quality ... we will set Singapore further apart from the competition and make us an even more compelling hub for education" ("Three Plans to Ensure Reputation of Private Schools", 10 September 2004). Consumers welcome the state's intervention; the PAP government has literally absorbed their interests and reflected them in its policies.

Singapore is also promoting itself as a medical hub—Singapore Medicine. To facilitate this strategy, medical centres and doctors are now allowed to advertise. The government is also considering removing restrictions imposed on local doctors that maintain a clear separation between medical and non-medical treatments. These restrictions are meant to protect unsuspecting patients from predatory doctors, who may drum up business for profits rather than cater to the needs of patients ("A Facelift for Singapore's Health Tourism", 15 October 2004). For example, the government is now reviewing legislation to see whether spas could offer dental treatment.

As Singapore faces competition from Thailand and Malaysia in the region, the government is willing to be flexible and change legislation to boost the fledgling medical tourism sector. In contrast to the Singapore Education scheme where standards are being raised, the Singapore Medicine scheme has loosened control on the medical profession by allowing services such as spas and cosmetic treatment to become part of the medical industry.

While many doctors frown on such services, the Singapore government wants to cater to the demands of tourists. But it is debatable if the loosening up of the medical industry will better serve the needs of both local and foreign consumers.

Undoubtedly, the educational and medical health industries in Singapore welcome assistance from the authorities to promote their services overseas. The government has changed regulations for the private educational and medical sectors, so as to assure an increased number of foreign consumers.

While tourists cannot organize themselves against lousy educational services in Singapore, the Singapore government acts on their behalf. Such state-sponsored activism benefits local residents too. However, it is questionable if it will help consumers when the medical industry is loosened up to include more services. In both cases, the policies will enrich Singapore's economy.

TOURISM AND SINGAPOREAN SOCIETY

The PAP government has constantly invoked the concepts of "survival" and "pragmatism" in the ideological and institutional entrenchment of public policies and popular consciousness. The term "Singapore Inc." is frequently used by researchers to describe how Singapore is ruled and run by the PAP; economic development takes precedence in most policy decisions in Singapore.

The ruling elite claims that public institutions, social life, and private businesses need to be engineered towards Singapore's economic development or else the country will not survive.

The industrial relations dispute between SIA and one of its independent-minded pilot unions which I used by way of example at the beginning of this chapter is indicative of this view.

The extent to which the Singapore government is able to push through its tourism agenda on the grounds of economic growth shows that Singaporeans have generally accepted the pragmatic arguments. Such acceptance comes with coercion and persuasion of various tourism stakeholders, including local civil society actors. The three tourism-related examples used in this chapter provide a number of important insights into the particular nature of state-civil society relations in Singapore.

First, considering that Singapore had more than 8 million visitors in 2004, and a population of only 4 million people (STB 20 January 2005), tourists have become a feature in local life. While individual tourists may come and go, as a group they form a permanent, albeit fluid, constituency. As non-citizens, however, tourists cannot organize themselves in the Singapore civil society. Instead, their interests have been absorbed by the Singapore state.

Parliamentarians regularly raise the interests of tourists in parliament. For instance, PAP MP Mr Ang Mong Seng said that Singapore needs to attract more tourists from China.

In order to do so, he suggested that Singapore should increase the use of Chinese signage: "in order to attract the Chinese tourists, we have to use their language so that they could feel at home when they are in Singapore" (Singapore

Parliament Hansard, 13 March 2004). Opposition MP Mr Low Thia Khiang agreed.The then Minister of State for Trade and Industry, Dr Vivian Balakrishnan, replied that the Chinese market is important for Singapore tourism, and efforts are being undertaken to attract them, including extending the period of visa validity for Chinese tourists, making it easier for the Chinese to apply for visas, stepping up marketing, and getting the relevant authorities to install Chinese signage (Singapore Parliament Hansard, 13 March 2004). In other words, tourists are effectively being represented in Singapore's parliament through the seduction of their economic might.

Second, it is difficult to imagine a "pristine" and "untouched" Singapore that is different from a socially engineered and touristified Singapore. In fact, many products initiated for tourism have become part of local life. For instance, in 1984 the STB introduced festive illuminations along Singapore's main shopping belt—Orchard Road—for Christmas. Subsequently, from 1985, Chinatown is now lit for Chinese New Year, Little India for Deepavali (Hindu festival), and Geylang Serai for Hari Raya Puasa and Hari Raya Haji (Muslim festivals).

While these illuminations attract locals and concentrate festive shopping activities in the respective areas, they allow tourists to experience the festivals. Today, Singaporeans wait in anticipation for these illuminations; the STB has not only helped Singaporeans celebrate their ethnic identities, it has entrenched the Singaporean ethnic model and allowed tourists to experience aspects of Singapore's ethnic festivals. Local identities are constructed, asserted, and reified through tourism; tourism agendas are embedded in Singaporean culture and society.

Third, and closely related to the second point, socially engineered categories may generate civil energies. For instance, the STB is heavily involved in the re-invention of Chinatown. Some Chinese Singaporeans, however, disagree with the tourism-inspired vision for the area. An STB officer revealed to me that many Chinese Singaporeans, including those in the independent Heritage Society, took offence to the original plan to theme Chinatown into the five elements—water, fire, earth, metal, and wood—as entrenched in a traditional Chinese worldview.

While the authorities wanted to introduce more Chinese elements into the district, many Singaporean Chinese wanted to return Chinatown to what it was in the past without the new elements. While such protests were healthy and the STB eventually withdrew the five-element theme, the master plan remains. The lesson learned, according to my STB respondent, is that "it is important to consult local residents".

In this instance, the socially engineered ethnic category "Chinese" had been taken seriously by Singaporeans, and grassroots energies were being generated within Singapore's CMIO ethnic framework. Fourth, on the grounds of being economically pragmatic, the PAP government has opened up civil and social spaces that were once closed. The PAP government advocates that individuals in Singapore should make choices and be given more responsibility for their actions.

This is a move away from the nanny-state mentality. The government wants to replace the strait-laced image of Singapore with an image of a more tolerant and open city.

This move has been partly motivated by the demands of tourism. Sanctioning gambling to attract tourists is just one example. Another example relates to attitudes towards sexuality. During a parliamentary sitting on 13 March 2004, a few MPs voiced their concerns about changes in sexual attitudes. PAP MP Mr Ahmad Khalis bin Abdul Ghani said:

We have seen discernible moves towards greater easing up of our social scene. The main reason for this easing up is to present Singapore as a more happening place to woo tourists and foreigners. [... Some people] are concerned that such moves promote the idea that sexual promiscuity is acceptable, and therefore, this may undermine our family values. [... I believe...] we do not quite need bar-top dancing or such other types of items to woo more tourists and foreigners. (Singapore Parliamentary Hansard, 13 March 2004)

The then Minister of State for Trade and Industry, Dr Vivian Balakrishnan, replied that he agrees that Singaporeans "must not lose our values, and we must not lose our compass" and he continued:

There was an article that Professor Richard Florida wrote, entitled "The Rise of the Creative Class".... His research found that cities, which are able to embrace diversity, are able to attract and foster a bigger creative class. These are key drivers in a knowledge-based economy. The larger lesson for us in Singapore is that we need to shift our mindset so that we can be more tolerant of diversity.

To achieve this, we have begun to take small but important steps to signal that we need a new respect for diversity and openness to ideas. So these examples that the Members cited, *e.g.*, night spots to open 24 hours, bar-top dancing, and bungee jumping, are just part of that signalling process. (Singapore Parliamentary Hansard, 13 March 2004)

Thanks to tourism, the PAP government is loosening social controls and giving people opportunities to choose and take responsibility for their own social and personal actions. It remains questionable to what extent this will translate into a more active civil society.

The PAP government has invoked the freedom of choice argument, and future civil society arguments can tap into this precedence.

The government has also invited civil groups to help manage any negatives that may arise of the two casinos in Singapore, for instance—social and civil spaces are undoubtedly being sanctioned and created. (Gomez, "International

NGOs", in this volume, and Hobson, "Considering 'Green' Practices", in this volume, however, show that there are still many limits to the ability of government-sanctioned civil spaces to contribute to the growth and development of Singapore civil society.)

Fifth, while the Singapore government is protecting the needs of tourists, it is also supporting many local businesses, such as those in the education and medical industries. The STB is able to provide incentives for private companies to follow their lead.

The various STB strategies are efficient and are able to boost the local economy but such state-sponsored initiatives may stifle private initiatives. (2) The Singapore approach is not only pragmatic; it is efficient in providing seamless tourism experiences; the negative aspect seems to be that the private sector has more incentive to follow than to lead, a complaint I heard from two STB officers.

In using Giddens' "Third Way", Burns (2004) paints a bipolar view of tourism planning. The first view—"leftist development first"—focuses "on sustainable human development goals as defined by local people and local knowledge. The key question driving development is 'What can tourism give us without harming us?'" The second view—"rightist tourism first"—aims to "maximize market spread through familiarity of the product.

Undifferentiated, homogenized product depends on a core with a focus on tourism goals set by outside planners and the international tourism industry" (ibid.). In trying to bring different interests together, and to manufacture consensus, the Third Way conceptually bridges the two poles, although in practice, how this works out remains to be seen and tested. But as this chapter shows, Singapore has its own Third Way in tourism planning.

The PAP government has created a bureaucratic state structure that makes different government agencies work together.

It has empowered the STB to develop tourism products and realise a vision that not only serves tourists but also the locals. From the consideration of efficiency and effectiveness, the Singaporean system is able to draw cooperation amongst different parties.

Private sector cooperation is garnered through incentive schemes, such as financial support for products that reflect the STB's goals. The leadership and visions of the STB are supported by other state institutions. This means that the STB has become a powerful organization that has the ability to distribute resources.

To make Singapore an attractive tourism destination, tourists have become a de facto constituent in Singapore, as their interests are absorbed and represented in parliament. Many tourism products in Singapore match various social engineering programmes in the country; locals and tourists are subjected to the same messages and experiences.

Consequently, some civil groups that challenge STB's initiatives are organized along Singapore's social engineered categories (for example, being Chinese in the CMIO ethnic model). Regardless, social and civil spaces are being opened up for the sake of tourism. In sum, tourists are being Singaporeanized and Singapore touristified.

This chapter is the product of ongoing investigation of the Singapore tourism industry since 1996. Primary and secondary data were collected for this study.

Besides documented materials from the STB, the mass media, and the Singapore Parliament Hansard in-depth interviews and discussions were conducted with officers of the STB, operators of tourism attractions, and tour agents. Since some of the issues raised can be construed as sensitive, my respondents have requested that their identities be kept anonymous.

6

The Rise of Indigenous Cultural Tourism

The nineteenth century Aboriginal corroboree performed for non-Indigenous settler audiences was Australia's pre-eminent prototypical Indigenous cultural tourism product. Options for the development of this product by both Aborigines and settlers were fashioned by competing and complementary strategies of various colonial interest groups. The implementation of these strategies acted directly to restrict supply of traditional corroboree performances and access to markets. Producers had to find new socially acceptable genres, such as minstrelsy and temperance entertainments in order to reproduce their product.

This necessarily resulted in product transformation, but enabled continuity of a performance tradition to the present day. The Tjapukai Aboriginal Dance Theatre and the Bangarra Dance Theatre are but two modern inheritors of this tradition.

Come Share Our Culture, the title of the Northern Territory Tourism Commission's first Indigenous tourism information brochure (NTTC 1993), sums up the core invitation extended by Australian Indigenous cultural tourism to consumers. However, there are different types of Indigenous cultural tourism enterprises, each allowing a different kind of interaction between host and guest, and, in consequence, a different kind of 'sharing experience'.

These types of Indigenous cultural tourism can be characterised in terms of degrees of intimacy. Within ranges along this continuum, various types of tourism enterprises, defined by their core business, may be distinguished in terms of exhibiting low, medium and high levels of intimacy.

The lowest level of intimacy is provided by forms of indirect tourism, where no face-to-face encounter takes place, and where the cultural experience is entirely brokered. One example is the provision of themed tourist accommodation, in which an Indigenous group may simply hold equity.

But in Australia the major example of Indigenous indirect cultural tourism is in the purchase of Aboriginal and Torres Strait Islander art and craft from non-Indigenous retailers in capital cities. In Australia, the overwhelming majority of Indigenous peoples in remote areas involved in the tourism industry are represented by this area of indirect tourism: the distant sale of art and craft products, and the licensing of reproduction rights.

The typical Indigenous cultural tourism enterprise exhibiting a medium level of intimacy is the Indigenous-owned art and craft retail outlet. There is a face-to-face encounter between the Indigenous salesperson and the customer, but it is necessarily restricted in scope, being framed by an arena of commercial transactions. The explicit focus of the encounter is upon the prospective sale/purchase, rather than on imparting a cultural experience and the sharing of cultural knowledge.

Indigenous cultural tourism enterprises displaying high levels of intimacy are typically those that bring or invite tourists into their communities or onto their traditional lands. They include, for example, interpretive guided tours of sites by traditional owners, and the equivalent of 'farm-stay tourism' experiences in Indigenous communities or homelands.

While the overall encounter between host and guest is structured by these enterprises' commitment to delivering the attractions and highlights promised in their brochures with continuous face-to-face encounters, there are generally more opportunities for unstructured interaction and free-flowing questioning and discussion between host and guest, opportunities that obviously increase with the extension of the time frame.

As these categories relate to core business activities, they may not necessarily be exclusive to a particular enterprise. A retail art and craft store or space may offer a higher level of intimacy between host and guest groups than that normally offered by retail transactions through fostering highly interactive encounters between their clientele and performing artists and musicians. The framing offered by the retail space tends to make such encounters, however, relatively brief. A guided tour of a jointly-managed national park may also, as part of the tour package, offer occasions for lower levels of intimacy in the provision of hotel accommodation, souvenir sales, formal lectures, and staged dance performances.

Generally, in moving from low intimacy level to high intimacy level ventures two important shifts may be observed. Firstly, there is the shift in emphasis from product to person; from 'making a sale', and 'putting on a show' to 'being on show' oneself. Depending on the degree of Indigenous control of the process, 'being on show' may oscillate from 'being exhibited' to 'exhibiting one's being'; choosing to communicate one's way of 'being-in-the-world'.

Secondly, there is the shift along a continuum, from presenting culture as object or, in Bourdieu's terms (1986:243), cultural capital in its 'objectified state', to culture as subject, expressed by cultural capital in its 'embodied state'. The history of the presentation of Indigenous Australian cultures in its objectified state can be traced through studying changes in the actual objects, which document in themselves processes of tradition and transformation.

The history of the presentation of Indigenous cultures in its embodied state, as exemplified in dance performances, is not so easily traced, and therefore must be constructed out of the overall historical record of host-guest interaction.

In the tourism marketplace references to 'Indigenous cultural tourism' often refer to tour operations conducted by Indigenous persons offering medium to high levels of intimacy, as their core tourism product is the sharing of Indigenous cultural knowledge and practice. Such ventures invite visitors to experience aspects of a different way of life, and a different way of seeing this different way of life. The embodiment of this culture, and of this difference, is the people themselves. What is said and what is done by the host group is, for the guest group, mediated by whom they perceive the host to be, and historically determined by where they perceive the host to live.

Indigenous cultural tourism can be seen as a modern 'touriculture', the cultivation of the symbolic landscape for a non-traditional market. For Australian Indigenous peoples, this landscape acts as the foundation and 'anchorage' of all myth that underpins cultural production.

As the berndts state in the speaking Land:

... it is, then, the land which is really speaking—offering,to those who can understand its language, an explanative discourse about how it came to be as it is now, which beings were responsible for its becoming like that, and who is or should be responsible for it now. The Speaking Land must be heard. But what it says may be understood only if we know its language.

This language is a semiotic system. 'The whole land is full of signs: a land humanised so that it could be used and read by Aborigines who were/are intimately familiar with it, and read as clearly as if it were bristling with notice-boards'. The source of traditional meaning for Indigenous Australian cultural tourism products has been the symbolic landscape, and ultimately the land itself. Notably, as a consequence, without access to this source and the knowledge it allows to be transmitted, reproduction of the traditional forms of these meanings becomes difficult.

In Australia, as the actions of British colonisation proceeded, Indigenous cultural tourism increasingly acted to express covert control by Indigenous individuals over their domains. The framing of the supply of cultural tourism performance became the struggle for physical and cultural survival given rapid depopulation, separation of families and denial of access to traditional lands, goods and services. The nature of the historical demand for such products was to be uneven and contested in non-Indigenous society, ranging from promotion to appropriation to restriction through the application of policies of social control; consequently their supply was to be similarly uneven.

The current interest in Indigenous cultural tourism has masked this fact, that it is an industry with a long history; a knowable past. While in the late twentieth century it developed as an out-working of the decolonising process of returning some Indigenous land, it was initially shaped in response to demands from a colonial market as a re-working of an Indigenous pre-colonial trade in art, song and dance.

Prior to European contact, there was an extensive traditional market for all forms of artworks, weapons and utensils, one that came to be consumed by an evolving non-traditional tourist market. The traditional marketplace consisted of a trade in ritual, songs and dances between groups and within groups.

Butlin has commented on the latter, in particular the importance of 'intergenerational transfers of knowledge' as a dynamic element in the Indigenous economy. Traditionally, these transfers were accompanied by payment by younger to older men, for example. Butlin sees them as encompassing 'more than just the productive activities of hunting and gathering or even resource management. The intergenerational transfer of ritual and myth, both lore and law, is vital.

As education for life, such transfers go beyond the realm of the secret-sacred, and include what non-Indigenous observers may regard as meaningless 'leisure time activities' in which older men schooled the young in games and sports. 'Entertainment' and 'sport' have been nominated by Sutton as examples of 'domains of relative autonomy' of Aborigines that 'tend to be concentrated in areas conceived of by outside interests largely as private affairs, not as part of the public domain'.

One of the main attractions for Indigenous peoples in meeting guests' demand for cultural performances and survival skills was because in their domain these were not trivial, but related directly to 'focal and basic stages on which the Aboriginal public, political, and economic life is lived out ... not a side-show ... [but] core activities for people and core activities for whole communities'. Nineteenth century settler-defined domains of 'entertainment' and 'sport' provided a space for the growth of the 'corroboree', the first, and still one of the major, forms of organised Indigenous cultural tourism in Australia. Encouraged by some parts of settler society and contested by others, this performance event heralded latter-day commercial Indigenous Australian cultural tourism ventures.

SEEING CORROBOREES

Corroborees were primarily dance accompaniment to songs; that is, the verbal content was at least as important as the morphology, the form of the corroboree. The multiplicity of Indigenous languages, and settler ignorance of even local languages shifted this balance; with the tourist corroboree, the form became all-important. This was not necessarily disadvantageous. If the spectators were unable to know the meaning of the words, they could all the more easily impute a significance of choice to the overall performance.

Settler corroboree-audiences were well aware that there was an Indigenous significance, which was hidden from them, in what they were seeing and hearing.

'It is not clear what a corroboree is intended to signify', wrote J.D. Woods in his A Narrative of the Visit of HRH The Duke of Edinburgh KG to South Australia (1868:87). 'Some think it is a war dance—others that it is a representation of their hunting expeditions—others again, that it is a religious, or pagan observance, but on this even the blacks themselves could or would give no information'.

Few translations of corroboree songs in South Australia and Victoria appeared in the first half of the nineteenth century. Where corroboree songs were faithfully translated, they often appeared, wrote W.A. Cawthorne in 1844, to be 'taken from some of the most trivial circumstances. To a European they would appear quite nonsensical'. Cawthorne's confidant, George French Angas, noted 'the frequent repetition of a few words, such as, "Water, water, where is water? There is water, welling out of the ground;" but this, of course, is sung in their own dialect'.

Strehlow, however, writing of the Arrernte of Central Australia, has argued that their Ltata songs, 'the true "corroboree" songs done for pleasure and amusement', were not entirely unrelated to sacred dances. The connection was in the allusive meaning of the words of the songs. The degree of coded meaning in the allusions meant that the meaning was often only 'intelligible to the singers who know the sacred myth'.

In this way, as the Berndts have noted, the existence of 'inside' and 'outside' words could hide the 'true' meaning of songs from some who apparently understood the language of the song. Even the 'pantomime' style of corroboree, a major source of commenting upon and critiquing the new settler society, could encode hidden meanings. Corroboree performers, declared Massola (1971:64), often 'mimicked, with veiled allusions, the activities of certain of their tribesmen'. They could do this even when they 'imitated the movements and calls of different animals', because of the totemic associations between animals and a people. As Strehlow has shown, some of these associations required ritual knowledge.

Assuming the encoding of hidden meanings in at least some tourist corroboree performances, it is possible that these performances may have served to maintain ritual knowledge and traditions. These meanings, even where offered by the hosts, were not generally assimilated by the guests. Primarily this was a language difficulty, of course.

Given that most settler audiences lacked Indigenous language skills, choreography rather than song content was the most accessible feature of corroborees. Second, it was a cultural difficulty: the guests were unable to access the coded meanings. Therefore morphology became the primary determiner of meaning, often guided by the established articulation of a people with place.

For nineteenth century corroboree audiences in both newly established and well-established locations, tourist corroborees evolved as a joint invention by Indigenous and non-Indigenous settlers that articulated a sense of place. This articulation of a sense of place oscillated between two poles: experienced initially as new colony and home country, and later as bush frontier and settled metropolis.

This articulation was to mesh with the peripheral place occupied by the 'Primitive' in European thought, and the historical distinction made by modern tourism between places visited by the 'tourist' and the 'traveller' (Buzard 1993: passim). The logical consequence of this articulation for its practitioners was the manifest determination of the Primitive's authenticity.

The new Australian colonists inhabited the socially insecure world that was the Indigenous peoples' domain. They experienced displacement from the old country and interpreted the corroboree in terms of the society they had lost. In this milieu, settlers perceived the domain in which they found themselves as Indigenous, not-yet-settled and thus not-yet-civilised, and their corroboree performances were perceived as authentic, despite the European trappings that may have been adopted.

There was, however, a further factor. New settlers' displacement was accentuated by the Antipodean inversions of their new surroundings. Added to this strange confusion and confutation of the known and normal was the apparent disorganisation of Indigenous Australian society—its lack of centralised authority and common language. Perceived incoherence of the new environment was thus experienced simultaneously with social and psychological ramifications of physical displacement.

In this unpredictable, unknown world, settlers could take some comfort in the fact that, to them at least, Aborigines all danced the same. The "'corrobory', their universal and highly original dance ... [was] from its uniformity on every shore, a very striking feature in their character", commented the explorer Thomas Mitchell (1834:4-6). In particular, the 'shake-a-leg' action of male corroboree performers was reported from Sydney in the eighteenth century to virtually everywhere explorers were to penetrate in the nineteenth century. It was even observed underwater: ... the dance consisted chiefly of the performers leaping two or three times successively out of the sea, and then violently moving their legs so as to agitate the water into a foam for some distance around them'.

This 'universal accompaniment' meant that Aboriginal dance for visitors could be read as undifferentiated across the continent by colonists as 'the corroboree'. The 'corroboree', as performed for colonial audiences, demonstrated that here was one people in one country. It became a familiar, and thus reassuring and welcome aspect of the social landscape.

Later, the 'civilization' of this domain, with the consequent removals of Indigenous peoples, led to these performances often being seen as 'inauthentic' in published reviews. In this manner, colonial perceptions of a corroboree's 'authenticity' emerged as a response to a sense of place, in terms of a projection of the viewer's own sense of displacement from home. 'Inauthenticity' correlated with the colonial transformation of nature into property consequent upon Indigenous removal, and subsequent social marginalisation. Imagining the corroboree as opera and ballet

Massola has characterised southeastern Australian corroborees as having been 'an artistic and aesthetic expression in no way different to our own theatrical performances', in some cases 'a type of ballet'.

In the late 1820s, Mitchell watched a corroboree at Bathurst in which 'the Aborigines imitated various animals, such as dingoes and the way in which they would catch and kill kangaroos'. As a finale they even imitated the wind by humming while waving a bough of a tree. To Mitchell it 'was a greater treat than any ballet he had ever seen on the stage at Covent Garden'.

Similarly, during her visit to Port Phillip in 1839, Lady Jane Franklin wrote to her husband of the 'Corroberry—their Arranmilly, or dance' which reminded her 'of the kickers and spinners on the Opera Boards'. This locating of the corroboree as ballet or opera reflected the non-Indigenous sense of displacement, of inhabiting an insecure, still Indigenous, space. It defined their sense of distance that here (in the colonial space) the ballet, the theatre was Indigenous, or more ominously, still Indigenous, as settlers looked forward to the establishment of metropolitan forms of theatre and dance.

This imagining helped settlers perceive the land of the corroboree as, after all, not so outlandish; as assimilable, since what was happening was a form of their own metropolitan experience. The colonists at this time sought the perception of sameness, not difference. As Manning Clark (1963:II 21) commented, 'so what did it matter if the white man's social gatherings left much to be desired: what did it matter if nothing like the splendour and gaiety of a ball in England could be exhibited in NSW for many years to come, when they had their own source of pride, and joy, and wonder, and mystery?'

No doubt Indigenous performers picked up, and played to the 'opera' and 'ballet' references. By 1856 in Victoria, the corroboree, having already been imagined as pantomime and ballet, was brought onto the stage by theatre producers of Christmas pantomimes.

The Ballarat review of the 1860 Ararat Aborigines' corroboree performance at Ballarat's Royal Theatre, reproduced in the Melbourne Argus also favourably noted that 'strict time kept together with their various steps, completely astonished the audience'. But, like that of the Queen's Theatre performance, the Royal's corroboree appears not have been repeated. Whatever the cause, there is no question that the socioeconomic environment of these independent players was restrictive. Mission policy depended upon having sedentary Indigenous groups firmly under their control. The dangerous independent livelihood that corroboree performances potentially provided was compared to rabbit-shooting, and had a double danger by reinforcing the notion that traditional cultural practices had value, and should be upheld. Indigenous peoples were seen as requiring 'protection' from engaging in such free trade in their cultural capital. It would take until the end of the twentieth century for Indigenous dance-theatre groups, such as Tjapukai Aboriginal Dance Theatre and Bangarra Dance Theatre to stage regular corroboree performances in mainstream theatre settings. According to the latter's Russell Page, 'The Bangarra Dance Theatre is a modern day corroboree'.

The missionaries were assisted by the changes in public perception as to the 'authenticity' of 'traditional Aboriginal practices' by those Indigenous residents of settled areas. As Spencer's and Gillen's newspaper reports of their 1901 expedition to Central Australia confirmed, the 'true' corroboree lay beyond the northern frontier, where 'authentic' Aborigines could still be found (Register 5 July 1901; Advertiser 29 May 1901). In the meantime, in the southern settled areas, Aboriginal corroboree performers in the late nineteenth and early twentieth centuries were to occupy the theatrical domain equivalent to their increasingly marginalised social position. In settlement areas where Indigenous groups could hope to occupy only proletarian roles, corroboree performances were relegated to proletarian forms of theatre.

For Indigenous settler-corroboree performers, there were advantages in representing themselves using the new modalities of English music hall, American vaudeville and blackface minstrel entertainment. Like many settler-corroboree performances, both vaudeville and the exceedingly popular blackface minstrel shows of the second half of the nineteenth century included short recital pieces, non-sense songs, mimed scenes, short plays, and displays of agility, such as feats of dancing, juggling, contortion, and acrobatics. Moreover, the corroboree easily shared in the ethos of the minstrel show, which emphasised 'defying and mocking authority' and 'making fun of the rich and prominent' through skits and lampoons. Minstrelsy's morphology was also echoed by the temperance movement entertainments. Mission-dwelling Aborigines found that traditional forms of corroboree entertainment could be absorbed and reinvented in Blue Ribbon Army or Band of Hope performances. Short plays and sketches and recitals were also readily adopted as the format of such temperance entertainments. Thus we have the Mt Barker Courier's description (18 June 1886) of a commercial corroboree performance in 1886 being given by 'Salvation Army natives'.

In 1894 the Point McLeay Mission formed a Glee Club that, in December 1895, performed at the Aborigines Friends Association AGM where it filled the Adelaide Town Hall with record crowds (Jenkin 1979:226).

The Glee Club's popularity led to the Aborigines Friends Association AGMs continuing to be held in the Adelaide Town Hall. In 1898, a massive exhibition of mats and baskets and other local products was added. The sales success of these items led to mat and basket weaving becoming included in the Point McLeay Mission school curriculum in 1904. In 1908, weekly tours began operating to the Mission for summer holidaymakers at Goolwa, the tourists being treated to singing performances. Some 2000 tourists visited over the summer of 1908-9, and many bought traditional woven articles as souvenirs. In December 1909 there were more fund-raising concert performances at Adelaide, along with speeches by David Unaipon and Philip Rigney, which echoed the prevalent fashion for minstrelsy entertainment combining sentiment with heartfelt political speeches.

This 'peroration', said the Advertiser, 'fitted the situation, and should have been, if it was not, appreciated by the thoughtful in the audience'. It 'fitted the situation' because through Ruth's performance, it directly linked the 'pathos and sadness of the life of the colored people of another country' to the Indigenous experience.

As a political speech, remonstrating with the audience, it was also fitting in the sense of not being out-of-place in the minstrel format, a socially acceptable format for protesting injustice. In 1910, Point McLeay Mission Aborigines performed at the Tasmanian State Centenary celebrations, at the request of the Tasmanian Government. Claiming all the Tasmanian Indigenous population had been exterminated, the Tasmanian Government asked South Australia to provide an Indigenous group to act as Tasmanians in the pageant's re-enactment of the first landing by Europeans at Hobart. Painted up and dressed in 'possum' skin rugs, the Ngarrindjeri reportedly most vigorously played their part in a sham battle corroboree opposing the planting of the British flag on 'their' soil. They also put on many other performances including boomerang throwing, contrasting them with magnificent choral singing in church services that 'astonished the Tasmanians'.

Perhaps it was the success of their Tasmanian tour that led to Point McLeay Mission's performance of a corroboree at the Commercial Travellers Club Charity Fancy Dress Football Carnival at the Adelaide Oval the following year. By 1911 the public was well aware of the new frontier of the Northern Territory and Spencer's and Gillen's eyewitness press reports on Central Australian corroborees revived public interest in the genre as it was felt a 'proper corroboree' cannot be seen except 'in the faraway haunts of the blacks'.

With 'twenty full-blooded natives' giving 'as perfect a reproduction of their old war dances as the laws of decency and their personal ability permit', the performance was meant to be a reminder of the dangers facing new settlers in the north of the State, but what in South Australia could only be an 'old-time corroboree', a 'novelty which should prove popular' as fancy dress football.

In such ways, marginal, mobile, gypsy forms of theatre were to dominate mainstream, sedentary forms for Indigenous performers for most of the twentieth century. Initially, non-Indigenous audiences saw corroborees as opera or ballet, when the Indigenous 'lords of the soil' were still in possession of their lands. But once displaced to become landless labourers, Indigenous persons were forced to turn to minstrelsy and vaudeville genres to re-frame their public performances. As vaudeville too became sedentary theatre for mainstream audiences, they shifted again to tour country towns at shows and rodeos and in sideshow boxing tents. These shifts acted to reinforce the representation of Indigenous peoples as 'nomads' and 'drifters', feckless wanderers over land, justifying and rationalising dispossession.

By the early twentieth century the corroboree performed in southern settled areas was often of the 'sham battle' kind. The playing out for non-Indigenous audiences of 'native war dances', far removed geographically and historically from the ever-present and real threat on the frontier, of an imagined threat, represented in a safe simulation. The corroboree was an incantation summoning up a lost frontier and its lost community.

On the other side of the frontier at the turn of the century, in Central Australia, in the wake of the Horn expedition and the growth of scientific interest in 'the Aborigine' as a remnant of the Stone Age, the demand for Aboriginal performance became subordinate to the rush to collect Aboriginal objects. These were mainly carved stone or wooden tjurungas, called 'corroboree stones', for sale to southern collectors and museum collections.

This interest saw a shift in South Australia, amongst those with a scientific or intellectual interest in Indigenous cultures, from experiencing intangible culture, such as corroborees, as collectable, to the construction of a collection of tangible objects, 'corroboree stones'. This shift created a secondary market, whereby tangible culture could be purchased or stolen by non-Indigenous wholesalers on the frontier for on-sale to non-Indigenous retailers and other buyers such as museums. Even on the frontier, however, at the level of the wholesaler, such as the prospector R.T. Maurice whose chief interest was to beat his rival Gillen to the best specimens, the corroboree became a means of adding value to corroboree stones by according meaning to them.

But an 'eyewitness account' in this context was insufficient, a 'mere travellers tale'. Given the cutthroat market-place of tjurunga-collecting, proof was required. Photography provided the process of assaying the intangible cultural interpretation of tangible objects. The by-product of the assay, the photograph, as an object to interpret an object, itself became saleable. Indigenous peoples in Central Australia quickly adapted to this new market. As early as 1895, Gillen wrote to Spencer that a 'deputation of greasy Udnaorigurta' Aborigines had approached him with the offer 'that they are prepared to allow me to photograph a corroboree this afternoon in return for a blowout of flour, tea and sugar'. 'Corroboree stone' collecting was sometimes accompanied by forced disclosure by Aboriginal informants. This led to Aboriginal reprisals against those disclosing. For example, the Horn Expedition's Aboriginal guide, Racehorse, forced to reveal the location of Luritja 'corroboree stones', was later executed by irate traditional owners. As Mulvaney (1989:139) commented, it was ironic 'that those in positions of authority who attempted to administer Indigenous affairs with a rough sense of justice, undermined the authority of clan elders and the fabric of Aboriginal society'.

The pilfering of these objects, which played a vital role in the ritual transmission of knowledge, inspired the 'collection' of 'every one he could locate' in the region by M.C. Cowle on behalf of the Sub-Protector of Aborigines, Frank Gillen. While, in 1927, Spencer stated 'It is regrettable that the true nature of the objects thus hidden away in a cave was not known at that time ... The loss of Churinga is the most significant evil that could befall any local group', no effort had been made to restore possession since 1897 when Gillen had confessed to him that 'there must be no more ertatulnga robberies. I bitterly regret ever having countenanced such a thing'. But while he had told Cowle to return some of them, Cowle continued to collect for Spencer's museum, sometimes through the interrogation of prisoners and the use of prison labour.

Winnecke and Stirling used the corroboree precedent to rationalise the theft, stating that they had 'left a number of tomahawks, large knives and other things in their place, sufficient commercially to make the transaction an equitable exchange'. Thus as scientific interest shifted from embodied cultural capital to objectified cultural capital, from person to product, a 'commercial' reckoning of the barter 'transaction' was readily imputed. In contrast, Indigenous groups mourned the loss of these objects as they did their relatives; a reckoning of product as person.

While the institutional, scientific and Governmental focus on collection of cultural materials was to be reflected by the tourism trade in souvenir boomerangs, coolamons, woomeras, spears, didjerdu and other carvings, it meant an opting out of the market for intangible cultural goods, such as the corroboree, which continued more firmly in the tourist domain. For hosts, this domain was relatively benign, affording an easier regulation over degrees of cultural disclosure.

Thus, even on the frontier, with its lack of a sizeable paying audience, by the end of the nineteenth century the word 'corroboree' became in equal parts guest convention and host invention. The true 'corroboree' was one Aboriginal people performed for visitors for a commercial consideration, as against the ceremonial and ritual dances they performed only for themselves. But as has been seen in Arrernte ltata songs, the latter could easily inform the former. That the former distinction was readily apparent by 1886, but the latter distinction not yet perceived, can be seen in the contribution by the South Australia Museum Director, E.C. Stirling, to the Report on the Work of the Horn Scientific Expedition to Central Australia.

In tourism terms, the response of Stirling, as an adventure traveller far 'off the beaten track', is understandable. Made aware that there are performances that outsiders, like him, may witness, and other 'secret' 'mysterious' performances that are kept hidden from outsiders, 'even Mr. Gillen', Stirling ranks the former as 'inferior'. But, as he finds himself only able to witness such performances, he goes on to reassure his readers that 'lest the statement of the inferior significance of these corroborees should unduly minimise their importance, that even these are very elaborate performances'.

Stirling's differentiation and his response to it encapsulated the in-built self-contradictions of antitourism in its urge to get off the beaten track in quest for an unattainable ideal. What is most superior to see is that which is prohibited from being seen. In the 'high degree of intimacy' situation, however, with its invitation to 'come share our culture', there is a certain, if uneven, guest expectation, that one is to be treated as an insider. Thus the difficulty occurs when hosts disclose or have disclosed to guests that what the latter are seeing is a partial disclosure, the one open to 'outsiders'.

The tantalising offer of 'forbidden fruit' may be a part of the chemistry of such interactions, but the revelation of exclusion accentuates the divide between host and guest and counters the sense of being hosted. Being kept outside the ring of those with inside knowledge, counters the 'authenticity' afforded by being on the other side of the frontier, and inside a guest-recognised Indigenous domain.

There is also the undercutting of the equilibrium of the capital exchange by the disclosure of non-disclosure. Stirling, for example, does not highlight but neither does he hide the fact that in performing for 'a few sticks of tobacco' or, as they did at Alice Springs, 'on promise of suitable reward', what his hosts were doing was to put on a show for visitors for a fee. But for Stirling the satisfaction of seeing 'a great show' performed in a dominantly Indigenous domain, offset the pangs of inauthenticity afforded by it being a staged paid performance.

Thus 'balletic' perceptions of corroborees by non-Indigenous observers remained active within the Indigenous domain, although they had long left the non-Indigenous 'settled' domain. In the late nineteenth and early twentieth century in settled Australia, dispossession, removal, denial of employment and self-employment through social control policies of government and mission agencies denied any possibility of independent Indigenous performers pursuing the mainstream theatrical stage.

The closure of options, acted to funnel and shunt Indigenous theatre into what was literally a sideshow tradition. Indigenous football and cricket players cum athletes cum corroboree performers found their niche in the rural fair, sporting or ploughing festival sideshows. Some Aborigines pursued acrobatic careers in roving vaudeville or burlesque bush shows. Some became famous as stars of touring colonial circuses, such as Ashton's trick rider, Mongo Mongo, and Combo Combo, the contortionist.

By the early twentieth century, stationary forms could be found in the Government settlement and Mission Station corroboree performances given to tourists. But the mobile forms—the circuses, tent troupes, wandering minstrel bands and travelling shows—provided an alternative forum of respectability, a locus of identity and, framed by exotic company, a measure of authenticity that was being denied to them by the advancing frontier. Indigenous performers were to affiliate socially and in some cases formally join such groups. This affiliation was to challenge, albeit not always successfully, the placing of a boundary around Indigenous and non-Indigenous geographical and social space.

Historically, the tourism industry, in its quest for experiencing the Other, has always encouraged an articulation of peoples with place, reinforced through destination marketing. This dove-tailed with the long European tradition that had it that, if inhabited, the most extreme places were occupied by the most extreme of peoples. The outlands were the home of the outlandish; the wilderness, the habitat of wild peoples. The inverse was seen to be equally true, with a place mirroring the perceived primitiveness of its inhabitants.

Thus for non-Indigenous settlers in early twentieth century Australia, the 'authentic Aborigine' was seen as one living beyond the frontier, not in the 'civilised' settled coastal regions. Consequently, the articulation of Indigenous peoples with wildness and wilderness in the non-Indigenous conception has left Indigenous peoples in more urbanised areas with the onus of proving their own authenticity, or being encouraged by the tourism market to emulate the accepted authenticity of 'The Outback Aboriginal'.

There has been an increasing recourse to using conservation areas to provide a link to the wildness and wilderness that has been lost or subsumed. For Indigenous communities seeking to demonstrate, gain or reinforce rights to their traditional lands, cultural tourism continues to combine the satisfying vision of economic self-reliance with a much deeper need. Cultural tourism has become a currency for Indigenous peoples to realise their land needs and to re-connect with their cultural heritage. Indigenous cultural tourism continues to express for both host and guest, in different ways, belonging to the land, and the longing to belong.

Rural mythology has historically provided an important focus for cultural explanations of Australian national identity. Since the early 1960s, however, rural myths-especially those represented through the Australian Legend-have been subjected to searching critiques from different positions within and outside the academy. Research using theoretical models interested in the politics of identity exposed the racial and gender bias of the rural legends associated with key Australian writers from the 1890s, in particular. At the same time, the apparent adoption of a form of identity politics in government policies related to migrants and the Indigenous community, along with a simultaneous enthusiasm across the political spectrum for privatisation, deregulation, and globalisation, enabled a populist identification of the academic and intellectual class promoting these critiques with politicians, their policy advisers, and the forces of global capital.

Commentators in the metropolitan press and the academy have tended to argue that the new 'racist' and anti-intellectual political force mobilised by Pauline Hanson's One Nation phenomenon represented an outdated Anglo-Celtic conservatism, which could be sourced to provincial cultures and their affinities with the Australian Legend. Paul Kelly has characterised Hansonism as 'an echo of our Anglo-Celtic origins; the claims of the once mighty bush to define the Australian Legend; a descendant of the romanticism and racism of Henry Lawson whose hold on national identity was once so comprehensive ... the latest manifestation of our reflex to distrust authority, abuse our elites and damn our leaders'.

Phillip Adams called it a 'mess movement of bigotries, disappointments, indignations, resentments, neo-fascism, old fascism, Christian fundamentalism, conspiracy theories, hopelessness, hysteria and good old-fashioned belly-aching'. Adams's essay is rhetorically interesting because it uses the metaphor of a shopping-bag lady to ridicule Hanson and her supporters and, while the caricature is entertaining, it also suggests both an intellectual and a class-based contempt for 'ordinary Australians' which analyses of opinion polls, and the One Nation party itself, found were part of the problem that Pauline Hanson and her followers were addressing.

The academic response to One Nation and its claims upon the authentic traditions of the Australian Legend has sometimes taken a similar path to the metropolitan press by setting up an ethical opposition between Anglo-Celtic culture, and Aboriginal or multicultural Australia. The unfashionable identification of Anglo-Celtic Australia with an Australian Legend tarnished by the critiques of the last forty years has been played out at the level of discursive style where style, as it is in Adams, is a display of a linguistic competency that guarantees the subject's implicit claim to the forms of distinction required to participate as an intellectual in the public sphere.

Richard Nile's Introduction to The Australian Legend and Its Discontents, for example, deploys 'Henry Lawson' as a trope for a particular version of the Australian Legend, critiqued as a set of images that helped to licence a narrow and outdated version of Australianness. Nile's essay, 'Tell Them that Henry Lawson is Dead', includes subheadings such as 'He Died Without a Bottle of Beer in His Hand' and 'There's Something About Henry', and thus works rhetorically and logically to dismiss Lawson's contemporary value.

Lawson seems particularly unfashionable now, but it needs to be recognised that arguments against him have received regular airings from left-wing nationalists and their opponents since Lawson's earliest reception in the 1890s. The need to discredit Lawson through exposes that take the form of biographical anecdote or rum quotation has long been a symptom of the threat that his reputation has posed to preferred versions of Australianness.

The longevity of the Lawson Legend can, in some ways, be explained by the persistence of historical attempts to incorporate, or to erase, his potential for dissidence. The establishment's early assessment of the need for such incorporation recognised the political significance of the popular purchase of his reputation. A significant omission in more recent academic critiques of both the Lawson and the Australian legends has been an investigation of the detailed contexts of this popular reception.

Lawson's place in the Australian social imaginary has never had much to do with a consistent logic within his oeuvre, or the biographical and historical facts obscured by his myth, and his symbolic significance in this country is never going to be settled by a set of simplistic assertions. As Ghassan Hage points out, academic arguments lack the power to decide questions of social identity, because identity is the fantastic product of symbolic powers. The stature of Henry Lawson in the cultural history of Australia is due to the historical utility of his reputation for licensing different forms of social identity.

Hage's analysis of the causes behind the feelings of disempowerment that have helped generate the new racism suggests that it has much to do with a shift in the forms of cultural capital required to claim a governmental authority over the national space. His work is useful for my purposes because it understands the new racism as a spatial crisis related to the symbolic operation of social identity.

Those critics who have sought to silence the racism that has sprung from this sense of disempowerment by seeking to ridicule their reliance upon a cultural heritage insufficiently useful for a (post)modern, cosmopolitan and multicultural country take a position in the debate that simply exacerbates the situation. The Lawson legend remains an important part of the national imaginary for some Anglo-Celtic sections of the Australian population who are denied the economic, cultural or political capital required to manage the pace of change in recent Australian society.

LOCAL CLAIMS ON AN AUSTRALIAN LEGEND

This region represents a suggestive sample of the contemporary popular use of Lawson's reputation and the rural mythologies that might be articulated with it for a number of reasons. This is where Henry Lawson spent his childhood, and the area provided the identifiable locations for many of his earlier works.

Mudgee is a regional town supported by a number of industries including wine, sheep and cattle grazing, fruit and vegetable growing, and tourism. It lies within the federal electorate of Gwydir, the seat of the National Party leader and Deputy Prime Minister John Anderson, where One Nation received 21per cent of the primary vote in the 1996 Federal election.

Local history in this region has often taken the form of a memorial to the famous writer. More recently, however, it has developed into a programme for the recovery of local memory and a related affirmation of a sense of community identity. These regional values sometimes run counter to the prevailing moods and intentions of the public memories of the nation, and the heritage tourism profile of the area consequently represents a process of negotiation between quite different constituencies—a theme that has been at the centre of much of the recent sociological work on globalisation and localisation.

The connections of the past of this region with a nationally-recognised rural mythology are put to a variety of uses by the local community. While there remains, here, much that I would still wish to critique, there is enough social value on show to suggest that some caution is needed before rural heritage in general, and its long suffering apostle Henry Lawson, in particular, are dismissed.

A celebrated pioneering history plays an important part in the commemorative activities of the area in which the famous writer was raised. The 'Roaring Days' of the great gold rushes represent one of the most significant in the national account of European settlement. During the 1870s and 1880s, the tailend of this significant historical period combined with the picturesque qualities of a specific local geography to inspire an exemplary son of the region. Henry Lawson and his work are both productive of, and the products of, a place, and these valued cultural relations provide that place with important associations. During this century, English-speaking cultures have made a habit of preserving regions as the immortalisation of their famous writers: Stratford has its Shakespeare, the English Lakes have their Romantic poets, and the United States's New England has its Thoreau. It is in this tradition that Eurunderee, the area of Lawson's youth and the subject of his work, has been remade as one of Australia's settler sites.

Lawson's habit of drawing upon the topography and social history of his youth in the Mudgee area has provided the region with rich cultural-historical associations. These associations allowed this space to achieve a particular place in debates over the status of the national culture in the period between the wars. After Lawson's death, the Lawson Societies, the Fellowship of Australian Writers (FAW), public intellectuals, and left-wing political interests were involved in campaigns to consecrate 'The Lawson country'.

The Lawson societies, the FAW, and public intellectuals such as Vance and Nettie Palmer, were motivated by a perceived need to respond to public and professional perceptions that Australia lacked the historical traditions required to sustain a sophisticated national culture. The promotional impetus provided by Lawson's State Funeral, the Domain Memorial Campaign, and his still significant public popularity, made him an ideal figure upon which to base a case for the national culture, and when the cultural nationalists' cause involved the national poet, they were able to secure aid from left-wing political figures for whom Lawson remained a useful political weapon.

Until recently, co-operation with initiatives from Sydney represented the characteristic mechanism of the Mudgee region's involvement in the preservation of its Lawson associations. In fact, the need to recognise a local connection with the celebrity of Lawson initially stemmed from a sense of shame caused by mistaken admiration from the metropolitan press. In 1921, when Mudgee opened Lawson Park as a memorial to William Lawson (no relation), the first European to stumble across and claim the land of the Wiradjuri people, it was incorrectly seen by some as a progressive recognition of Henry Lawson.

The local paper is quick to point out that it was fit and proper to recognise a dead explorer-settler before a living poet. The 'relative unimportance' of letters when compared to the 'finding and development and settlement of the Mudgee lands', and the 'gold ... sheep ... grain ... and the fortunes that have been made', meant that the Mudgee Guardian could safely reassure its readers that 'nothing so ambitious as an obelisk or a statue' need be contemplated. Not, at least, until the poet was actually dead.

THE SOCIAL PURCHASE OF LOCAL HISTORY

Some sixty years later another generation of Mudgee residents appeared to register the reluctance of the local establishment to recognise a poet while wine and honey were bringing in the money that really counted. Norman McVicker, Brendan Dunne, Betty McLean, Peter Mansfield and Carl Werchon formed the Eurunderee Provisional School Foundation, Inc. in 1989 to restore the small timber school that now occupied the site of the famous Old Bark School in which Lawson had been educated in the 1870s, as a memorial to the famous writer and the local community in which he was raised.

'Much of his best works were related to here', McVicker told the local press, 'and we ... wanted to save that'. The restoration was staged and conducted as a significant community event, and it used volunteer labour and local donations of money and of material and historical artefacts. In this way the one-room school was restored to its 'original' Federation colours, and an interior display established to represent the three important periods in its history: 1876, 1900 and 1970.

Although the building housed school memorabilia, McVicker was keen to distinguish it from a museum. It was to be a place that would permit the school children of today to 'imagine' themselves in the different historical periods that have formed the district, and the generations that have constituted its communities.

'Henry Lawson' is concerned to name the local pioneering families and catalogue their occupations, and this is a characteristic emphasis of the Foundation's commemorative activities. Lawson is valuable because of his national celebrity, and the potential tourist dollars associated with his fame, but he is also valuable as a repository of the area's forgotten social history. Fame can provide a powerful stimulus for local memories.

Celebrity gives quotidian things an enhanced significance, and often leads to the recollection of events more usually considered forgettable. Lawson's careful preservation by metropolitan, regional, and a number of interconnected familial cultures can thus be used by the locality to recover its own lost references. Through Lawson, Eurunderee might recover an authoritatively local sense of its past. Commemoration is, therefore, a familiar affirmation of the local settler history of pioneering families, and their establishment of a civil community.

The interest initially generated by the project led to a weekly column by McVicker in the Mudgee Guardian. Entitled 'Tales From the Wallaby Track ... In Search of Henry Lawson's Eurunderee', the column regularly reported the progress of the Foundation's restoration of the school complex and its rediscovery of the social history of the area. Writing in the column in November of the inaugural year, McVicker summarises the interests of the Foundation and its community activities: 'Our entire field of endeavour has been to establish and document the facts about Henry Lawson's Eurunderee years, the inter-relationship of the pioneer families and their association with Eurunderee as Lawson knew it and wrote about it'.

This mission is often interpreted as a monument to Lawson, within whose work Eurunderee is itself commemorated for posterity: 'Eurunderee is full of Lawson associations, its reality reinforced by the stories and poems which he wrote about the little world he knew. "Eurunderee", itself is his "Memorial". When our identifying signs are in place, Eurunderee will finally be recognised as "The Real Henry Lawson Country"'.

This shift in emphasis from Lawson to Eurunderee is a feature of the local initiative: Lawson and his work are memorials for Eurunderee. Remembering Henry Lawson thus adopts the form of the historical recovery of a local community history, and 'The Wallaby Track' accordingly thanked local residents and widely-dispersed expatriates for their regular donations of authentic artefacts, which had been safely preserved through the generations of a family.

Newer residents were also able to write themselves into the history of the area through their support for the Foundation and their respect for the community value of their places. One of the more interesting features of this recovery is a welcome sense of the multicultural character of original settlement, although it needs to be said that that character remains European, and hence fails to upset the articulation of local heritage with whiteness and its custodial role over the spatial imaginary. The Eurunderee Provisional School Foundation, Inc. and the weekly 'Wallaby Track' column together orchestrated an ongoing community interest and initiative in the recovery of the forgotten stories of its past. They provided an occasion for remembering, and a safe haven for artefacts, records, and oral memory. Often the Foundation republished well-known texts, which it then recontextualised as the signs of the significant locale now safely in its keeping. Lawson's poems 'The Roaring Days', 'The Lights of the Cobb and Co' and 'Eurunderee', together with the story 'The Loaded Dog' were represented in a tourist pamphlet as markers of the area.

The national celebrity of Henry Lawson and his associated geographies are thus represented in local terms, according to local interests. In this way the citizenry of the region can acquire a particular type of local authority, which well arms them for any disagreements with the metropolitan expertise of professional historians and educators. When a staff writer for the Sydney Morning Herald chided the people of Mudgee for their belated recognition of Lawson, he drew a non-committal response. When the writer accused them of attempting to 'sanitise his life story', however, he was promptly rebuked. 'We are proud of what the Foundation has achieved' wrote McVicker, 'we have documented and recorded only facts'.

An important part of his defence was the restatement of the Foundation's purely local interest. Other agents have concerned themselves with Lawson's later life, whereas the 'entire field of endeavour' of the Foundation has been to 'establish and document the facts about Henry Lawson's Eurunderee years, the inter-relationship of the pioneer families and their association with Eurunderee as Lawson knew it and wrote about it.

Nothing more-nothing less'. Reporting on the Henry and Louisa Lawson conference, which was held in 1991 at the Prince of Wales Opera House in Gulgong under the auspices of the Centre for Australian Language and Literature Studies at the University of New England, McVicker was again concerned to position local authority in relation to professional disciplines.

'Some of the subject matter was, to the layman, unbelievably esoteric', he wrote. 'I left the conference wondering whether Louisa and Henry would have understood the discussions', he added.

TOURISM AND THE DARK PAST OF THE LOCAL

The Foundation's efforts to recover the social history of the region always stood side by side with an affirmed commercial interest in the tourist potential of this history's more celebrated associations. McVicker, who identified himself as a man who 'for thirty years was closely associated with the [tourism] industry', regularly reported tourist news in 'Tales From the Wallaby Track'. In October 1989, immediately following the restoration of the school, the column reported the opening of the newly signposted 'Wallaby Track' by the Mudgee Shire Tourist Officer.

Two weeks later the success was announced of the first minibus tour of the 'Track' with McVicker as guide. One year later, the columnist described his partipation in many subsequent tours, and the growing interest in 'the childhood days of Henry Lawson and the pioneer doings of the early settlers in Eurunderee'.

The Foundation's proprietary interest in the tourist value of Mudgee's Lawson associations is partly driven by the need to convince local authorities of its potential, and partly by the need to secure the identification of the Foundation with its inevitable success. It implicitly recognises that schemes for the generation of social capital need to connect with an economic bottom line if they are to secure material resources. The surprising need to establish the potential of history is due to the area's already affirmed tourist identity as the Land of Wine and Honey—an identity that potentially restricts the flow of resources to the campaign to identify the local geography as Lawson country.

This is not a case of a depressed rural town desperately turning to cultural tourism for salvation. The success of Mudgee as a wine area, and of its particularly wide range of rural industries, has drawn increasing tourism and significant development in the town. Therefore this drive to re-establish Lawson as a complementary tourist property expresses the anxieties of certain sections of the community about the overly commercial ways in which tourism was representing the area.

The success of the campaign for recognition confirms the Foundation's worth to the regional economy, and legitimises the cultural arguments it has used to justify its wide range of initiatives. The subsequent success of these representations has, in turn, provided social, political, and economic capital for the restoration of artefacts, and the recovery of the local memories through which they might productively be re-associated.

The limited multiculturalism of Eurunderee's late nineteenth-century social history is enabled through those forms of pioneering mythology that have been widely criticised as claims to a place that erase Indigenous peoples. While it may have been possible to erase Indigenous presence without fear of contradiction in times past, however, the ethical purchase of Indigenous issues make such practices increasingly dubious-particularly in those cases where the local is forced to cater to the global, in the interests of generating revenue from tourism.

Tourist trading of the local inevitably entails its representation for the cosmopolitan tastes and expectations of the traveller, and this means that it has to register their expectations. Therefore, when McVicker organised a tour of the Wallaby Track for a group of Country Press Association members and their wives, he was quickly confronted with the absence of Indigenous reference in the Foundation's tourist narrative. The Press Association members' recognition of the priority of Indigenous possession and their associated curiosity about the Aborigines' associations of the area contradicts the settler claims of discovery and originality that so often feature in pioneering festivals, and McVicker moved quickly to produce a special issue of 'Tales From Along the Wallaby Track' on the Wiradjuri people. The Foundation's pamphlet, 'The Wiradjuri Story: Aborigines of Henry Lawson Country', represents a particularly interesting representation of black history.

In some ways it might be described in the (pejorative) words of Geoffrey Blainey, as a 'black armband' view of Indigenous history. The early settlers' violent dispossession of a 'healthy, moral' Indigenous community, which was living in spiritual harmony with a Land they understood, is seen as indefensible. The affirmed ethical character of the Wiradjuri is considered a function of their sophisticated association with the local place, and the Foundation's own search for local origins can thus be represented as the expression of comparable ethical substance.

Tony Bennett has argued that Aboriginal sites and artefacts have been officially appropriated so that the national time might be extended into a deeper and hence more legitimate past. The Foundation's pamphlet can certainly be seen as an attempt to consolidate the local 'settler' claim to place by appropriating the legitimacy of the indigene, and it needs to be said that for all its good intentions, the Foundation fails to connect the Indigenous history with the claims of a contemporary Indigenous population.

Ultimately, the booklet reverts to Prime Minister John Howard's tactic of consigning settler atrocities and their undeserving victims to the past: 'Their lands, their kinsmen and their lifestyle had been ruthlessly destroyed by greed. In the wake of despair came the diseases of the white man, alcohol-and finally death.

By 1850 the Wiradjuri had been completely dispossessed and were virtually extinct'. The discourse of nostalgic lament has been a feature of the liberal response to Indigenous genocide since the nineteenth century, and the Eurunderee Provisional Foundation's representation of the local Indigenous claims to place ultimately remain conservative. Nevertheless, they stop a fair way short of the forms of red-necked regional racism that we saw associated with Hansonism's Anglo-Celtic Conservatism.

We are no longer living in the nineteenth century, and Indigenous claims are now regularly represented in the mainstream media as a part of an ongoing active political struggle. The Foundation's acknowledgment of the ethically desirable local associations of the Wiradjuri is there to be claimed by interested political agents. The potential for the reconciliation process of the conjunction of interest in erased Indigenous places and lost settler associations has been a theme of recent work by Australian historians such as Peter Read. The widespread experience of lost place which characterises immigrant cultures is a resource which might more productively be used in this way.

Heather Goodall's work on rural community history reveals some willingness by pastoralists to reconnect their history with those of Indigenous Australians in a self-interested effort to enable their own ongoing struggles with rival industries and environmental disasters. The need for local Mudgee interests to cater for a cosmopolitan taste in order to confirm the tourist value of their heritage paves the way for a similar recognition of native association. The articulation of the Indigenous past with the local project of reclaiming the lost settler history also associates the Foundation's activities with the moral legitimacy of the increasingly powerful metropolitan narrative of Indigenous dispossession. This is important, for in the sphere of tourism at least, the boot is on another foot, and the regional settler identities that have so often erased native association are now themselves being consigned to the cosmopolitan nation's colourful past.

Nevertheless, the tourist's interest in the Wiradjuri is not reported in 'The Wallaby Track' column because it is thought to disable the local claim to originality. It is used to confirm the importance of the Foundation's search after local truths. This is why McVicker is careful to point out that the trip was not a 'junket', but a genuine expression of interest in authentic local origins.

The need to make this argument is of course an expression of anxiety. The tourist presentation of the local social history is inevitably directed towards its involvement in the originating moment of the national literary heritage, and the mention of this origin is primary. The authentic origin of a national celebrity is the grand narrative, and it is only through the articulation of the local with such a narrative that local social memory is capitalised for the tourists.

THE COUNTRY AS ANOTHER TIME

In discussing the tourist promotion of the historical Rocks redevelopment in Sydney, Bennett argues that the area has been transformed into a 'centre of origins in the sense of being not merely the first area of settlement but one which contains the seeds of future and broader developments'. The transformation of the Rocks adopts the rhetorical forms of 'consensus nationalism which, in overlaying the various objects and buildings encountered, enables them to function as origins of the subsequent unfolding of the nation's history told as the gradual rise of a free, democratic, multicultural citizenry'.

If there is a comparable rhetoric for the transformation of the Eurunderee area into the Lawson country, it is the liberal pioneering myth. The Foundation gives little emphasis to the class struggle that was expressed through the battles over the Land Acts throughout the late nineteenth century, and the pioneering myth tends to work in conjunction with the conservative nationalist version of Australian literary culture to redeploy the political struggles of the settlers as a more familiar contest with isolation and environment.

The densities of local memories and their multiple authorial locations partially protect the local from the loaded forms of erasure practised by the official institutions of public culture, but the local is not immune from the flattering imaginings of a pioneering legend and its idealisation of quotidian struggles. The use of Lawson to get at local memories is reversed for tourists, who are presented with local memories as signs of the national celebrity. This reversal can shed the complicated idiosyncrasies of the local account, and allow the easy consumption of the region.

As recent studies of tourism and globalisation have shown, local significance can seldom function for the tourist in the ways that it might for the local citizenry. To make a tourist commodity out of a local past requires the adoption of the rhetorical tropes of the national heritage and these tropes, as Bennett describes them, are there to be found in both the literature of the local Tourist Information Centre, and the Foundation's packaging of local memories for tourist consumption.

In the discourses of tourist promotion that address the cosmopolitan consumer, the country becomes a pastoral form of the past that functions as a refuge from what Les Murray would call 'this metropolitan century'. As Bennett puts it, 'The more the structure of the past is subject to the exigencies of tourism, the greater the likelihood that it will focus on the country rather than the city, and on the nineteenth rather than the twentieth century. It will, as a consequence tend to offer the great majority of Australians an imaginative diversion from their present conditions of existence rather than affording a familiarity with the more immediate histories from which those conditions effectively flow'. Those local social memories would be appropriated through their articulation with the public memory and the marketing rhetoric of the tourism industry was rendered inevitable by the Foundation's need to find a place for their Lawson narrative within the region's already established tourism strategies.

The predominant tourist identity of the Mudgee area was, and largely still is, drawn from the region's distinctive rural industries: as noted, Mudgee is the 'Land of Wine and Honey'. Ruth Barcan has pointed out the way in which 'big things' (for example, the big cow, the big banana) 'create some regional identities at the cost of others, since tourist identities work best when they are distinct, relatively singular and easily reproducible visually'. Thus 'Difference gets subsumed under the marketing logic of brand recognition'.

It is easy to discern a note of self-justification in McVicker's celebration of the tourist triumphs of the 'Wallaby Track' and the Eurunderee Provisional School, which is perhaps directed towards local reluctance to accept that the land of wine and honey might at the same time be Henry Lawson Country.

Parochial rivalries and local tensions aside, the importance of a discourse of time and place to the marketing strategies of the wine industry meant that Henry Lawson was always going to be easily accommodated by the vignerons. It is the spirit of the place that was the genius of Lawson's art, and that same spirit of place is now creating the award-winning tastes of Montrose Wines' Poet's Corner. Wine is not a drink, it is a culture, and this culture needs to be distinguished by a geography that is rich in natural and historical associations.

The fusion of nature and culture provides a wine with a style, which it offers in the form of a taste. Style is the enabling trope of the publicity narratives of wine, because it represents a superior way of life. The national historical and cultural associations of the Mudgee area therefore provide Mudgee wine with the deep time and the rich place of a distinguished reputation. To buy and taste the wine of Poet's Corner is therefore a form of communion with a historically significant place.

Montrose wine has Mudgee and Henry Lawson in a bottle, and both the local mythologies and the national heritage are in this way transformed into a commodity for consumption and exchange.

Tourist maps of the district's wineries are thus inscribed upon the historical map of Lawson Country, and the tourist cannot only travel, survey, imagine, feel, and experience the national heritage, they can taste it as well. It is therefore no surprise that the local wine industry has come to the Henry Lawson party as a prominent sponsor of the historical and cultural activities of the Eurunderee Provisional School Foundation and the Henry Lawson Society of NSW, which is based in the nearby town of Gulgong.

Montrose Wine's publicity narrative was printed on the back page of the entry form for the annual Henry Lawson Society of New South Wales/Montrose Wines Poet's Corner's Award for the best poem based upon a contemporary Australian subject or theme. The judging and the exhibition of entries was held at the Montrose Winery during the 1994 Mudgee Wine Festival in September of that year.

This complementary relation between wine and culture is one that the 'Tales From the Wallaby Track' column comes increasingly to encourage, as history is gradually admitted to the tourist profile of the region. The role played by mythological figures such as Henry Lawson and pioneering myths similar to the Australian Legend in the constitution of contemporary Australian identities have much more to do with the strategic conditions in which local spaces encounter the cosmopolitan cultures of postmodernity than with privileged professional readings of the discursive detail of particular textual estates.

It is the strategic detail of these local contests that we are going to have to deal with if we are to follow David Carter's call to find 'new ways to make pluralism as popular as populism', and this study suggests that we are going to be much more successful at this if we find a way of engaging with a cultural heritage that provides a proportion of our citizenry with the symbolic capital required to feel a part of the nation. There is a disturbing similarity between the ways in which the local volunteer society consigned the native claim to place to a regrettable past, and the manner in which cosmopolitan Australia represents the times and places of its regional and rural cultures.

Questions of race, place and identity are always a question of capital, and if we are going to alleviate the racial tensions in this country, then we are going to have to find an innovative and productive way of capitalising the diverse forms of identity now party to the Australian social contract. For a politically significant number of Australians, that is going to mean a dynamic, creative and more specific critical engagement with rural mythology, the Australian Legend-and maybe even poor old Henry Lawson.

7

The Tourist Industry

Tourism is defined as the act of travel with the intentions of recreational pleasure. The World Tourism Organization defines a tourist is someone who travels at least 50 miles or 80 kilometers away from their home, for the purpose of entertainment and pleasure.

There are a variety of ways that a traveller can get to their intended destinations. Shorter distances may be reached by automobile or bus, where longer distances can be reaches by airplane, train or boat. A newer form of travel that has recently become available involves having *outer space* as an option. From a tourism viewpoint, the division of the world into tourist-generating and tourist-receiving countries is not as sharp as one might imagine.

Tourism is a give and take traffic, which presupposes an exchange of tourism arrivals between countries although to varying extents. Nevertheless, economic realities show that the industrial states with the highest standard of living (mostly Western) are the main tourist generators in the world. Statistics show that 75per cent of the world tourism traffic is generated by twelve Western countries only, which get at the same time about 84per cent of the international tourism movement. Developing countries in Africa, the Middle East, Asia and Latin America get about 7per cent, if we leave room for countries in-between like Japan, Australia and those of Eastern Europe.

India is a country having a great potential of tourism during vacation in the country. Tourism in the country has received a major boost in the past decade. There are lots of options in the country appealing tourists from world over. The country has right potential of tourism and attractions to captivate all kinds of tourists even the most negative tourist.

Adventure tours, cultural expeditions, wildlife expedition, beach tourism, pilgrimage tours, heritage tourism, medical tourism, monsoon tourism, rural tourism, etc are prime elements of tourism in India that enthralls a great influx of tourists from all over the world. Traveling in different parts, states and cities of India gives tourists cultural and geographical richness of the country.

Geographically, the country of India has been divided in the four parts – North India, East India, West India and South India. And part is known for own charm of culture and rich tourism potential. The country of India has 28 states and 7 union territories. Each state of India has its own charm and fascination and gives tourists something new and something extra. Rajasthan, Jammu and Kashmir, Uttar Pradesh, Uttarakhand, Himachal Pradesh, Goa, Maharashtra, Kerala, Tamil Nadu, Andhra Pradesh, are some of states of India known for their rich tourism potential.

These popular states of India offer tourists real charm of India tourism combing together culture and heritage tourism, adventure tourism, hill station tourism, beach tourism, rural tourism, monsoon tourism and medical tourism.

If you are interested in heritage of India you, travelling through Indian states like Rajasthan, Uttar Pradesh, Maharashtra, Andhra Pradesh, Kerala, etc can be exciting experience.

If you are interest in wildlife tourism exploring wildlife destination like Ranthambhore, Sariska, Gir Forest, Corbett, Bharatpur, Kanha, Pench, Panna, Bandhavgarh and Periyar can be thrilling experience you will love to cherish whole life long.

If you are interested hill tourism, nature tourism or adventure tourism then go to states like Assam, Sikkim, Himachal Pradesh, Jammu and Kashmir, etc; you will have truly a memorable experience of Inde tourisme. If you are beach lovers then Goa and Kerala have some finest beaches in the world where you can make your vacation in a cheerful way enjoying awesome beach tourism and fun activities.

If you want to take a deep insight of rich culture and great Indian hospitality you should visit Rajasthan – the royal state of Rajasthan and Delhi with the capital city New Delhi. Rajasthan is widely known for it rich culture, great hospitality and glorious past. Delhi has some of magnificent monuments like Red Fort, Jama Masjid. Taj Mahal in Agra is not to be missed attraction of Inde voyage.

Varanasi, Pushkar, Ajmer, Amritsar, Vaishno Devi, Tirupati, Shirdi, Khajuraho, Deoghar, Rajgir, Bodhgaya, Konark, etc are popular destinations known for their religious significance. Kerala, Goa, and Uttarakhand have some of world class ayurvedic and spa resorts offering excellent accommodation and ayurvedic and spa experience as well with modern amenities.

The royal state of Rajasthan has some of world famous heritage hotels where tourists find ethnic and age old ambiance with modern amenities. In general, India is a perfect destination for perfect vacation with right tourism potential. And tourism in India during India vacation never fails to grab the attentions and steal the heart of tourists and vacationers.

TRAVEL ELEMENTS

When traveling, tourists must keep in mind and plan for:

- Accomodation: a place to stay while traveling, whether it is a hotel, motel, apartment, resort, inn, hostel or guest house.
- Foods and beverages.

- Tours: getting to know the surrounding area that has been visited. This can be achieved through a walking tour, bus tour, coach tour, boat tour, even by helicopter.
- Souvenirs: bringing home a memory from the trip, such as a postcard, shot glass, keychain or snow globe.

Other elements of tourism might involve insurance, safety, security, culture, language and currency exchange. Many tourists travel for a number of reasons, including relaxation, escape, adventure, as well as experiencing new and different cultures.

Cultural heritage tourism or heritage tourism is a niche element of the overall tourism spectrum. It is meant to gain an appreciation of the past or something we have got in legacy. It is one of the oldest forms of travel, and involves heritages of all kinds – colonial heritage, urban renewal, religious tourism, genealogy, industrial heritage, and ethnicity. Thus a visit to Cellular Jail in Port Blair, or to Haldighati and Ellora Caves constitute heritage tourism in the Indian context.

Heritage tourism is difficult to segregate from other elements of tourism. Tourists interested in other areas, like adventure, religion and leisure also visit different Indian heritage sites; with monuments like Taj Mahal, Humayun's Tomb, Red Fort, Sarnath, Kaziranja, Tirupati, Varanasi, Rameshwaram, and Ajanta being quite popular. UNESCO has identified 27 heritage sites in

India as world heritage, and has collaborated with state government authorities to develop several themed itineraries, like linking Buddhist holy places, legends of Shiva, yoga, and ayurvedic healing.

More than five million foreigners visited India in 2007, and out of these, at least, three million visited heritage sites in India. Number of domestic tourists outnumbered foreign travelers by more than 60 times in 2007. The share of cultural heritage tourism in the overall tourism figures in India, be it domestic or foreign travelers, is over 60 per cent, according to various estimates.

India needs quite a lot of effort and professional touch to keep its heritage sites intact. While government authorities have been mainly responsible for this, heritage management in India has started seeing the participation of big players like Tata, Oberoi, Indian Oil Corporation, and others, on the lines of European countries and the US. Heritage hotels, another colour in the spectrum of heritage tourism, are quite popular among tourists, with celebrities like Amitabh Bachchhan and Richard Gere also voicing their preference for them. Barring most of major hotel players like Taj, Oberoi, and ITC, there are several heritage hotels owned by the descendants of former rulers and aristocrats.

Not everything is, however, honky dory in the field of heritage tourism. Services at heritage sites are nowhere compared to those at similar sites in countries like Italy, UK, China and Spain. Foreign tourists often feel cheated as they pay several times more entrance fees compared to Indians. They often feel disappointed by the shabby treatment they receive at the hands of the vendors, whose only agenda seems to be to extract the maximum possible money from the tourists. Tourists are also miffed at the lower levels of services offered by several heritage hotels, tour operators, transporters and others.

Be it the exquisite marble inlay work of the Taj Mahal or the titillating sculptures of the Khajuraho temples or the excellent fusion of science and art in Konark Sun Temple, Indian heritage sites manifest their richness everywhere. Taj Mahal, the most popular heritage of India, alone attracts some 2.5 million tourists every year.

According to various estimates, heritage tourism contributes well over 60 per cent to the overall share of tourists in India, both domestic and foreigners. An interesting aspect of this, however, is that almost 80 per cent of foreign tourists visiting India restrict themselves to the Golden Triangle (Delhi-Jaipur-Agra) and Rajasthan, areas quite rich in heritage monuments.

This comes as a surprise considering places like Bihar, Tamil Nadu, Kerala, Andhra Pradesh, Uttar Pradesh, Madhya Pradesh have so many beautiful heritage monuments. This, however, also spells huge untapped opportunities heritage tourism presents. Even if a fraction of the potential of these states is tapped, it can do wonders. Aditya Nath, managing director, Apass India Leisure Solutions, a Delhi-based tour operator, says, "A package for the Golden Triangle can easily be sold.

Everyone wants to make easy money. Convincing tourists to visit other places will require more efforts." Nath says, "Rajasthan looked at heritage tourism as an opportunity to shed its BIMARU (Bihar, Madhya Pradesh, Rajasthan, and UP) tag. Better marketing strategy backed by focus on infrastructure development and creating safe environment for tourists in the state have proved the differentiator."

Rajasthan has been systematic in promoting its heritage sites. It has been flexible with time as well. While till a few years ago the state was busy promoting better known places like Jaipur, Udaipur and Jaisalmer, now attempts are successfully being made to market lesser known places, often in hinterlands, like Sawai Madhopur, Kumbhalgarh, Kota, Sariska, Alwar, Bundi, Barmer, and Dungarpur.

Required Factors

In order to travel, a person must possess four essentials:

- Disposable Income: money that can be spent on pleasure items.
- Time.
- Means of transport.
- Accommodation arrangements.

The history behind tourism and travel first referred to wealthy people who were interested in visiting distant parts of the world in order to view historic buildings or other works of art, as well as to learn a new language or sample foreign foods. The terms tourist and tourism were first recognized in 1937 by the League of Nations, whose definition involved a person who traveled abroad for more than 24 hours.

Types of tourism

There are different types of tourism that can be enjoyed. Some are listed below:

- Adventure tourism: involves travel to rugged regions so that tourists can participate in adventure sports such as hiking or climbing mountains.
- Cultural Tourism: involves visiting historical or intersting cities, such as Paris, Shanghai, Beijing or Warsaw. This is when tourists engage in cultural experiences, like visiting an art museum, theater or opera.
- Ecotourism: involves traveling that does not pose a threat to the environment, such as safariing in Kenya.
- Gambling Tourism: visiting destinations for the purpose of gambling, to places such as Las Vegas, Atlantic City or Monte Carlo/
- Sport Tourism: involves travel with the thought of a particular sport in mind, such as a ski trip during the winter season.

World events, the economy, tastes and trends and the technology of travel—all of these and more have an effect on global tourism. And despite a decline in American travel in recent years, the web site peopleandplanet.net reports, "By some measure, tourism may already be the world's largest industry, with annual revenue approaching $500 billion." A major in tourism will get you a foot in the door to this ever-booming industry. And the sky's the limit—quite literally—on where you go from there. Tourism majors aim to discover the world's top destinations and how best to encourage people to visit them.

From the dreamy, steamy islands of the South Pacific to Sweden's Icehotel, you'll learn how to make guests feel welcome and enjoy a safe and memorable stay. A tourism major covers the whole spectrum of travel—you'll study everything from the booking of flights to facilitating operations at a resort hotel.

You'll use the tourism industry's most prevalent electronic databases and discover how to navigate other travel-related computer programmes and systems.

Count on learning how to market and sell travel destinations and products, including how to promote tourism in new places and how to sustain interest in classic tourist destinations. In addition, you'll examine how Internet technology is affecting the Tourism industry and how to use this technology most advantageously. Your tourism major should also touch on the effect tourism has on the environment—and how certain aspects of the industry are working to minimize those effects.

Tourism is more global than ever and this major will explore the role it plays in the world—how it affects cities and countries both economically and culturally. You'll learn where the industry has been and where it might go in the future. (Is a moon resort really viable? *You'll* be able to tell *us*.) Before you graduate, you should be a pro at giving knowledgeable and friendly customer service and managing all aspects of the travel experience. After college, you'll have the skills you need to pursue a career for an airline, a travel agency, or many other sorts of travel service organization.

Tourism is an interdisciplinary major and your course work will draw from accounting, marketing, communication and other business courses, as well as courses in geography and specific elements of tourism.

Tourism Overview in 2005-06

Tourism in India has registered significant growth in the recent years. In 1951, International Tourist Arrivals stood at around 17 thousand only while the same has now gone up to 3.91 million in 2005. The upward trend is expected to remain firm in the coming years. Tourism is the third largest net earner of foreign exchange for the country recording earnings of US $ 5731 million in 2005, a growth of 20.2per cent over 2004. it is also one of the sectors which employs the largest number of manpower.

The first ever Tourism Satellite Accounts for India compiled by NCAER for the year 2002-03 showed that tourism employed 38.8 million persons, directly and indirectly, which was 8.3per cent of the total employment in the country and who contributed 5.8per cent of the GDP. These figures are estimated to have increased to 41.85 million employed in 2003-04 with a GDP contribution of 5.9per cent. Various studies have also shown that tourism generates the highest employment per unit of investment for the skilled, semi-skilled and unskilled. The World Travel and Tourism council (WTTC) has identified India as one of the foremost growth centers in the world in the coming decade.

While the growth in tourism has been impressive, India's share in total global tourism arrivals and earnings in quite insignificant. It is an accepted fact that India has tremendous potential for development of tourism. The diversity of India's natural and cultural richness provides the basis of a wide range of tourist products and experiences, which embrace business, leisure, culture, adventure, spirituality, eco-tourism and many other pursuits.

Apart from acknowledging the traditionally recognized advantages of developing tourism for the promotion of national integration, international understanding, earning of foreign exchange and vast employment generation, it can play a major role in furthering the socio-economic objectives of nation.

The Ministry of Tourism adopted a multi-pronged approach in order to achieve this growth. Providing a congenial atmosphere for tourism development, strengthening the tourism infrastructure and hospitality related services, integrated development of identified destinations and circuits, integrating elements of tourism, emphasizing on culture and clean civic life marketing of tourism products a focused manner along with a branding exercise and 0positioning India as a high value destination in the new key markets and giving thrust on the human resource development activities have been the hallmarks of this strategy.

The focus of product development in the States also underwent a change by enhanced outlays for 'destination development up to an amount of ₹. 5 crore and 'circuit development' up to an amount of ₹. 8 crore. A new proposal was moved to allocate up to ₹. 50 crore for individual destinations with high tourist footfalls in order to totally redesign the experience of the tourist through greater organization and provision of civic facilities

The important initiatives taken by the Government to improve the flow of foreign tourists into the country and thereby increasing the country's share in the world tourism included the following:-

- Beginning of cruise tourism by an international shipping firm.
- Direct approach to the consumers through electronic and print media through the "Incredible India" Campaign called "Colours of India".
- Creation of World Class Collaterals.
- Centralized Electronic Media Campaign.
- An integrated campaign in South East Asia to promote Buddhist sites in India.
- Direct co-operative marketing with tour operators and wholesalers overseas.
- Greater focus in the emerging markets particularly in the region of China, South Korea, Japan and South East Asia.
- Participation in over 185 Trade Fairs and Exhibitions all over the world.
- Optizmizing Editorial PR and Publicity.
- Use of Internet and Web marketing.
- Generating Tourist Publications.
- Re-enforcing hospitality programmes including grant of air passages to invite media personnel and tour operators on familiarization tours to India to get first hand knowledge on various tourism products.
- Launching of Road Shows in key source markets of Europe, America, South East Asia and the Middle East.
- Focusing on growth of hotel infrastructure particularly budget hotels.
- Enhancing connectivity through augmentation of air capacity and improving road infrastructure to major tourist attractions.
- Introduction of the Medical Visa.
- Guidelines formulated for the classification of Time Share Resorts, Serviced Apartments, Guest Houses and Home Stay accommodation.

Impressive strides were made in the field of Human Resource Development. The Institute of Hotel Management continued to be the backbone of manpower training for hospitality industry in the country. The Diploma courses offered by these Institute were upgraded to a Degree course. The scheme of 'Capacity Building for Service Providers' also continued to be implemented for providing basic skills to unorganized sector service providers engaged in activities having direct interaction with the tourists. The first Phase of the "Atithi Devo Bhava" Programme was completed during which over 26,000 stakeholders in seven cities were trained.

The allocation of plan funds was raised from ₹.500.00 crore in 2004-05 to ₹.786 crore in 2005-06. The new priorities and initiatives have been actuated with a sound backing of a National Tourism Policy. With the significant positive trends in the year 2005, the Tourism industry is poised for a brighter 2006.

Urban Tourism

The demand for travel to cities has greatly increased over the last few decades. While many travel for business or convention purposes, others are traveling on leisure time to learn about other cultures, to develop their specific interests and to seek entertainment. But what exactly are the specific elements of the urban tourism product that determine the attractiveness of a city for visitors?

Christopher Law examines the relationship between tourism and urban areas. He distinguishes between primary, secondary and additional elements of a city's tourism resources. Primary elements provide the main reasons why tourists visit cities.

Secondary elements such as accommodation and shopping as well as additional elements like transportation or tourist information are also very important for the success of urban tourism, but are not the main attractor of visitors. The following are key elements that can enhance the visitor friendliness in urban areas.

Historic attributes of buildings, streetscapes, neighbour-hoods and special landmarks emphasize the local character of an area. Historic districts are generally very pedestrian friendly with a mix of attractions and amenities that are easily accessible. Beyond their educational component, they also generate a sense of place and provide the urban visitor with memorable experiences. Thus, cities blessed with heritage as a selling point are advantaged when looking to develop their tourism product.

Approximately 80 per cent of Europe's population lives in towns and cities, making Europe the world's most built-up continent and the **urban** question one of the major issues for future years. **Urban** conurbations mirror the problems that face European society as a whole: traffic gridlock, pollution, lawlessness and unemployment. They are not just the main places in which wealth is created and the focus of cultural and social development, however, but places where people live and work, shop and enjoy leisure pursuits.

Renewed interest in **urban tourism** since the beginning of the 1980s has brought about a sharp upturn in this kind of **tourism.** Various interlinked factors have undoubtedly played a part in this: the need to breathe life back into and rehabilitate the historic centres of towns and cities, wider-ranging and more diversified cultural pursuits, consumers' interest in the heritage and **urban** development and their search for things to do and for spending opportunities. The fact that people are taking more, but shorter, holidays, the advent of the single market and the general increase in mobility have also helped to build up **urban tourism** in Europe.

The broader range of activities and leisure pursuits that visitors are seeking is extending what is on offer. This diversification is also due to a growing awareness of **tourism** among political decision- makers who are increasingly keen to promote it as a key factor in economic development bringing wealth and employment. **Tourism** is being seen as a cornerstone of a policy of **urban** development that combines a competitive supply able to meet visitors' expectations with a positive contribution to the development of towns and cities and the well-being of their residents.

Integrated quality management (IQM) offers an opportunity to act on both these fronts: economic development, on the one hand, and **urban** development, on the other. It does this by offering visitors a unique and original experience and by trying as far as possible to satisfy residents' rightful aspirations for harmonious economic and social development which shows concern for the environment.

Taking 15 case studies of European **urban** tourist destinations as a starting point, this publication highlights factors that have helped to make such strategies successful, looks at methods and procedures and shows what resources have been implemented and what results have been obtained. This publication is for everyone, whether in the public or private sector, involved in managing **urban** destinations.

Not just those in charge of or providers of tourist services or products in destinations, but also those responsible for **urban** development (planning and **urban** development departments, development and environmental agencies, *etc.*). The case studies and recommendations may also provide food for thought for local, regional and national public authorities, the **tourism** industry and in particular SMEs which are the driving force behind and the cornerstones of an **urban** destination's quality initiatives.

The publication also looks at the ways in which **tourism** enterprises can help individually or collectively to improve a destination's quality. **Urban** destinations from the whole of the European Economic Area that are being promoted as tourist destinations, have been studied. They include small towns and large cities, towns with a tradition of **tourism** and towns where **tourism** is a more recent development, as well as towns active in various **urban tourism** markets (cultural cities, leisure centres, business centres, trade fair and conference towns). Residential towns and towns with fewer than 20 000 inhabitants were excluded as case studies.

This publication is the result of a study conducted by the Belgian contractor OGM ('Organisation Gestion Marketing') for the **Tourism** Unit of the Enterprise Directorate-General of the European Commission. Information gathered from European, national and regional organisations and an assessment of the replies to a self-evaluation questionnaire sent out to 171 **urban** destinations in the European Economic Area provided a starting point for identifying and selecting the 15 case studies.

A panel of experts initially selected a long list of 28 destinations which, following further examination, were reduced to a final list of 15 destinations for detailed study (in particular through a visit to the destination). The 15 destinations finally selected reflect the diversity of European **urban** tourist destinations from the point of view of their location, size, openness to and reliance on **tourism** and the progress that has been made with quality initiatives and the ways in which such initiatives can be implemented, as well as their objectives and strategies. While these may not be unique situations, they do illustrate real experiences and can in no way be considered to be models.

Waterfronts

Not matter if it is for transportation, industry, or entertainment, urban waters have always attracted people out of necessity or pleasure. Lately, cities and private investors are paying increased attention to waterfronts because they pose a variety of opportunities for tourism, economic and community development.

San Antonio (TX) is probably one of the most classic examples in the US for successful riverfront development. San Antonio's capitalized on the city's main attraction, the water, which creates aesthetic and entertainment value while at the same time generating tourist dollars for the city.

Convention Centers and Exhibitions

Convention Centers and Exhibitions are often regarded as one of the staples of city tourism. In some cities, up to forty per cent of those staying overnight have come for this type of business tourism. Convention Centers and Exhibitions are perceived to be strong growth sectors in which the visitor spends an above average amount and which operate for most of the year.

Employment, publicity, image improvement and urban regeneration are benefits that generally justify the big financial investment for those centers. Besides these advantages, it is important to remember that the conference business cannot be separated from the rest of the tourism industry particularly because most participants are also seeking urban amenities in an exciting environment.

Festivals and Events

Festivals and Events have become an increasingly popular means for cities to boost tourism. They range in size and scale from one time events like the World Exhibition or the Olympics to annual events like Folk Music Festivals or Gallery Nights. Spectacles like that are important, however, their impact upon the city's tourist industry depends on the attendance and the type and number of outside visitors

Special Visitor Districts

Special visitor districts are places where a combination of visitor attractions such as cultural, amusements, or sports facilities is clustered in one location. These districts are not merely a strategy to attract tourists and provide better amenities for local residents, but one that can be used to facilitate urban renewal.

Special visitor districts enable visitors to move easily from one attraction to another and, if this is known in advance, may encourage more visitors to come to the city due to a critical mass of attractions).

In many parts of the world, special visitor districts have been the anchor for regenerated dockland zones. In Baltimore, for instance, the Inner Harbour was planned with three such attractions: an aquarium, a science museum and a viewing platform at the top of the World Tr ade Centre. According to the Baltimore Area Convention and Visitors Association, the total number of out-of-town visitors was almost 12 million. These guests spent an estimated $2.9 billion.

Tourism Employees

Friendliness is probably one of the most important sociocultural features of the tourism product. Professionalism and excellence of service offered to visitors start with friendliness. Key factors in visitor's decision to visit a place are friendly, hospitable people. That's what people remember and that's what they come back for. Responsibility for the "Welcome", however, does not rest solely with tourism employees.

Each and every person working and living in the city, who has contact with visitors, should market themselves to the kind of visitors needed to bring more dollars to restaurants, hotels, museum and other entertaining places. If urban tourism wants to continue to grow and prosper, everyone, from the cab driver to the storeowner and the resident, should act as a tourism agent and provide their guests with positive memorable experiences.

Retail and Catering Facilities

Although shopping and restaurants are regarded as a secondary element of tourism, it is still an important part of the tourism economy since visitors spend a significant amount of time and money on shopping and eating. Shopping, for instance, has for some visitors become a leisure activity where they tour stores with no specific purpose in mind.

For others, it is more like a sport where they go from store to store and see if there are different goods on sale at the destination compared to home. Cities that add retail stores or restaurants to their downtown or to special facilities like airports, train stations, or casinos, experience positive economic impacts that not only apply to one location, but spill over and trickle down to other areas of the city.

Requirement of Visa

Foreigners desirous of visiting India can do so after obtaining a visa from the Indian Mission in the country of their residence. They should posses a valid National passport-except in the case of nationals of Bhutan and Nepal, who may carry only suitable means of identification. Any foreigner who wants to enter into India must have a valid visa affixed on his or her passport. This can be obtained from the Indian Consulate in your country. Foreign nationals of Indian origin, their spouses and children can obtain visas from the Consulate. Foreign nationals of Indian origin, their spouses and children can obtain Entry Visas valid upto 10 years.

Tourist Visas can be obtained for six months, one year and 10 years. Visas of the appropriate type should be obtained by students, businessmen, journalists and others who want to visit India for professional purposes.

All types of visas are valid for the indicated period from the date of issue (and not repeat not from the date of first entry into India). Post-dated visas are not issued at any case. All applicants for Entry and Tourist visas are required to fill out an application form and provide one recent passport size photograph. Applicants for Business, Research, Journalist and some other types of visas are required to submit two forms duly filled in and two pictures.

Visas can also be issued to persons who normally do not live in the jurisdiction of this Consulate (this also includes people holding Tourist/Business visas) after obtaining clearance from the Indian Mission under whose jurisdiction the applicant normally resides. This however takes a few weeks. The applicant may, however, pay an additional charge for clearance by fax or telex.

Persons desiring to go to a restricted area should fill in special forms and apply well in advance as clearances are required before a permit can be issued to travel to these places. It takes at least 6 to 8 weeks to receive the Government of India's clearances in such cases.

Firm letters of admission from Universities, recognized Colleges or Educational Institutions in India are required for issuance of Regular Student Visas. Applicants are also required to produce satisfactory evidence of financial support. In case of admission in a medical or a para-medical course, the applicant has also to produce a 'No Objection Certificate' from the Ministry of Health, Government of India, to obtain a Student Visa.

Applicants for Student Visas who want to pursue graduate or post-graduate studies in Engineering/Technology are required to produce a similar 'No Objection Certificate' from the Ministry of Human Resource Development (Department of Education). Provisional Student Visas for a period of 6 months can however be issued on production of a Provisional Admission Certificate issued by a University/recognized Educational Institution in India. It can be changed to a regular student visa in India itself subject to completion of the formalities listed above. However, no change of institute/purpose is allowed.

The entry of foreigners, stay, movements and departure is regulated by the Acts passed by the Indian Parliament and rules framed hereunder by the Central Government from time to time. Foreigners who enter India should have a valid passport, visa or other accredited travel documents. All foreigners should enter India through authorized check post or airport only. They are subjected to immigration check at the airport or check post.

All foreigners who enter India or depart from India either by air or sea shall furnish a true statement of particulars setting it out in form 'D' embarkation card. The civil authority under Foreigners Order 1948 has powers to impose restrictions on the movement of any foreigner in India.

The authority can also refuse a foreigner entry into India if he/she does not posses a valid passport, or is insane or is suffering from any infectious disease or has been convicted for an extradition offence or if his/her entry is prejudicial to the interest of the country. All foreigners who desire to stay in India beyond 180 days have to register themselves at the Foreigners Registration Office within two weeks of their arrival. Those who intended to stay for less than 180 days but ended up staying longer also have to register themselves. Any violation of this provision makes them liable for prosecution under section 5 of the Registration of Foreigners Act, 1939.

The State Registration Officer in the State capital functions as the liaison office between the Foreigners Registration Officers (FRO) and the government. The Foreigner Registration Officer is the primary agency to regulate the registration, movement, stay, departure and also for recommending the extension of stay in India. A foreigner who enters India on a valid visa shall report before the Foreigners Registration Officer within two weeks of arrival and get himself registered.

He has to produce 6 sets of photos, passport copies, visa page, *etc.* Thereafter the FRO will issue registration certificate and a residential permit upto the validity of the visa period. A foreigner coming to India on a tourist visa valid for 6 months need not register his name. However this depends on the condition noted on the visa.

Children of foreigners under 16 years of age residing in India need not register their name as they are exempted from Registration (Exemption) Order 1957. But they will be issued a residential permit for their stay in India. They should also obtain extension for their stay from time to time.

Foreigners who wish to stay in India beyond the visa period should apply for extension of stay 90 days before his Residential Permit is due to expire. The Central Government has delegated limited powers to the FROs to grant extension of stay to foreigners and in all other cases the following documents are to be sent to the State government.

- Application duly filled and signed by the foreigner in duplicate.
- Photostat copy of the valid passport along with visa page.
- HIV certificate issued by a recognized medical institution.
- Copy of the registration certificate and residential permit.
- Financial guarantee given by an Indian citizen on a ₹. 10 stamp paper.
- Photostat copy of the bank account and remittance and letter given by the bank manager.
- Police report in English issued by the jurisdictional police station where the foreigner resides.
- Receipt for having paid the prescribed fee to the RBI under head of account OAS-0070.
- In case of businessmen, the agreement between the firm and the Government of India.
- In case of employment visa, letter of consent of the firm where the foreigner is employed.

Exemption from Registration

Foreigners coming to India on tourist visas for 180 days or a shorter period are not required to register themselves with any authority in India. They can move about freely in the country, except to restricted/protected areas and prohibited places.

Individuals without nationality or of undetermined nationality (stateless person; IRO refugees, persons receiving legal or political protection, holder of Nansen passport *etc.*) should have valid passport, identity documents or sworn affidavit with visa for which they should apply at least two months in advance.

LAND PERMIT FACILITY

Tourists may note that no Landing Permit Facility is available to any foreign tourist landing without a visa. A limited facility exists only for group tours consisting of 4 or more members and sponsored by a travel agency recognized by the Government of India. Children below the age of 12 years of foreigners of Indian origin may be granted a landing permit by the Immigration authorities up to a period of 90 days to see their relatives, in case they happen to come without a visa.

Tourist Group

A tourist group arriving by air, ship or by a chartered or scheduled flight may be granted a collective landing permit for a period upto 30 days by the

Immigration authorities on landing, provided the group is sponsored by a recognized travel agency, a predrawn itinerary is presented along with details of passport *etc.* of the members and the travel agency gives an undertaking to conduct the group together.

Extension of Visa

Facility exists for an extension of tourist visa beyond six months. In such a case, however, the foreigners' Registration Officer throughout the country and obtain an extension of visa from him. All formalities of registration under the law would have to be fulfilled.

Other Types of Visas

If a foreigner wishes to come to India for a purpose other than tourism, he should come after obtaining an appropriate visit out of the following:

- *Business Visa*: A foreigner can obtain from an Indian Embassy abroad a multiple entry business visa valid for one year or five year but with a cumulative stay in India of not more than 180 days, provide he wishes to come for some business.
- *Student Visa*: A student visa can be obtained from the Indian Embassy on the production of proof of administration and means of sustenance while in India, *etc.* The visa is valid for one year but is extended in India for the duration of the course.
- *Conference Visa*: Delegates coming to attend International Conferences in India can be granted "Conference Visas" to cover the conference as well as tourism in India. Delegates are advised to apply to the Indian Embassies well in advance.
- Foreigners wishing to undertake trekking, botanical expeditions, mountaineering expeditions, canoe-rafting, *etc.*, in a team may be granted visas for the required duration on presentation of full details of he touring members, nature of the event, area to be visited and any other tourist information that may be asked for by the Indian Embassy.
- Sports teams or individual sportsmen wishing to participate in international sports events being held in India may apply to an Indian Embassy/Mission for the grant of visa for the necessary duration. Requests for such visas may be made well in advance.
- Foreign journalists, media men, documentary and feature filmmakers may obtain necessary visas after due formalities from the Indian Embassy.
- *Yoga*: Visa for study of Yoga, Vedic Culture, dance, music *etc.* Foreigners wishing to come to India to study these subjects are required to apply well in advance with all necessary particulars. The Indian Embassies may grant visas for a period of one year which may be extended on an annual basis in India.

Currency Regulations

There are no restrictions on the amount of foreign currency or travellers' cheques a tourist may bring into India provided he makes a declaration in the Currency Declaration Form given to him on arrival. This will enable him not only to exchange the currency brought in but also to take the unspent currency out of India on departure. Cash, bank notes and travellers' cheques up to U.S.$10,000 or equivalent need not be declared at the time of entry.

Any money in form of travellers' cheque, draft, bills, cheques, *etc.* in convertible currencies which tourists wish to convert into Indian currency should be exchanged only through authorized money changers and banks who will issue an encashment certificate.

This certificate is required at the time of re-conversion of any unspent money into foreign currency. Tourists are warned that changing money through unauthorized persons is not only illegal but also an offence under Foreign Exchange Regulations Act 1973.It also involves the risk of receiving counterfeit currency.

Customs Formalities and Regulations

The usual duty free regulations apply for India.

- Alcoholic liquor and wine upto 1 litre each.
- 200 cigarettes or 50 cigars or 250 gms. of tobacco.

Visitors are generally required to make oral baggage declaration in respect of baggage and foreign currency in their possession. Visitors in possession of more than US$ 10,000 or equivalent thereof in the shape of travellers' cheque, bank notes currency notes are required to obtain a Currency declaration Form before leaving Customs. They should fill in the Disembarkation Card handed over to them by the airlines during the course of the flight. There are two channels for Custom clearance:

Green Channel: for passengers not having any dutiable articles or unaccompanied baggage.

Red Channel: for passengers having dutiable articles or unaccompanied baggage or high value articles to be entered on Tourist Baggage RE-Export Form.

Immigration

Passport: Citizen of all countries require a valid national passport or valid travel documents and valid visa granted by Indian Mission abroad for entering India Except Nepalese or Bhutanese citizens who when proceedings from their respective countries need no passport or visa should possess suitable documents for their identification.

Illegal immigration is a serious political problem in India, with widely differing estimates of the number of such migrants. In places this has led to outbreaks of xenophobic violence, particularly against those perceived to be

Bangladeshi. In 2003, former Indian Defence Minister George Fernandes alleged that there are there are more than 20,000,000 illegal Bangladeshi immigrants in India. The Government of Bangladesh claims that "there is not a single Bangladeshi migrant in India".

It is extremely hard to distinguish between illegal Bangaldeshis and local Bengali speakers. The Hindu has reported a case where Bangladeshis have been able to secure ration and voter identity cards.

Assam spent ₹.1.7 billion between January 2001 and September 2006, which resulted in identification of 9,149 foreigners, only 1,864 could be deported back to Bangladesh. This amounts to ₹. 180,000 spent to deport an illegal Bangladeshi. India is building a fence along its entire border with Bangladesh.

The Centre for Women and Children Studies estimated in 1998 that 27,000 Bangladeshis have been forced into prostitution in India. Ahmedabad Crime Branch (ACB) has investigated a prostitution racket run by a Bangladeshi couple living in Ahmedabad. It believed over 500 women had been coerced into prostitution by illegal Bangladeshi agents in Gujarat.

Indian newspapers reported that "the state government has reports that illegal Bangladeshi migrants have trickled into parts of rural Bengal, including Nandigram, over the years, and settled down as sharecroppers with the help of local Left leaders. Though a majority of these immigrants became tillers, they lacked documents to prove the ownership of land".

Allegations exist that other parties such as the Bharatiya Janata Party and the Indian National Congress have discriminated against Bengali-speaking Muslims.. Even though it must be noted that the number of Bengali-speaking Muslims has increased multifold since independence, suggesting that many of these Bengali-speaking Muslims are maybe illegal Bangladeshi immigrants.

In August 2008, the Delhi High Court dismissed a petition by a Bangladeshi national against her deportation. The High Court ruled that the illegal Bangladeshi immigrants "pose a danger to India's internal security".

Arrival Formalities

If the visa for stay in India is more than 180 days, registration Certificate and Residential Permit should be obtained from the nearest Foreigners' Registration Office within 7 days of arrival. Personal appearance is absolutely necessary at the time of registration, extension or exit as required by the Law of the Land. Four photographs/pictures are also required for registration. The foreigners are registered at Foreigners' Registration.

The foreigners registered at Foreigner's Registration Office are required to report change of their addresses. Departure from India All persons except nationals of Nepal and Bhutan leaving by roads or rail have to fill an Embarkation Card at the time of departure. All tourist visitors holding Registration Certificate are endorsed by the appropriate registration authorities before departure.

Registration Certificates and Residential permits are to be surrendered at the Registration Office.

None for holders of Entry Visas (Except tourist/Transit Visa Holders). All visitors holding Registration Certificate have to obtain, before departure, exit endorsement from the Regis-tration Officer of the district in which they were registered

INCOME TAX CLEARANCE

If a person not domiciled in India intends to stay in the country for more than 120 days, an Income Tax Clearance' certificate is required in order to leave the country. This document will prove that the person's stay in India was financed by his own money and not by working or selling his goods.

The foreign section of the Income Tax Department at Delhi, Calcutta, Madras and Bombay issues these certificates on being shown the person's passport, visa extension form and the currency exchange receipts, which have been used by the person.

FOREIGN TRAVEL TAX

Passenger embarking on journey to any place outside India from a Customs airport/seaport will have to pay a Foreign Travel Tax (FTT) of `. 500 and `. 250 on journeys to Afghanistan, Bangladesh, Bhutan, Burma, Nepal, Pakistan, Sri Lanka and the Maldives. No tax is payable on journeys performed by ship from Rameshwaram to Talaimanar and in case of transit passenger, provided they do not leave the Customs barrier.

Transit passenger travelling by air who have to leave the airport on account of mechanical trouble provided they continue their journey by the same aircraft and the same flight number by which they arrive are also exempted from FTT. Transit sea passenger leaving the ship for sightseeing, shopping etc, during the ship's call at any of the Indian ports will not be required to pay FTT.

INLAND AIR TRAVEL TAX

An Inland Air Travel Tax is leviable at 10 per cent of the basic fare on all passengers paying their airfare in foreign exchange will be exempted from payment of this tax.

In addition infants, cancer patients, blind persons and invalids (those on stretchers) are also exempted from this tax after fulfilling certain conditions stipulated in the relevant notifications.

GUIDES

Trained English speaking guides are available at fixed charges at all important tourist centres. The Government of India Tourist Offices can be contacted by tourists for these. French, Italian, Spanish, German, Russian and Japanese speaking guides are available at some cities.

Please consult the nearest Government of India Tourist Office. Unapproved guides are not permitted to enter protected monuments and tourists are, therefore, advised to ask for the services of guides who carry a certificate issued by the Department of Tourism/Archaeological Survey of India.

HEALTH REGULATIONS

Foreign tourists should be in possession of Yellow Fever Vaccination Certificate conforming to International Health Regulations, if they are originating or transitting through Yellow Fever endemic countries (Africa and South America).

INTERNATIONAL AIRPORT FACILITIES

The international airports offer a range of services ensuring that the traveller on business can continue working while waiting to catch an international connection, or when transferring between international flights.

These include gourmet restaurants, business centres and are equipped with state of the art equipment including word processors and telefax. Airports also provide the tourist with such facilities for leisure as duty-free and handicrafts shopping, informal snack bars, nursery and baby care rooms and even an art gallery. Duty-free prices in the airport shops are very competitive, offering you bargains on international merchandise.

INLAND TRAVELS

Indian Airlines

Ranked as the world's second largest domestic IATA airlines outside USA, Indian Airlines commands a large and modern fleet of A300, A320 and B737 aircraft. Indian Airlines (IC) network, spanning the country's 3,000 km from Leh in the north to Thiruvananthapuram in the south and about the same from east to west, covers all important places of tourist interest linking 55 cities in India and 17 in fourteen neighbouring countries: Afghanistan, Bangladesh, Maldives, Nepal, Pakistan, Singapore, Sri Lanka and Thailand. Also included is Kuwait and Kuala Lumpur.

Fares: IC offers a variety of special fares aimed at encouraging tourist travel within the country. These include:

Discover India, US$750, permits unlimited travel within India for 21 days.

India Wonderfares, US$300, permits unlimited travel within India for 21 days.South India Excursion, 30 per cent discount on US$ tariff for travel on specific South Indian Sectors.

Youth Fare, 25 per cent off on US$ tariff for all tourists between the ages of 12 and 30. Reservations: Reservations on IC can be made from any where abroad in a matter of minutes through the SITA Airlines Communications System which is linked to the airline's Real Time Computer Reservation System.

IC has inter-line agreements with over 120 airlines worldwide and the offices of any of these airlines or their agents have been enabled to issue tickets on IC flights. To facilitate group tourists in obtaining reservations, IC is guaranteeing confirmed seats to all foreign tour groups of 10 or more passengers provided booking is requested more than four months in advance on all Airbus and selected B737 tourist services.

Private Airlines

Jet Airways and Sahara Airlines are two major private carriers. They operate metro routes, tourist circuits and also offer special fares to discover India. Smaller airlines like Archana and Jagsons in the north and Gujarat Airways in the west provided feeder services to smaller towns. Jet and Sahara have either their own offices or representative offices in major countries abroad.

Railways

The Indian Railways system is the largest in Asia and the second largest it the world among systems under a single management. Daily, ore than 11 million people or more than 1.4 per cent of India's population board the trains.

Everybody more than 1 million tonnes of freight traffic are lifted by Indian Railways. Nearly 11,000 trains crisis-cross about 62,500 kilometers of rail route, connecting 7,084 railway stations scattered over the far-flung parts of the vast country.

Indrail Pass

Indian Railways have introduced the facility of Indrail Passes which offer all budget visitors the facility to travel as they like over the entire Indian railway system without any route restriction and within the period of validity of he ticket. Indrail passes are sold only to foreign nationals and Indians residing abroad holding valid passports.

Payment is accepted only in US Dollars and Pound Sterling. A tourist travelling on Indrail pass is exempt from paying reservation fees, sleeper charges and extra supplementary charges for travelling by Superfast trains which are otherwise chargeable in the case of ordinary tickets.

RESTRICTED AND PROTECTED AREAS

Military installations and areas, defence organisations and research organisations are considered protected areas, where permits are generally not given to foreigners.

PHOTOGRAPHY RESTRICTIONS

Photography is prohibited in places of military importance, railway stations, bridges, airports and other military installations.

EXPORT OF ANTIQUITIES

Antiquities include sculpture, painting or other works of art and craftsmanship, illustrative of science, art, crafts, religion of bygone ages and of historical interest which have been in existence for not less than one hundred years. Also manuscripts, or other documents of scientific, historical, literary or aesthetic value in existence for not less than seventy five year art treasures not necessarily antiquities but having regard to the artistic and aesthetic value cannot be exported out of India.

For farther clarification on the antiquity of an artefact, the tourists can contact the authorities and get information on the Acts and Rules governing Antiquities and Art Treasures Act, 1972. Govt. of India is concerned about the conservation of its endangered and rare fauna. With this view, export of all wild animals indigenous to the country and articles made from such listed animals like skin, pelts, furs, ivory, rhino horns, trophies etc have been totally banned.

Tourists are also advised to acquaint themselves with the provisions of Convention on International Trade of endangered species of wild fauna and flora. All the member countries of the convention allow import of the articles covered by convention on the strength of a certificate of export from the country of origin.

CLIMATE

India has three major seasons: winter, summer and the monsoon. The winter months (November-March) are pleasant throughout India with bright sunny days. In the northern plains, the minimum temperature may vary between 4 to 10 degree Celsius and there is snowfall in the hills. In the west, south and the east, however, December and January are pleasantly cool, never really cold. The summer months (April-June) are hot in most parts of India and it is during this season that hill resorts such as Shimla, Musoorie, Nainital, Kullu and the Kashmir valley, Darjeeling, Shillong, Octacamund, Kodaikanal, Pachmarhi and Mount Abu provide cool retreats.

The south-west monsoon usually breaks about the beginning of June on the west coast and reaches elsewhere later. With the exception of the south-eastern areas, India receives the major share of its rainfall from the north-east monsoon between mid-October and December-end. Traditionally, India had been popular in the winter months. However, with easy availability of air-conditioned hotels, transport and leisure facilities (such as dining and shopping), the summer months too have become popular and India has become a year-round tourist destination.

The climate of India defies easy generalisation, comprising a wide range of weather conditions across a large geographic scale and varied topography. Analysed according to the Köppen system, India hosts six major climatic subtypes, ranging from desert in the west, to alpine tundra and glaciers in the north, to humid tropical regions supporting rainforests in the southwest and the island territories. Many regions have starkly different microclimates. The nation has four seasons: winter (January and February), summer (March to May), a monsoon (rainy) season (June to September), and a post-monsoon period (October to December).

India's unique geography and geology strongly influence its climate; this is particularly true of the Himalayas in the north and the Thar Desert in the northwest. The Himalayas act as a barrier to the frigid katabatic winds flowing down from Central Asia. Thus, North India is kept warm or only mildly cold during winter; in summer, the same phenomenon makes India relatively hot. Although the Tropic of Cancer—the boundary between the tropics and subtropics—passes through the middle of India, the whole country is considered to be tropical.

As in much of the tropics, monsoonal and other weather conditions in India are unstable: major droughts, floods, cyclones and other natural disasters are sporadic, but have killed or displaced millions. India's long-term climatic stability is further threatened by global warming. Climatic diversity in India makes the analysis of these issues complex.

During the Late Permian (some 260–251 Ma), the Indian subcontinent was part of the vast supercontinent Pangaea. Despite its position within a high-latitude belt at 55–75° S (as opposed to its current position between 5 and 35° N), latitudes now occupied by Greenland and parts of the Antarctic Peninsula, India likely experienced a humid temperate climate with warm, frost-free weather, though with well-defined seasons. Later, India joined the southern supercontinent Gondwana, a process beginning some 550–500 Ma.

During the Late Paleozoic, Gondwana extended from a point at or near the South Pole to near the equator, where the Indian craton (stable continental crust) was positioned, resulting in a mild climate favourable to hosting high-biomass ecosystems.

This is underscored by India's vast coal reserves—much of it from the late Paleozoic sedimentary sequence—the fourth-largest reserves in the world. During the Mesozoic, the world, including India, was considerably warmer than today. With the coming of the Carboniferous, global cooling stoked extensive glaciation, which spread northwards from South Africa towards India; this cool period lasted well into the Permian.

Tectonic movement by the Indian Plate caused it to pass over a geologic hotspot—the Réunion hotspot—now occupied by the volcanic island of Réunion. This resulted in a massive flood basalt event that laid down the Deccan Traps some 60–68 Ma, at the end of the Cretaceous period. This may have contributed to the global Cretaceous-Tertiary (K-T) extinction event, which caused India to experience significantly reduced insolation.

Elevated atmospheric levels of sulphur gases formed aerosols such as sulfur dioxide and sulfuric acid, similar to those found in the atmosphere of Venus; these precipitated as acid rain. Elevated carbon dioxide emissions also contributed to the greenhouse effect, causing warmer weather that lasted long after the atmospheric shroud of dust and aerosols had cleared.

Further climatic changes 20 million years ago, long after India had crashed into the Laurasian landmass, were severe enough to cause the extinction of many endemic Indian forms. The formation of the Himalayas resulted in blockage of frigid Central Asian air, preventing it from reaching India; this made its climate significantly warmer and more tropical in character than it would otherwise have been.

India is home to an extraordinary variety of climatic regions, ranging from tropical in the south to temperate and alpine in the Himalayan north, where elevated regions receive sustained winter snowfall. The nation's climate is strongly influenced by the Himalayas and the Thar Desert.

The Himalayas, along with the Hindu Kush mountains in Pakistan, prevent cold Central Asian katabatic winds from blowing in, keeping the bulk of the Indian subcontinent warmer than most locations at similar latitudes. Simultaneously, the Thar Desert plays a role in attracting moisture-laden southwest summer monsoon winds that, between June and October, provide the majority of India's rainfall.

Four major climatic groupings predominate, into which fall seven climatic zones that, as designated by experts, are defined on the basis of such traits as temperature and precipitation. Groupings are assigned codes according to the Köppen climate classification system.

A tropical rainy climate covers regions experiencing persistent warm or high temperatures, which normally do not fall below 18 °C (64 °F). India hosts two climatic subtypes that fall under this group. The most humid is the tropical wet monsoon climate that covers a strip of southwestern lowlands abutting the Malabar Coast, the Western Ghats, and southern Assam. India's two island territories, Lakshadweep and the Andaman and Nicobar Islands, are also subject to this climate. Characterised by moderate to high year-round temperatures, even in the foothills, its rainfall is seasonal but heavy—typically above 2,000 millimetres (79 in) per year.

Most rainfall occurs between May and November; this is adequate for the maintenance of lush forests and other vegetation throughout the remainder of the year. December to March are the driest months, when days with precipitation are rare. The heavy monsoon rains are responsible for the extremely biodiverse tropical wet forests of these regions.

In India, a tropical wet and dry climate is more common. Significantly drier than tropical wet zones, it prevails over most of inland peninsular India except for a semi-arid rain shadow east of the Western Ghats.

Winter and early summer are long, dry periods with temperatures averaging above 18 °C (64 °F). Summer is exceptionally hot; temperatures in low-lying areas may exceed 50 °C (122 °F) during May, leading to heat waves that can each kill hundreds of Indians. The rainy season lasts from June to September; annual rainfall averages between 750–1500 millimetres (30–59 in) across the region. Once the dry northeast monsoon begins in September, most precipitation in India falls on Tamil Nadu, leaving other states comparatively dry.

A tropical arid and semi-arid climate dominates regions where the rate of moisture loss through evapotranspiration exceeds that from precipitation; it is subdivided into three climatic subtypes. The first, a tropical semi-arid steppe climate, predominates over a long stretch of land south of Tropic of Cancer and east of the Western Ghats and the Cardamom Hills. The region, which includes Karnataka, inland Tamil Nadu, western Andhra Pradesh, and central Maharashtra, gets between 400–750 millimetres (16–30 in) annually.

It is drought-prone, as it tends to have less reliable rainfall due to sporadic lateness or failure of the southwest monsoon. North of the Krishna River, the summer monsoon is responsible for most rainfall; to the south, significant post-monsoon rainfall also occurs in October and November. In December, the coldest month, temperatures still average around 20–24 °C (68–75 °F). The months between March to May are hot and dry; mean monthly temperatures hover around 32 °C, with 320 millimetres (13 in) precipitation. Hence, without artificial irrigation, this region is not suitable for permanent agriculture.

Most of western Rajasthan experiences an arid climatic regime. Cloudbursts are responsible for virtually all of the region's annual precipitation, which totals less than 300 millimetres (12 in). Such bursts happen when monsoon winds sweep into the region during July, August, and September. Such rainfall is highly erratic; regions experiencing rainfall one year may not see precipitation for the next couple of years or so. Atmospheric moisture is largely prevented from precipitating due to continuous downdrafts and other factors.

The summer months of May and June are exceptionally hot; mean monthly temperatures in the region hover around 35 °C (95 °F), with daily maxima occasionally topping 50 °C (122 °F). During winters, temperatures in some areas can drop below freezing due to waves of cold air from Central Asia. There is a large diurnal range of about 14 °C (57 °F) during summer; this widens by several degrees during winter.

East of the Thar Desert, the region running from Punjab and Haryana to Kathiawar experiences a tropical and sub-tropical steppe climate. The zone, a transitional climatic region separating tropical desert from humid sub-tropical savanna and forests, experiences temperatures that are less extreme than those of the desert. Average annual rainfall is 30–65 centimetres (12-26 in), but is very unreliable; as in much of the rest of India, the southwest monsoon accounts for most precipitation. Daily summer temperature maxima rise to around 40 °C (104 °F). The resulting natural vegetation typically comprises short, coarse grasses.

Most of Northeast India and much of North India are subject to a humid sub-tropical climate. Though they experience hot summers, temperatures during the coldest months may fall as low as 0 °C (32 °F). Due to ample monsoon rains, India has only one subtype of this climate, *Cfa* (under the Köppen system). In most of this region, there is very little precipitation during the winter, owing to powerful anticyclonic and katabatic (downward-flowing) winds from Central Asia.

Humid subtropical regions are subject to pronounced dry winters. Winter rainfall—and occasionally snowfall—is associated with large storm systems such as "Nor'westers" and "Western disturbances"; the latter are steered by westerlies towards the Himalayas. Most summer rainfall occurs during powerful thunderstorms associated with the southwest summer monsoon; occasional tropical cyclones also contribute.

Annual rainfall ranges from less than 1,000 millimetres (39 in) in the west to over 2,500 millimetres (98 in) in parts of the northeast. As most of this region is far from the ocean, the wide temperature swings more characteristic of a continental climate predominate; the swings are wider than in those in tropical wet regions, ranging from 24 °C (75 °F) in north-central India to 27 °C (81 °F) in the east.

India's northernmost areas are subject to a montane, or alpine, climate. In the Himalayas, the rate at which an air mass's temperature falls per kilometre (3,281 ft) of altitude gained (the adiabatic lapse rate) is 5.1 °C/km. In terms of environmental lapse rate, ambient temperatures fall by 0.6 °C (1.1 °F) for every 100 metres (328 ft) rise in altitude. Thus, climates ranging from nearly tropical in the foothills to tundra above the snow line can coexist within several dozen miles of each other.

Sharp temperature contrasts between sunny and shady slopes, high diurnal temperature variability, temperature inversions, and altitude-dependent variability in rainfall are also common. The northern side of the western Himalayas, also known as the trans-Himalayan belt, is a region of barren, arid, frigid, and wind-blown wastelands. Most precipitation occurs as snowfall during the late winter and spring months.

Areas south of the Himalayas are largely protected from cold winter winds coming in from the Asian interior. The leeward side (northern face) of the mountains receives less rain while the southern slopes, well-exposed to the monsoon, get heavy rainfall. Areas situated at elevations of 1,070–2,290 metres (3,510–7,510 ft) receive the heaviest rainfall, which decreases rapidly at elevations above 2,290 metres (7,513 ft). The Himalayas experience their heaviest snowfall between December and February and at elevations above

1,500 metres (4,921 ft). Snowfall increases with elevation by up to several dozen millimetres per 100 metre (~2 in; 330 ft) increase. Elevations above 5,000 metres (16,404 ft) never experience rain; all precipitation falls as snow.

The India Meteorological Department (IMD) designates four official seasons:

- Winter, occurring between January thru March. The year's coldest months are December and January, when temperatures average around 10–15 °C (50–59 °F) in the northwest; temperatures rise as one proceeds towards the equator, peaking around 20–25 °C (68–77 °F) in mainland India's southeast.
- Summer or pre-monsoon season, lasting from March to June (April to July in northwestern India). In western and southern regions, the hottest month is April; for northern regions, May is the hottest month. Temperatures average around 32–40 °C (90–104 °F) in most of the interior.
- Monsoon or rainy season, lasting from June to September. The season is dominated by the humid southwest summer monsoon, which slowly sweeps across the country beginning in late May or early June. Monsoon rains begin to recede from North India at the beginning of October.
- Post-monsoon season, lasting from October to December. South India typically receives more precipitation. Monsoon rains begin to recede from North India at the beginning of October. In northwestern India, October and November are usually cloudless. Parts of the country experience the dry northeast monsoon.

The Himalayan states, being more temperate, experience an additional two seasons: autumn and spring. Traditionally, Indians note six seasons, each about two months long. These are the spring (*Sanskrit: vasanta*), summer (*grîcma*), monsoon season (*varcâ*), early autumn (*œarada*), late autumn (*hemanta*), and winter (*œiœira*). These are based on the astronomical division of the twelve months into six parts. The ancient Hindu calendar also reflects these seasons in its arrangement of months.

Once the monsoons subside, average temperatures gradually fall across India. As the Sun's vertical rays move south of the equator, most of the country experiences moderately cool weather; temperatures change by about 0.6 °C (1.35 °F) per degree of latitude. December and January are the coldest months, with mean temperatures of 10–15 °C (50–59 °F) in Indian Himalayas. Mean temperatures are higher in the east and south, where they reach 20–25 °C (68–77 °F).

In northwestern India, virtually cloudless conditions prevail in October and November, resulting in wide diurnal temperature swings; as in much of the Deccan Plateau, they range between 16–20 °C (61–68 °F). However, from

March to May, "western disturbances" bring heavy bursts of rain and snow. These extra-tropical low-pressure systems originate in the eastern Mediterranean Sea. They are carried towards India by the subtropical westerlies, which are the prevailing winds blowing at North India's range of latitude.

Once their passage is hindered by the Himalayas, they are unable to proceed further, and they release significant precipitation over the southern Himalayas. The three Himalayan states (Jammu and Kashmir in the extreme north, Himachal Pradesh, and Uttarakhand) experience heavy snowfall; in Jammu and Kashmir, blizzards occur regularly, disrupting travel and other activities.

The rest of North India, including the Indo-Gangetic Plain, almost never receives snow. However, in the plains, temperatures occasionally fall below freezing, though never for more one or two days. Winter highs in Delhi range from 16 °C (61 °F) to 21 °C (70 °F). Nighttime temperatures average 2–8 °C (36–46 °F). In the Punjab plains, lows can fall below freezing, dropping to around "6 °C (21 °F) in Amritsar. Frost sometimes occurs, but the hallmark of the season is the notorious fog, which frequently disrupts daily life; fog grows thick enough to hinder visibility and disrupt air travel 15–20 days annually.

Eastern India's climate is much milder, experiencing moderately warm days and cool nights. Highs range from 23 °C (73 °F) in Patna to 26 °C (79 °F) in Kolkata (Calcutta); lows average from 8 °C (46 °F) in Patna to 14 °C (57 °F) in Kolkata. Frigid winds from the Himalayas can depress temperatures near the Brahmaputra River. The two Himalayan states in the east, Sikkim and Arunachal Pradesh, receive substantial snowfall. The extreme north of West Bengal, centred around Darjeeling, also experiences snowfall, but only rarely.

In South India, particularly the hinterland of Maharashtra, Madhya Pradesh, parts of Karnataka, and Andhra Pradesh, somewhat cooler weather prevails. Minimum temperatures in western Maharashtra, Madhya Pradesh and Chhattisgarh hover around 10 °C (50 °F); in the southern Deccan Plateau, they reach 16 °C (61 °F).

Coastal areas, especially those near the Coromandel Coast, and low-elevation interior tracts are warm, with daily high temperatures of 30 °C (86 °F) and lows of around 21 °C (70 °F). The Western Ghats, including the Nilgiri Range, are exceptional; there, lows can fall below freezing. This compares with a range of 12–14 °C (54–57 °F) on the Malabar Coast; there, as is the case for other coastal areas, the Indian Ocean exerts a strong moderating influence on weather.

Summer in northwestern India lasts from April to July, and in the rest of the country from March to June. The temperatures in the north rise as the vertical rays of the Sun reach the Tropic of Cancer. The hottest month for the western and southern regions of the country is April; for most of North India, it is May. Temperatures of 50 °C (122 °F) and higher have been recorded in parts of India during this season.

In cooler regions of North India, immense pre-monsoon squall-line thunderstorms, known locally as "Nor'westers", commonly drop large hailstones. Near the coast the temperature hovers around 36 °C (97 °F), and the proximity of the sea increases the level of humidity. In southern India, the temperatures are higher on the east coast by a few degrees compared to the west coast.

By May, most of the Indian interior experiences mean temperatures over 32 °C (90 °F), while maximum temperatures often exceed 40 °C (104 °F). In the hot months of April and May, western disturbances, with their cooling influence, may still arrive, but rapidly diminish in frequency as summer progresses. Notably, a higher frequency of such disturbances in April correlates with a delayed monsoon onset (thus extending summer) in northwest India. In eastern India, monsoon onset dates have been steadily advancing over the past several decades, resulting in shorter summers there.

Altitude affects the temperature to a large extent, with higher parts of the Deccan Plateau and other areas being relatively cooler. Hill stations, such as Ootacamund ("Ooty") in the Western Ghats and Kalimpong in the eastern Himalayas, with average maximum temperatures of around 25 °C (77 °F), offer some respite from the heat.

At lower elevations, in parts of northern and western India, a strong, hot, and dry wind known as the Loo blows in from the west during the daytime; with very high temperatures, in some cases up to around 45 °C (113 °F); it can cause fatal cases of sunstroke. Tornadoes may also occur, concentrated in a corridor stretching from northeastern India towards Pakistan. They are rare, however; only several dozen have been reported since 1835.

The southwest summer monsoon, a four-month period when massive convective thunderstorms dominate India's weather, is Earth's most productive wet season. A product of southeast trade winds originating from a high-pressure mass centered over the southern Indian Ocean, the monsoonal torrents supply over 80per cent of India's annual rainfall. Attracted by a low-pressure region centered over South Asia, the mass spawns surface winds that ferry humid air into India from the southwest.

These inflows ultimately result from a northward shift of the local jet stream, which itself results from rising summer temperatures over Tibet and the Indian subcontinent. The void left by the jet stream, which switches from a route just south of the Himalayas to one tracking north of Tibet, then attracts warm, humid air.

The main factor behind this shift is the high summer temperature difference between Central Asia and the Indian Ocean. This is accompanied by a seasonal excursion of the normally equatorial intertropical convergence zone (ITCZ), a low-pressure belt of highly unstable weather, northward towards India. This system intensified to its present strength as a result of the Tibetan Plateau's uplift, which accompanied the Eocene–Oligocene transition event, a major episode of global cooling and aridification which occurred 34–49 Ma.

The southwest monsoon arrives in two branches: the Bay of Bengal branch and the Arabian Sea branch. The latter extends towards a low-pressure area over the Thar Desert and is roughly three times stronger than the Bay of Bengal branch. The monsoon typically breaks over Indian territory by around 25 May, when it lashes the Andaman and Nicobar Islands in the Bay of Bengal. It strikes the Indian mainland around 1 June near the Malabar Coast of Kerala.

By 9 June, it reaches Mumbai; it appears over Delhi by 29 June. The Bay of Bengal branch, which initially tracks the Coromandal Coast northeast from Cape Comorin to Orissa, swerves to the northwest towards the Indo-Gangetic Plain. The Arabian Sea branch moves northeast towards the Himalayas. By the first week of July, the entire country experiences monsoon rain; on average, South India receives more rainfall than North India.

However, Northeast India receives the most precipitation. Monsoon clouds begin retreating from North India by the end of August; it withdraws from Mumbai by 5 October. As India further cools during September, the southwest monsoon weakens. By the end of November, it has left the country.

Monsoon rains impact the health of the Indian economy; as Indian agriculture employs 600 million people and composes 20per cent of the national GDP, good monsoons correlate with a booming economy. Weak or failed monsoons (droughts) result in widespread agricultural losses and substantially hinder overall economic growth. The rains reduce temperatures and replenish groundwater tables, rivers, and lakes.

During the post-monsoon months of October to December, a different monsoon cycle, the northeast (or "retreating") monsoon, brings dry, cool, and dense Central Asian air masses to large parts of India. Winds spill across the Himalayas and flow to the southwest across the country, resulting in clear, sunny skies. Though the India Meteorological Department (IMD) and other sources refers to this period as a fourth ("post-monsoon") season, other sources designate only three seasons.

Depending on location, this period lasts from October to November, after the southwest monsoon has peaked. Less and less precipitation falls, and vegetation begins to dry out. In most parts of India, this period marks the transition from wet to dry seasonal conditions. Average daily maximum temperatures range between 28 °C and 34 °C (82–93 °F).

The northeast monsoon, which begins in September, lasts through the post-monsoon seasons, and only ends in March, carries winds that have already lost their moisture while crossing central Asia and the vast rain shadow region lying north of the Himalayas. They cross India diagonally from northeast to southwest.

However, the large indentation made by the Bay of Bengal into India's eastern coast means that the flows are humidified before reaching Cape Comorin and rest of Tamil Nadu, meaning that the state, and also some parts of Kerala, experience significant precipitation in the post-monsoon and winter periods. However, parts of West Bengal, Orissa, Andhra Pradesh, Karnataka and North-East India also receive minor precipitation from the northeast monsoon.[46]

Shown below are temperature and precipitation data for selected Indian cities; these represent the full variety of major Indian climate types. Figures have been grouped by the four-season classification scheme used by the IMD; year-round averages and totals are also displayed.

Climate-related natural disasters cause massive losses of Indian life and property. Droughts, flash floods, cyclones, avalanches, landslides brought on by torrential rains, and snowstorms pose the greatest threats. Other dangers include frequent summer dust storms, which usually track from north to south; they cause extensive property damage in North India and deposit large amounts of dust from arid regions. Hail is also common in parts of India, causing severe damage to standing crops such as rice and wheat.

In the Lower Himalaya, landslides are common. The young age of the region's hills result in labile rock formations, which are susceptible to slippages. Rising population and development pressures, particularly from logging and tourism, cause deforestation. The result, denuded hillsides, exacerbates the severity of landslides, since tree cover impedes the downhill flow of water. Parts of the Western Ghats also suffer from low-intensity landslides. Avalanches occur in Kashmir, Himachal Pradesh, and Sikkim.

Floods are the most common natural disaster in India. The heavy southwest monsoon rains cause the Brahmaputra and other rivers to distend their banks, often flooding surrounding areas. Though they provide rice paddy farmers with a largely dependable source of natural irrigation and fertilisation, the floods can kill thousands and displace millions. Excess, erratic, or untimely monsoon rainfall may also wash away or otherwise ruin crops.

Almost all of India is flood-prone, and extreme precipitation events, such as flash floods and torrential rains, have become increasingly common in central India over the past several decades, coinciding with rising temperatures. Mean annual precipitation totals have remained steady due to the declining frequency of weather systems that generate moderate amounts of rain.

Tropical cyclones, which are severe storms spun off from the Intertropical Convergence Zone, may affect thousands of Indians living in coastal regions. Tropical cyclogenesis is particularly common in the northern reaches of the Indian Ocean in and around the Bay of Bengal. Cyclones bring with them heavy rains, storm surges, and winds that often cut affected areas off from relief and supplies. In the North Indian Ocean Basin, the cyclone season runs from April to December, with peak activity between May and November. Each year, an average of eight storms with sustained wind speeds greater than 63 km/h (39 mph) form; of these, two strengthen into true tropical cyclones, which have sustained gusts greater than 117 km/h (73 mph). On average, a major (Category 3 or higher) cyclone develops every other year.

During summer, the Bay of Bengal is subject to intense heating, giving rise to humid and unstable air masses that morph into cyclones. The 1737 Calcutta cyclone, the 1970 Bhola cyclone, and the 1991 Bangladesh cyclone rank among the most powerful cyclones to strike India, devastating the coasts of eastern India and neighboring Bangladesh.

Widespread death and property destruction are reported every year in the exposed coastal states of West Bengal, Orissa, Andhra Pradesh, and Tamil Nadu. India's western coast, bordering the more placid Arabian Sea, experiences cyclones only rarely; these mainly strike Gujarat and, less frequently, Kerala.

Cyclone 05B, a supercyclone that struck Orissa on 29 October 1999, was the deadliest in more than a quarter-century. With peak winds of 160 miles per hour (257 km/h), it was the equivalent of a Category 5 hurricane. Almost two million people were left homeless; other 20 million people lives were disrupted by the cyclone. Officially, 9,803 people died from the storm; unofficial estimates place the death toll at over 10,000.

Indian agriculture is heavily dependent on the monsoon as a source of water. In some parts of India, the failure of the monsoons result in water shortages, resulting in below-average crop yields. This is particularly true of major drought-prone regions such as southern and eastern Maharashtra, northern Karnataka, Andhra Pradesh, Orissa, Gujarat, and Rajasthan. In the past, droughts have periodically led to major Indian famines. These include the Bengal famine of 1770, in which up to one third of the population in affected areas died; the 1876–1877 famine, in which over five million people died; the 1899 famine, in which over 4.5 million died; and the Bengal famine of 1943, in which over five million died from starvation and famine-related illnesses.

All such episodes of severe drought correlate with El Niño-Southern Oscillation (ENSO) events. El Niño-related droughts have also been implicated in periodic declines in Indian agricultural output. Nevertheless, ENSO events that have coincided with abnormally high sea surfaces temperatures in the Indian Ocean—in one instance during 1997 and 1998 by up to 3 °C (5 °F)—have resulted in increased oceanic evaporation, resulting in unusually wet weather across India. Such anomalies have occurred during a sustained warm spell that began in the 1990s.

A contrasting phenomenon is that, instead of the usual high pressure air mass over the southern Indian Ocean, an ENSO-related oceanic low pressure convergence centre forms; it then continually pulls dry air from Central Asia, desiccating India during what should have been the humid summer monsoon season. This reversed air flow causes India's droughts. The extent that an ENSO event raises sea surface temperatures in the central Pacific Ocean influences the degree of drought.

India's lowest recorded temperature reading was "45 °C ("49 °F) in Dras, Ladakh, in eastern Jammu and Kashmir; however, the reading was taken with non-standard equipment. Further south, readings as low as "30.6 °C ("23 °F) have been taken in Leh, also in Ladakh. However, temperatures on the Indian-controlled Siachen Glacier near Bilafond La (5,450 metres (17,881 ft)) and Sia La (5,589 metres (18,337 ft)) have fallen below "55 °C ("67 °F), while blizzards bring wind speeds in excess of 250 km/h (155 mph), or hurricane-force winds ranking at 12 (the maximum) on the Beaufort scale.

It was those conditions, not actual military engagements, that were responsible for more than 97per cent of the roughly 15,000 casualties suffered by India and Pakistan over the course of conflict in the region. The highest reliable temperature reading was 50.6 °C (123 °F) in Alwar, Rajasthan in 1955. This mark was also reached at Pachpadra in Rajasthan. Recently, claims have been made of temperatures touching 55 °C (131 °F) in Orissa; these have been met with some skepticism by the India Meteorological Department (IMD), which has questioned the methods used in recording such data.

The average annual precipitation of 11,871 millimetres (467 in) in the village of Mawsynram, in the hilly northeastern state of Meghalaya, is the highest recorded in Asia, and possibly on Earth. The village, which sits at an elevation of 1,401 metres (4,596 ft), benefits from its proximity to both the Himalayas and the Bay of Bengal.

However, since the town of Cherrapunji, 5 kilometres (3 mi) to the east, is the nearest town to host a meteorological office (none has ever existed in Mawsynram), it is officially credited as being the world's wettest place. In recent years, the Cherrapunji-Mawsynram region has averaged between 9,296 millimetres (366 in) and 10,820 millimetres (426 in) of rain annually, though Cherrapunji has had at least one period of daily rainfall that lasted almost two years. India's highest recorded one-day rainfall total occurred on 26 July 2005, when Mumbai received more than 650 millimetres (26 in); the massive flooding that resulted killed over 900 people.

Remote regions of Jammur and Kashmir, such as Baramulla district in the east and the Pir Panjal Range in the southeast, experience exceptionally heavy snowfall. Kashmir's highest recorded monthly snowfall occurred in February 1967, when 8.4 metres (331 in) fell in Gulmarg, though the IMD has recorded snowdrifts up to 12 metres (39 ft) in several Kashmiri districts. In February 2005, more than 200 people died when, in four days, a western disturbance brought up to 2 metres (7 ft) of snowfall to parts of the state.

Current sea level rise, increased cyclonic activity, increased ambient temperatures, and increasingly fickle precipitation patterns are effects of global warming that have impacted or are projected to impact India. Thousands of people have been deplaced by ongoing sea level rises that have submerged low-lying islands in the Sundarbans. Temperature rises on the Tibetan Plateau are causing Himalayan glaciers to retreat, threatening the flow rate of the Ganges, Brahmaputra, Yamuna, and other major rivers; the livelihoods of hundreds of thousands of farmers depend on these rivers. A 2007 World Wide Fund for Nature (WWF) report states that the Indus River may run dry for the same reason.

Severe landslides and floods are projected to become increasingly common in such states as Assam. Ecological disasters, such as a 1998 coral bleaching event that killed off more than 70per cent of corals in the reef ecosystems off Lakshadweep and the Andamans, and was brought on by elevated ocean temperatures tied to global warming, are also projected to become increasingly common.

The Indira Gandhi Institute of Development Research has reported that, if the predictions relating to global warming made by the Intergovernmental Panel on Climate Change come to fruition, climate-related factors could cause India's GDP to decline by up to 9per cent. Contributing to this would be shifting growing seasons for major crops such as rice, production of which could fall by 40per cent. Around seven million people are projected to be displaced due to, among other factors, submersion of parts of Mumbai and Chennai, if global temperatures were to rise by a mere 2 °C (3.6 °F).

Such shifts are not new. Earlier in the Holocene epoch (4,800–6,300 years ago), parts of what is now the Thar Desert were wet enough to support perennial lakes; researchers have proposed that this was due to much higher winter precipitation, which coincided with stronger monsoons. Kashmir's erstwhile subtropical climate dramatically cooled 2.6–3.7 Ma and experienced prolonged cold spells starting 600,000 years ago. Thick haze and smoke, originating from burning biomass in northwestern India and air pollution from large industrial cities in northern India, often concentrate inside the Ganges Basin. Prevailing westerlies carry aerosols along the southern margins of the steep-faced Tibetan Plateau to eastern India and the Bay of Bengal.

Dust and black carbon, which are blown towards higher altitudes by winds at the southern margins of the Himalayas, can absorb shortwave radiation and heat the air over the Tibetan Plateau. The net atmospheric heating due to aerosol absorption causes the air to warm and convect upwards, increasing the concentration of moisture in the mid-troposphere and providing positive feedback that stimulates further heating of aerosols.

Citizens of all countries, except Nepal and Bhutan, require a valid national passport or valid travel documents and a valid visa granted by Missions abroad for entering India. Nepalese or Bhutanese citizens need no passport or visa but should possess suitable documents for their identification when proceeding from their respective countries.

Foreigners desirous of visiting India can do so after obtaining visa from the Indian Mission in their country of their residence. They should possess a valid National Passport except in the case of nationals of Bhutan and Nepal, who may carry only suitable means of identification. Usually, a multi-entry visa, valid for a period of 180 days, is granted for the purpose of tourism.

The visa is valid from the date of issue. The facility also exists for the issue of collective visas to group tours consisting of not less than four members and sponsored by a travel agency recognized by the Government of India. Such groups may split into smaller groups for visiting different places in India after obtaining a collective "license to travel" from the immigration authorities in India. However, they must reassemble and depart as the original group.

Transit visas are granted by Indian Missions abroad for a maximum period of 15 days. Foreigners coming to India on tourist visas for 180 days or shorter period are not required to register themselves with any authority in India. They can move about freely in the country, except to restricted/protected areas and prohibited places. Nationals of Bangladesh are exempted from registration upto six months.

If their stay exceeds six months, they have to register themselves. Individuals without nationality (stateless persons; IRO refugees, persons receiving legal or political protection.) should have valid passports, identity documents or sworn affidavits along with the visa for which they should apply two months in advance. Family passports issued by other governments are recognized without discrimination.

Tourists may note the no *Landing Permit Facility* is available to any foreign tourist landing without a visa. A limited facility exists only for group tours consisting of four or more members and sponsored by a travel agency recognized by the Government of India. Children of foreigners of Indian origin below the age of 12 may be granted a landing permit by the immigration authorities' upto a period of 90 days to see their relatives, in case they happen to come without a visa.

A tourist group arriving by air, ship or by a chartered or scheduled flight may be granted a collective landing permit for a period of upto 30 days by the immigration authorities on landing, provided the group is sponsored by a recognized travel agency and a pre-drawn itinerary is presented along with details of passport *etc.* of the members and the travel agency gives an undertaking to conduct the group together.

As a rule no extension of stay is granted on a Tourist Visa. Other Types of Visas: If a foreigner wishes to come to India for a purpose other than tourism, he should come after obtaining one of the following visas.

A foreigner can obtain one from an Indian Embassy abroad. A multiple entry visa is valid for 5 years, provided he wishes to come for some business. Foreigners of Indian origin can obtain a 5 year multiple entry visa for business, to meet their relatives *etc.* A student visa can be obtained from the Indian Embassy on the production of proof of admission and means of sustenance while in India, *etc.* The visa is valid for one year but can be extended in India for the duration of the course. Delegates coming to attend international conferences in India can be granted Conference Visa to cover the conference as well as for tourism in India.

Delegates are advised to apply to Indian Embassies well in advance. Foreigners desirous of coming to India for taking up employment should apply for an Employment Visa, which are issued by Indian Missions abroad. Initially granted for a period of one year, it can be extended in India upto the period of contract. Recreation: Foreigners wishing to undertake any international sporting event, trekking, botanical expeditions, yoga, journalists, media men, documentary and feature film makers may obtain visas after due formalities from the Indian Embassy.

Customs Formalities and Regulations

Visitors are generally required to make an oral baggage declaration in respect of baggage and foreign currency in their possession. They are also required to obtain the Currency Declaration Form from the Customs. They should fill in the Disembarkation Card handed over to them by the airline during the course of the flight. For passengers not in possession of any dutiable articles or unaccompanied baggage. For passengers with dutiable articles or unaccompanied baggage or high value articles to be entered on the tourist Baggage Re-Export Form.

Currency Regulations

There are no restrictions on the amount of foreign currency or travelers' cheques a tourist may bring into India provided he makes a declaration in the Currency Declaration Form given to him on arrival. This will enable him not only to exchange the currency bought in, but also to take the unspent currency out of India on departure. Cash, bank notes and travelers' cheques up to US$ 1,000 or equivalent, need not be declared at the time of entry.

Any money in the form of travellers' cheques, drafts, bills, cheques, *etc.* in convertible currencies, which tourists wish to convert into Indian currency, should be exchanged only through authorized money changers and banks who will issue an encashment certificate that is required at the time of re-conversion of any unspent money into foreign currency. Exchanging of foreign currency other than banks or authorized money changers is an offence under Foreign Exchange Regulations Act 1973.

Arrival Formalities

If the visa, for stay in India, is for more than 180 days, a Registration Certificate and Residential Permit should be obtained from the nearest

Foreigners' Registration Office within 15 days of arrival. All persons including Indian nationals are required to fill in a Disembarkation Card, at the time of arrival. Four photographs are also required for registration. The foreigners registered at Foreigners' Registration Office are required to report change of their addresses.

Departure from India

All persons, except nationals of Bhutan and Nepal, leaving by air, road or rail have to fill in an Embarkation Card at the time of departure.

Exit Formalities

Every foreigner who is about to depart finally from India shall surrender his Certificate of Registration either to the Registration Officer of the place where he is registered or of the place from where he intends to depart or to the Immigration Officer at the Port/Check post of exit from India.

Health Regulations

Foreign tourists should be in possession of their Yellow Fever Vaccination Certificate conforming to International Health Regulation, if they are originating or transiting through Yellow Fever endemic countries.

Airports

The international airports in the metro cities offer a range of services ensuring that the traveller on business can continue working while waiting to board an international connection, or when transferring between international flights. These include restaurants, business centers, rest rooms and handy telephones booths. Business centers are equipped with state-of-the-art equipment including word processors and tele fax.

Airports also offer tourist dutyfree and handicrafts shopping, informal snack bars, nursery and baby care rooms and even an art gallery. Dutyfree prices in the airport shops are very competitive, offering you bargains on international merchandise.

Foreign Travel Tax

Passengers embarking on journeys to any place outside India from a Customs airport/seaport will have to pay a Foreign Travel Tax (FTT) of ₹. 500 and ₹. 150 on journeys to Afghanistan, Bangladesh, Bhutan, Myanmar, Nepal, Pakistan, Srilanka and Maldives. No tax is payable on journeys performed by ship from Rameshwaram to Talaimanar and in case of transit passengers, provided they do not leave the customs barrier.

Transit passengers traveling by air who have to leave the airport on account of mechanical trouble but continue their journey by the same aircraft and the same flight number by which they arrive are also exempt from FTT. Transit sea passengers leaving the ship for sightseeing, shopping *etc.* during the ships' call at any of the Indian ports will not be required to pay FTT.

During the 1990s, Turkey's inbound tourism industry underwent massive growth, catapaulting the country from a middle range tourist destination to one of the top 20 most popular tourist destinations in the world. Statistically, inbound tourism grew from 5.389 million in 1990 to 10.428 million in 2000. There has been considerable speculation about the reasons for Turkey's sudden burst of popularity at the end of the twentieth century.

The most credible explanation is that, during the 1990s, Turkey mounted an aggressive and professional promotional campaign to showcase the country's many compelling tourist attractions to its key source markets.

Geographically and culturally, Turkey straddles the two continents of Europe and Asia. Its largest city, Istanbul, bridges both continents. Turkey is a country of many paradoxes. Almost 99 per cent of Turkey's 66 million people are Muslim, but its political orientation is democratic, secular and Westernorientated. Turkey is a member of NATO and—unusually for a predominantly Muslim nation—enjoys cordial relations with Israel and has actively sought membership of the European Community.

Conversely, Turkey has often maintained tense relations with its neighbouring Arab states of Syria and Iraq to its south, problematic relations with Iran to its east, and there has been traditional tension in Greek-Turkish relations to Turkey's west. Historically, in the days of the Ottoman Empire (1500–1917), Turkey dominated much of what is referred to today as the Middle East, including Syria, Iraq, Lebanon, Israel and Egypt. The Ottoman Empire also dominated Bulgaria, Greece and parts of the former Yugoslavia to the west. In a region where political memories are long, there is lingering resentment between many Arab countries and their former Turkish overlords.

To its northeast, Turkey borders the two newly independent states of Armenia and Georgia, formed as a result of the collapse of the former Soviet Union. Relations with Armenia in particular are coloured by Armenian claims of genocide which allege that between 1 million and 1.5 million Armenians were killed by the Turkish army during World War I. The Turks hotly deny claims of genocide and state that the numbers involved were far smaller and most Armenian deaths resulted from a military response to Armenian insurgency during that war.

The establishment of an independent Armenian state in 1990, bordering on Turkey, has led to the first tentative attempts to resolve this historic chasm between the two countries. The collapse of the former Soviet Union enabled Turkey to establish diplomatic and economic relations with many of the predominantly Muslim republics in what was the southern part of the Soviet Union. The major source of recent and contemporary political conflict in the eastern and southern frontier regions of Turkey has been the challenge of

Kurdish separatism. The Kurds are a stateless ethnic group numbering 25 million, most of whom live at the confluence of Turkey, Syria, Iraq and Iran. The Kurdish plight has rarely been reported in the Western media and only came to prominence during the 1991 Gulf War when the United States-led coalition established a 'safe haven' for them in Northern Iraq, an area which has been variously attacked by Iraqi and Turkish forces.

Both countries accuse the Kurds of undermining their sovereignty. US government foreign policy towards the Kurds has at best been confusing: Kurdish nationalism is viewed positively by the US as a source of opposition to Saddam Hussein's regime in Iraq and viewed negatively when it is in conflict with its ally, Turkey.

Kurdish nationalist and territorial claims have long been consistently vague and subject to internal debate among the various Kurdish factions. Some Kurdish factions seek statehood, while others want autonomy in the countries in which they live or simply seek rights as a minority. Kurdish separatists have been in conflict with the governments of all the countries in which they reside.

The confrontation between Kurdish nationalists and Turkey, home to half the Kurdish population, has been especially bitter. Between 1991 and 2001 there were many instances of Kurdish orchestrated terrorism in Turkey aimed at attracting international attention to Kurdish nationalist claims. Some terrorist acts were targeted at tourists, which has presented a continuing problem for the Turkish government and Turkey's image as a safe and desirable tourist destination.

Although this chapter will focus on the impact of the 1999 earthquake on tourism to Turkey, Turkish tourism authorities have regarded Kurdish terrorism as an impediment to the uninterrupted growth of its tourism industry, though a lesser threat than natural disasters.

One of the compelling attractions of Turkey as a tourist destination has been the impact the cross-currents of human history have wrought upon the country's cultural landscape. Modern Istanbul is one of the great urban chameleons of history: it was known as Byzantium during the days of Roman dominance, and was a bulwark of emerging Christian power; after the fall of Rome and the rise of Islam, the city was named Constantinople, the capital of an empire which encompassed Egypt, the Levant and spread into Greece, Bulgaria and the Balkans. From the rise of the Ottoman Empire, it became known as Istanbul. The city was the setting for the rise of secular nationalism led by Kemal Ataturk at the end of World War I.

All over Turkey, there is evidence of indigenous societies and the influence of empires ranging through Greek, Hittite, Assyrian, Roman, Persian, Babylonian and Sumerian. St Paul (born the Jewish Saul of Tarsus in Southern Turkey) traversed Turkey during his journey throughout the Roman Empire to spread Christianity. It is said by some New Testament scholars that Jesus's mother Mary died in Ephesus. The Turkish town Catalhoyuk is claimed by Turks to be the oldest known human urban settlement on earth, dating back 9500 years—a title traditionally challenged by Jericho. Since the September 2001 discovery of a town in Israel on the shores of the Sea of Galilee dating back 23 000 years, both claims are now redundant. However, there is no dispute that the history of human civilization in Turkey is long, varied and fascinating.

The city of Troy, one of the world's most famous archaeological treasures, is located in western Turkey. Capadoccia, curious rock formations of conical peaks, were hollowed out as homes to thousands of people 4000 years ago in southern central Turkey. Nearby Pamukkale is a series of calcium-rich bleached thermal springs millions of years old, which have formed a series of terraced pools along the slopes of a mountain.

Geographically and scenically, Turkey is a country of immense contrasts and beauty. The mountainous east is dominated by the country's highest peak, Mt Ararat, fabled resting place of the biblical Noah's Ark. Turkey is girded by 8000 kilometres of coastline on the Black Sea, Sea of Mamara, Aegean Sea and the Eastern Mediterranean. Turkey's 775 000 square kilometres range from deserts to lush and fertile lands. In recent years, the Turkish Ministry of Tourism has become increasingly effective in communicating the variety and quality of the country's scenic, historical and cultural attractions.

The curse of Turkey's geographical location is that it is situated at the epicentre of a series of fault lines caused by the pressure exerted by three major plates of the Earth's crust. The Arabian, African and Eurasian plates literally squeeze Turkey from north, south and east.

The convergence of these tectonic forces on Turkey has caused frequent earthquakes over the centuries, some of which have been highly destructive and inflicted many thousands of casualties. During the twentieth century alone 96 major earthquakes in Turkey caused 100 000 deaths. The two most destructive earthquakes in Turkey during the twentieth century were the Erzinkan earthquake of 1939, which caused 32 000 deaths, and the Izmit earthquake of August 17, 1999, which resulted in 17 000 deaths. The Izmit earthquake is the focal point of this case study.

Turkey's tourism industry was one of the few success stories of Turkey's troubled economy during the 1990s. As described at the beginning of this chapter, inbound tourism numbers almost doubled between 1990 and 2000. Tourism receipts increased from US$2.705 billion in 1990 to US$7.636 billion in 2000. In 2000, the Turkish tourism industry employed at least 2.5 million people in Turkey, although unofficial estimates are double this figure when taking into account Turkey's large black economy (business conducted without records and in cash only to avoid taxes) and the many merchants who derive much of their living from selling goods and services to tourists. The tourism industry was estimated to contribute 2.1 per cent of Turkey's GNP in 1988. By

1997, tourism's contribution to GNP had more than doubled to 4.5 per cent, or 25 per cent of export earnings.

During the decade 1990–2000, tourism matured to become a significant and strategically vital element in Turkey's economy. The major source market was Europe. Turkey successfully marketed the destination worldwide and attracted a growing diversity of source markets. In 2000, the total inbound tourism numbers reached 10.428 million.

The largest single source market was Germany, primarily driven by the 'visiting friends and relatives' (VFR) market drawn from the 3 million Turks living in Germany at that time. Turkey's ease of access from Europe by road, rail, air and sea, coupled with the modest prices (by European standards) of its accommodation, shopping and internal transport, made it an increasingly popular destination for tourists of all types, ranging from backpackers to luxury travellers.

The growth of Turkish tourism during the 1980s was driven by government-funded developments and marketing initiatives based on a series of five-year plans. These included infrastructure development projects exemplified by the establishment of the Turkish Riviera based on the southern Mediterranean port of Antalya. In the city of Antalya, the opening of a series of casinos (the only legal casinos in the Muslim world) attracted large numbers of tourists from the former Soviet Union and Israel especially, who took advantage of low-priced package tours to the Antalya area.

The casinos were closed in the late 1990s due to religious opposition, but by that time the region was well established as a sun-and-fun resort area with or without the dubious attractions of legal gambling. As prices in Greece began to steadily increase, the high-quality, low-priced Mediterranean resorts of southern Turkey were marketed as an attractive alternative.

Turkish tour operators and developers established ski resorts and a well-defined series of tour programmes, which included many of Turkey's historical, scenic and cultural attractions. The industry diversified to promote eco-tourism and adventure tourism; Christian, Jewish and Muslim pilgrimage tourism; and educational, archaeological and historically-oriented tours. The international marketing of destination Turkey was coordinated by the Turkish Ministry of Tourism, based in the capital of Ankara. Turkish information offices were located in 23 countries by 2000. The activities of Turkish tourism offices were actively supported by the national carrier, Turkish Airlines, and a growing number of Turkish and internationally based tour operators, all of which were able to take advantage of marketing subsidies available from the Turkish Ministry of Tourism.

During the 1990s, the Turkish Ministry of Tourism was utilising the marketing consultancy services of international PR consultants PPK. The strategic and high-quality advertising of Turkey in leading publications and television stations in key source markets was improving destination awareness. The advertisements featured diverse images of Turkey to reinforce the message that Turkey was a destination that appealed to many market segments.

Certain niche marketing programmes were also developed, ranging from promotions to Christian pilgrims in the years leading to 2000 (Christianity's bi-millennial); business travellers from Russia and the Arab world; war veterans and their descendants, packages which had strong appeal to sections of the British and Australasian markets; golfing for the Japanese; and sporting and adventure travel options which appealed to the European and North American markets.

A special campaign was conducted to appeal to the large UK and European academic and schools tour markets, promoting Turkey's many pricecompetitive and well-preserved historical, cultural and archaeological sites. Turkey was increasingly incorporated into multi-destination European package tours.

At the luxury end of the market, Istanbul was featured as the true end of the line on the fabled Orient Express, which until the 1990s only went as far as Venice. Overall, the prime marketing message was the promotion of the diversification of Turkey's appeal as a destination and the capacity of its tourism infrastructure to meet varied tastes and budgets. During the 1990s, the Turkish government upgraded and expanded the main international gateway airports of Istanbul, Ankara and Antalya to more efficiently manage increased demand and also to improve the image of these gateway points.

Turkish Airlines services 113 destinations worldwide and plays an important role in Turkey's destination marketing. Its recent opening of a route from Istanbul to Shanghai is indicative of increasing awareness of the potential importance of a rapidly growing outbound market from China (PRC) which also has a government policy of 'approved destinations' based in part on a proviso that the approved destination must have a direct air link with China.

The Turkish Ministry of Tourism and Turkish tourism offices worldwide actively sponsored familiarisation trips and hostings for travel agents and travel journalists to assist in spreading the marketing message. The Ministry also sought to overcome the powerful negative images portrayed in the highly successful 1978 Hollywood film *Midnight Express,* which depicted two American tourists incarcerated on charges of drug smuggling in Turkey, and that affected a large segment of young American and Western European markets. The film, which depicted cruelty and corruption in Turkey, coloured negative Western—and especially American—images of Turkey for many years, a stereotype that the Turkish tourism industry was anxious to alter.

The growth of high-quality hotel and resort accommodation in Turkey's major cities, resort areas and tourist attractions was beginning to lure the big-spending but fickle markets of the United States and Japan, where travellers sought new and different destinations which offered high-quality accommodation and service. By 2001, Istanbul alone had 5000 five-star hotel rooms operated by most leading international hotel chains.

In their tourism marketing, Turkey's tourism authorities were careful, almost to the point of paranoia, to depict Turkey as a European destination and anxious to avoid being labelled or depicted as a Middle Eastern destination. Turkey did, however, accept being defined in certain markets—such as Eastern Asia and Australasia—as an Eastern Mediterranean destination, provided it was promoted in conjunction with primarily European countries in that region. This attitude was a marketing position and reflected Turkey's geopolitical alignments.

The overall picture of Turkish tourism during the decade 1990–2000 was one of considerable growth. The diversification of Turkey's tourism infrastructure and its weak currency meant that Turkey was a relatively inexpensive destination for foreign visitors, irrespective of the standard of travel, tourist services and accommodation required.

The key interruptions to Turkey's inbound tourism growth in 1991 were attributable to the Gulf War (Operation Desert Storm) and Turkey's actual and perceived proximity to the war zone. Although the war between the coalition and Iraq was officially over by early March 1991, there was an extended period of Turkish involvement in the Kurdish dominated region in northern Iraq.

In 1993, Turkey experienced internal political instability and there was an upsurge in Turkish-Kurdish conflict which impacted on tourism during that year. However, the largest downturn in Turkish tourism numbers during the decade was directly linked to the August 1999 earthquake, which occurred during the height of the summer tourism season and led to a substantial reduction in inbound tourism numbers in late 1999.

The August 1999 Izmit earthquake was one of the most destructive and costly natural disasters afflicting Turkey during the twentieth century, both in terms of human casualties and destruction of residential and industrial property. The exceedingly rapid recovery of tourism to Turkey after this wellpublicised disaster was partly because most of Turkey's major tourist attractions were spared damage from the quake but due mainly to the highly effective campaign to restore the tourism market after the disaster.

On August 17 at 3.00 a.m. local time, an earthquake measuring 7.4 on the Richter scale with an epicentre near the Turkish city of Izmit, 100 kilometres east of Istanbul in the Marmara region of northern Turkey, devastated a large area. Seismologists defined the earthquake as a *shallow quake.* This maximised the destruction to buildings. Casualties were estimated to be 20 000 dead and 50 000 injured. The region in which the earthquake struck was a heavily populated and highly industrialised region of the country. According to a UN report, 350 000 housing units and business premises were damaged or destroyed. Many of the dead and injured were buried in the rubble of their homes while they were sleeping.

The earthquake met with a massive international response of sympathy and support. In addition to the mobilisation of thousands of local rescue workers and medical professionals, rescue and medical aid teams from Israel, the United Kingdom, the United States, Greece, Kuwait, Germany and nineteen other countries arrived at the scene within 72 hours.

There was an international effort involving 64 countries to provide food, medical assistance, temporary shelter and clothing aid to the victims. Rescue and aid teams were hampered by the extensive damage to roads and bridges and the on-site difficulty of access to victims trapped among the rubble of collapsed multi-storey buildings. While the rescue efforts were both heroic and extensive, the reactive nature of response to the Izmit earthquake revealed an ongoing problem of disaster management in Turkey.

Turkey's vulnerability to earthquakes and floods has been a fact of life for thousands of years, yet there appears to have been little done to develop contingency plans and measures which could have assisted in casualty and damage minimisation. A common observation of rescue and relief teams, engineers, financial planners and others involved in assessing the impact of the Izmit earthquake was that there was little or no indication of readiness for earthquakes.

There was little evidence of legislation or enforcement of building regulations to protect structures against the impact of earthquakes. Most private residences and business premises were uninsured. Emergency facilities were poorly equipped or non-existent. There were few if any procedural guidelines to facilitate rescue or evacuation from danger zones. In fact, only since the 1980s had the Turkish government devoted resources to establish seismic stations and it was only as recently as 1998 that early warning systems for floods and other natural disasters were developed.

In November 1997, the Turkish government, in association with the United Nations Disaster Relief Programme, established the Disaster Management Implementation and Research Centre. The DMIRC was established concurrently with the foundation of the General Directorate of Disaster Affairs as a Branch of the Turkish Ministry of Public Works and Settlement. The two organisations were empowered to research and develop contingency plans to deal with disasters and establish early warning systems.

The General Directorate of Disaster Affairs had in fact proposed a series of building codes in early 1999, but by August 1999 they were not subject to legislation—and even if they had been, it would have been unlikely that more than a small fraction of existing structures could have been altered to meet the technical requirements. Turkey's rapidly growing population and residential and industrial building requirements were met by rapidly and poorly built, cheap and usually flimsy buildings. The Izmit disaster and the criticism levelled at the Turkish government's lack of preparedness by the United Nations, the

World Bank, the media and some of the rescue teams led to Turkey upgrading its disaster management infrastructure. In fact, the global effort to assist Turkey led to Ankara hosting the Global Disaster Information Network Conference in April 2000, which resolved to implement global cooperation in the prevention, contingency management, information-sharing, financing, and rescue and recovery procedures for major natural disasters.

The human cost of the Izmit earthquake was massive. However, the financial cost all but crippled the Turkish economy, which had been burdened by 50 per cent per annum inflation, poor balance of payments, massive external debt and a government hampered by ongoing deficit budgeting. The Izmit earthquake ruined much of Turkey's productive industrial heartland. The World Bank's assessment of the Izmit disaster suggested that the net cost of the earthquake would be in the region of US$3.6–6.5 billion, or between 1.5 and 3.3 per cent of GDP in 1999–2000. The assessment was based on increased output in unaffected regions and external financial support. The report was critical of Turkey's lack of preparedness for the disaster in relation to the paucity of enforceable building codes, poor insurance cover and a shortage of contingency measures.

It did, however, praise the Turkish government's preparedness to increase tax to finance social welfare measures to assist the 500 000 homeless and to provide social security, educational and medical services and housing to the families of the 20 000 killed and 50 000 injured. The report called on the Turkish government to establish a centralised fund for disaster relief.

The Centre for Strategic International Studies in Washington DC published a detailed paper by Rusdu Saracoglu, a former Governor of the Turkish Central Bank and Minister of State for the Economy. Saracoglu observed that, during the 1990s, Turkey had experienced high GNP growth coupled with high inflation and a large number of outstanding government and private-sector loans. He described the Turkish financial system as small and weak by world standards.

Saracoglu believed that Turkey needed to operate under tighter controls such as those enforced by the International Monetary Fund. A more disciplined fiscal system would lead to control of interest rates and reduction in inflation and government deficits. In his view, the Izmit earthquake was evidence that these measures needed urgently to be implemented by the government.

The Izmit earthquake generated a vast amount of media coverage, much of it sympathetic to Turkey and especially the plight of the victims. The rescue and recovery effort did a great deal to build bridges between Turkey and the nations involved in providing assistance. The Izmit earthquake was a scene of cooperation of rescue teams from Israel and Arab states and the extensive involvement of US military rescue teams reinforced the Turkey-United States alliance. The political dividend from the US perspective was Turkey's vocal and strategic support for the US 'war against terrorism' following the September

11, 2001 attacks against New York and Washington DC. Turkish support was politically valuable for the United States in seeking to galvanise support from predominantly Muslim countries.

A positive outcome was a thawing in relations between Turkey and Greece. The Greek government provided considerable assistance to Turkey and sent rescue teams. Turkish rescue teams reciprocated when Greece experienced a severe earthquake in 2000. Cultural links and other bilateral contacts increased between Greece and Turkey following the earthquake.

The initial impact of the Izmit earthquake was devastating and immediate. From all key source markets, there were cancellations and a reduction of forward bookings to Turkey. The media coverage at the time of the earthquake painted a picture of Turkish devastation. The normally sobre BBC reported that even central Istanbul was badly hit—though these reports were eventually revised when the actual extent of damage was realised.

The eastern outskirts of Istanbul were indeed affected by the quake, but not the central part of the city. The UK Foreign Office established an update line. On August 18, 1999, the Association of British Travel agents warned British travellers to 'reconsider' visits to Istanbul in the days immediately after the earthquake.

John Cunningham, reporting in *The Guardian* (London), summed up the response of many would-be tourists to the Turkish earthquake: 'after empathising with the victims ... is to wonder whether it is safe to go or holiday there'. His article went on to discuss the impact of disasters, be they terrorism, war or natural disaster, on all destinations. The blanket coverage of global media TV services including BBC, CNN and Deutsche Welle had a particularly profound and negative impact on tourism from Turkey's three largest source markets: Germany, the United Kingdom and the United States.

The impact was magnified when the largest Kurdish resistance movement PKK (Kurdistan Workers Party) issued statements in October 1999 warning tourists to avoid Turkey and threatened attacks on tourists who visited the country.

Although there was intense media interest in the Izmit earthquake at the time of the event, media coverage ran its course and waned within one month. Unlike some other countries discussed in this book, Turkey does not have a large permanent contingent of foreign correspondents and media coverage is subject to far stricter controls than in Western European countries or North America. Other stories such as the onset of the millennium and the great scare of the 'Y2K Bug' rapidly replaced the Izmit earthquake in Western media headlines.

Even the PKK's genuine threats against tourists, which were tactically timed to gain media coverage while world attention was focused on Turkey, failed to stir a great deal of media interest—much to the relief of the Turkish government and the chagrin of the Kurds. In the months between August and December 1999, inbound tourism figures were 30 per cent down on comparable months of 1998. Within a month of the earthquake, Turkish tourism authorities began the task of restoring the market.

The main tasks were:

- Highlighting the minimal earthquake damage to most visited tourist sites in the country and the tourist attractions of Istanbul;
- Encouraging the travel industry to demonstrate support for Turkey by urging their clients to visit;
- Stressing the overall safety of Turkey as a destination;
- Organising familiarisation visits by travel industry and tourism journalists to see Turkey first-hand and pass the message on to their clients/readers/listeners/viewers;
- Cooperate with allied tour operators in the various source markets to help disseminate a positive message about turkey.

The success story of the restoration of Turkey's tourism market in 2000 had a great deal to do with the professionalism of the Turkish Ministry of Tourism's marketing management and the onset of 2000, so frequently and incorrectly described as the 'New Millennium'.

The Turkish Ministry of Tourism was provided with strong moral and financial support by the Turkish government, enabling it to embark on a marketing restoration programme after the Izmit earthquake. The Turkish government recognised that tourism was a strategically important source of foreign exchange and goodwill. Turkish ethnic communities worldwide were encouraged to support the country during the emergency period and to assist in encouraging foreigners to visit.

The first priority for Turkish tourism offices was the mobilisation of media and travel agency hostings to Turkey facilitated by the Turkish Ministry of Tourism with the cooperation of Turkish Airlines and the major tour operators servicing Turkey. Television crews, journalists and travel agents were invited to see the extent of earthquake damage and then visit the main tourist areas to reinforce the message that they were largely untouched by the quake.

This strategy sought to convey a dual message of support for the victims of the quake by spending tourism dollars in Turkey. The Ministry also increased marketing subsidies to operators promoting Turkish tourism product.

The Turkish Ministry of Tourism established a crisis management team immediately after the earthquake to control press releases and messages tailored to the travel industry, the public and the media. The excellent Turkish Tourism web site was utilised to reinforce the prime messages that tourism infrastructure was undamaged, access to the country and popular sites was unaffected and that tourists were safe if they visited. While it is impossible to give a statistical measure of the success of these PR activities, there is no doubt that by January 2000 inbound tourism to Turkey had reached and surpassed the levels of the pre-earthquake period of 1999.

Turkey also actively promoted itself, sometimes in conjunction with Israel and Italy, as a key destination for Christian pilgrims during Christianity's bimillennial in 2000. During Pope John Paul II's series of visits to Christianity's holiest sites during the 2000 Holy Year declared by the Roman Catholic Church, Turkey was an integral part of the Pope's eastern Mediterranean itinerary.

Mr Erdal Aktan was appointed in 2001 to manage the Turkish Tourism Office in Australia. He had served in London during the early 1990s and was involved in the PR campaign to thank rescue teams in Turkey during 2000. As a gesture of the Turkish government's appreciation for their efforts Mr Aktan organised the hosting in Turkey of members of rescue teams from the 24 countries that provided rescue and medical teams during the earthquake crisis.

According to Mr Aktan, these hostings were warmly welcomed by the invitees and generated considerable positive publicity about Turkey in the countries which had provided the teams. The hostings also included reunions between rescuers and the people and communities they had assisted and helped publicise the recovery of devastated areas.

The Turkish Ministry of Tourism, with the assistance of its marketing consultants DDB Dreamworks, designed a new logo for Turkish tourism and released a new advertising campaign in 2000. The campaign focused on traditional themes of the diverse attractions of destination Turkey, but it also emphasised spirituality, 'green' and environmentally sensitive themes. The campaigns of 2001 were ethereal compared with the simple message of the 1990s, which was that Turkey was a jigsaw of attractions.

Considerable emphasis was placed on finding testimonials from people who had visited after the earthquake and whose opinions would carry weight in source markets. Concerts were staged in Turkey featuring European and American celebrities who could show their concern for the victims of the earthquake and then see Turkey and pass on the message to their audiences that it was safe to visit—a popular, mutually beneficial and effective public relations strategy.

The combination of creating a new marketing image, reassuring travellers and travel agents, and promoting a new millennial interest in Turkey all contributed to the acceleration of Turkey's tourism restoration. Overall, the combination of strategies was highly successful.

The other element which helped to achieve rapid recovery was the working alliance between the national tourism authority, airlines servicing Turkey (especially Turkish Airlines), and the Turkish and overseas tour operators marketing Turkey. Turkey's phenomenal growth as a destination during the 1990s provided considerable business for many private companies, hoteliers, charter carriers, and transport and tour operators servicing Turkey.

Apart from a genuine concern about speeding the recovery of Turkish tourism for all these businesses, there was a powerful element of enlightened self-interest to facilitate and accelerate the recovery.

Of the case studies in this book, the recovery of Turkey's tourism industry from the devastating Izmit earthquake was one of the most rapid and complete marketing restoration campaigns. While the Izmit earthquake represented a single incident, it was one of a series of earthquakes which Turkey, due to its geological structure, will regrettably continue to experience.

Turkey's strength, in common with that of Fiji, involved a well coordinated marketing campaign combining the resources of the government and private sector. A distinguishing factor of the Turkish recovery was the welltargeted and effective PR campaign directed at the travel industry from major source markets and the media. In the future, Turkey's position in a geologically and politically volatile part of the world will almost certainly require Turkey's tourist authorities to maintain their crisis management contingency plans in good working order.

8

Tourism Policy and International Organizations

So much has been said about globalization and the need for corrective policies at this crossroads in history, that the demand for solid institutions to design, apply and develop these policies has all too often been overlooked. It was only in the late 1990s, with the Asia-Pacific economic crisis, the situation in Russia and other countries of the former communist bloc - Bosnia, Kosovo or Chechnya - that the mainstream of thought was admitting to the need for second generation reforms, that is to say, policies aimed at reinforcing institutions.

Given this situation, theoretical thinking in tourism and actual tourism policies are still somewhat behind the times. The need for an explicit national tourism policy is at times questioned: such tourism powers as the United States have dismantled their central tourism agencies; others, like the European Union, assign their tourism policy to small departments with absurd budgets, inadequate staff resources and incoherent programmes.

In some countries, especially in those which have recently become active in tourism, interventionism is practised, while others employ the discredited if well-intentioned formula of leaving business to the businessmen, while the public administrations carry out the promotion.

The panorama is even more baffling at the international level. While all main agents of tourism - airlines, hotel chains, tour operators, tourism administrations, *etc.* - discuss and/or defend globalization, little is done to analyse its contents and implications. In this regard, much less has been done to propose frames and instruments of action for international tourism policy and, beyond that, global institutions committed to the development and coordination of world tourism.

In some cases, it seems that the concept of globalization is introduced to justify non-action or, more specifically, the dismantling of national and international *public* tourism policy. Somehow, the argument goes, the market forces will find a way, and it will be to the benefit of consumers.

In spite of that business philosophy, this chapter deals with public sector intervention, through a specific sectoral policy, tourism policy, which responds to at least two crucial issues:

- The significant contribution of tourism activity to the general aims of economic policy - development, stability, efficiency, *etc.*; and
- The large component of public goods in tourism activity.

An overview of explicit tourism policy implemented in the last decade shows an evolution in its content, from interventionist attitudes and a focus on promotional mechanisms, to the creation of frameworks that foster the competitiveness of tourism clusters and the use of broad scope instruments, quite similar to those present in industrial policy.

Globalization - or rather, the growing trend towards globalization - increases the need for national and interna-tional tourism policies. But the question of who are to be the decision-makers of such policies, and what will be their substance, needs to be examined. Multinational/transnational enterprises will obviously play a role, and it will be naturally concerned with the efficiency and profitability of international tourism.

Non-governmental organizations will also want to intervene to ensure that tourism is compatible with their own agendas, with specific cultural, environmental or social objectives in mind.

Thus, it is vital to analyse what is the role of governments and intergovernmental organizations in global tourism and what may be the adequate substance of international global tourism policy, regarding both the development of tourism and its contribution to global society.

GLOBALIZATION AND TOURISM: THE NEW AGE

In recent years, reference to globalization in the academic and professional world is constant. The notable interdependence between economies and the trend towards greater similarity of lifestyles are two conventional points of reference in the globalization concept. Nevertheless, globalization, under other names, is not a new concept but rather an acceleration of trends that have been active for decades and even centuries.

In fact, in the twentieth century, apart from technological advances and the political and social transformations of the past few decades, there had not been a great advance of this trend. It can even be said that financial and economic institutions in the second half of the nineteenth century were more internationalized than at the beginning of the twentieth century.

What is often understood as globalization comprises diverse economic, social and political phenomena. The intensification of commercial exchanges, marked by the progressive dismantling of protectionist barriers, the growing integration of financial markets, the presence of new industrialized countries and technological developments, especially in the area of know-how and information, are affecting both the national economies and the lifestyles of societies.

All of this is creating the basis for a global system or organization, distinctly characterized by a high level of economic, socio-cultural and environmental interdependence. In the latter area, some authors have pointed to the problems caused by the global warming, pollution and the danger of nuclear war as factors which accelerate globalization. The development of these and other phenomena on a global scale clashes with the entrenched policies and institutions designed for national frameworks, as public policies, debated and occasionally agreed upon in international fora as they may be, still lack the global dimension.In this context, it is not remarkable that tourism activity is both the cause and effect of accelerated globalization. It is useful to point out three essential elements of contemporary tourism:

- The extension of tourism demand throughout the world: the increase in intra- and inter-regional travel - although many strata of the population are still travelling only locally or are strangers to tourism.
- Similarity of tourism demand: convergence of consumer preferences, tastes and lifestyles - although the type of travel is segmented.
- Concentration and similarity of tourism supply: expansion of distribution systems, business mergers, *etc.* - although new specialists agents are appearing on the scene.

To all of this it must added without doubt the impact of new technologies on tourism, which is even more significant than that of changes in consumer taste or in institutional structures. The traditional tourism resources, the comparative advantages (climate, landscape, culture, *etc.*), are becoming less and less important compared with other factors in tourism competitiveness.

Information (or rather, the strategic management of information), intelligence (innovative capacity of teams within an organization) and knowledge (know-how, or a combination of technological skills, technology and organizational culture - *humanology*) now constitute new tourism resources and key factors in the competitiveness of tourism organizations (enterprises, destinations and institutions).

The major (most-visited) tourism destinations of the world are no longer the famous beaches or traditional cultural capitals, but rather man-made products, such as Orlando or Las Vegas. In fact, the greatest foreseeable competition in the medium term for the present tourism activity is not the appearance of new exotic resorts, but instead the massive use of the increasingly accessible and efficient information and communication technologies for new leisure products: virtual travel and experiences.

Tourism thus finds itself in a situation, which Kuhn (1962) would clearly define as a paradigm shift, and which is not casually related to or far from the globalization process of economy and society in general. The concept of a business paradigm, understood as a set of theories, values, attitudes, methods and instruments, rules and practices, is useful when analysing business strategy in given framework conditions.

Thus, it is increasingly seen that, in recent decades, mass tourism business strategies (the Fordian Era of Tourism) - and especially profit-making through economies of scale and the consequent standardization of rigid tourism packages - are giving way to a new paradigm shaped by the segmentation of the new consumer demands, new technologies, new forms of business production and management and new framework conditions.

This new post-Fordian business paradigm in tourism, which Fayos-Solà (1994) called the *New Age of Tourism*, has repercussions on business strategy, and also very profound ones on the policy and even the organization of tourism administrations.

The main objective of tourism policy is to improve the conditions under which tourism activity is carried out. In the Fordian era, increase in tourism activity required a quantitative type of action - which goal was maximizing the number of visitors. In this paradigm, the emphasis on attracting demand corresponded well to the then traditional type of economic policy, based on Keynesian mainstream thinking. Tourism receipts enhanced foreign currency earnings and the creation of employment, so that the success of this sectoral tourism policy allowed other economic policy objectives to be reached, especially those related to economic growth and full employment.

The Keynesian-style policies are based on handling the components of aggregate demand: consumption, investment, public expenditure and net exports (exports minus imports). In this intervention framework, tourism expenditure is considered as an item within exports. The income multiplier - *i.e.* the mechanism which explains how an increase of the variables of aggregated demand (investment, public expenditure and exports) creates an increase in income which exceeds the initial effort - has constituted the central explanatory and justifying mechanism of demand policies.

The transmissions and leakages in the multiplier chain depend on the marginal propensity to consume (the part of each increment in income destined to consumption), on the marginal propensity to import, and the average tax rate. These last two elements constitute leakages in the Keynesian model: the greater these two elements are, the less the multiplier effect in the domestic economy is.

Interior tourism expenditure (domestic plus incoming - traditionally considered under exports) favours the initial effort in the chain. Outgoing tourism expenditure (national less domestic - usually considered under imports) diminish, cancel or make this initial effort negative. The capacity of the national economy to supply the needs of tourism activity affects the marginal propensity to import, increasing or diminishing the final effect of income creation.

Within this theoretical framework we should emphasize how Keynesian-style economic policy makes full sense within a framework of nation-states, where the effects of these policies are highly predictable and controllable. However, this model lost validity after the financial and economic crises at the end of the 1970s, its theoretical base weakened by the difficulty of applying Keynesian formulas when facing wage-price spiralling inflation - stagflation - and a growing internation-alization of the economy.

The dismantling of international trade restrictions (tariffs, import duties, *etc.*) stimulated by the GATT strongly modified the preconceptions on marginal propensity to import. Imports have become less expensive and the previously described chain of induced consumption was easily channelled towards 'foreign' products. 'National' economic areas are now more receptive to foreign products. The leakages of the model described have increased considerably.

In addition, in international tourism markets the emergence of new destinations and products with competitive prices has been constant since these years, and is a strong threat to traditional destinations. With growing competition, it has been necessary to undertake the restructuring of traditional offers.

Within this setting, it is logical that tourism admini-strations since the 1980s have switched their emphasis to supply policies. The main aim of aggregated supply policies is to increase and improve the productive capacity of a country. Without abandoning supply policies, it is necessary to point out the change in perspective caused by this shift, since it was no longer only a question of creating internal or external demand, of improving demand conditions, of fostering their increase or moderation in accordance with the current economic cycle; or of tourism administrations concentrating on promotion.

From this time, the need to improve tourism production to meet with an ever growing competition was felt. This implied the dismantling of sub-sectors, enterprises and unproductive products, a greater research and development (R and D) effort in education and training, in the business quality clusters, in the infrastructure, public services and goods for the sector, *etc.*

This change, from a tourism policy based on demand to supply models, takes into consideration that the basic problem is not tourism demand, which will continue to grow according to all forecasts. Globalization and the increased competition in tourism markets after the 1980s has required a consistent improvement in the price/product-characteristics ratio, that is to say, a continuous striving towards quality and efficiency. The Spanish case provides a good example of the new approach to tourism policies, which prioritizes action on the quantity and, especially, quality of tourism supply, making available to businessmen the necessary mechanisms to increase competitiveness:

- Improving know-how by fostering R and D , tourism education and training, and information management;

- Diversifying the supply, with new products and destinations;
- Physical modernization of installations and infrastructure;
- Improving business clusters, encouraging action by ancillary businesses, associations and the *coopetition* (cooperation-competition) between private agents and the public sector;
- Improving promotion, with greater quality (responding to promotion needs of the actual, existing supply) and efficiency;
- Conservation and regeneration of tourism areas; and
- Improving horizontal (interdepartmental) and vertical (local-regional-state-intergovernmental) coordination of public administrations for tourism policy.

Globalization, governance and the nation-state: implications for national tourism policies

As several authors have pointed out, the discussion on globalization often covers up highly ideological visions of the future; there is no true evidence that globalization has gone beyond the acceleration of political, economic and cultural internationalization processes which began in many cases centuries ago, and in any case, it does not appear to be totally just to use this concept to defend a radically anti-political vision of the world in the twenty-first century.

It is obvious that the debate on globalization has rekindled extreme right and left ideological points of view. For the former, globalization will offer new hope (after the failure of the monetary experiences of the 1970s and 1980s) for a world where free trade, world capital markets and transnational organizations can fully use productive resources without the clumsy interference of governments.

For the radical left (also affected by the fall of state socialism and the anti-imperialist movements of past decades), globalization of capitalism indicates the uselessness of social-democratic style 'welfare' initiatives carried out at a national level.

If we examine the general role of the state at present before defining its tourism policy functions, it is quite obvious that its capacities have been redefined. The *sovereignty*, exclusive control (excluding other authorities) of a territory no longer exists. The capacity to 'defend' its citizens from macro-conflicts has been questionable since the era of nuclear arms.

The claim to standardize and control culture within borders is also no longer justifiable; citizens of the world establish cultural affinities and links through means of communications that escape the control of nation-states and almost any censoring attempt. Finally, and this has been remarked previously, economic internationalization makes it practically impossible to carry out autonomous economic policies.

But all this does not signify either the disappearance of the political role of nation-states, or a great change in international relations. Perhaps it should be recalled that in the first place the very sovereignty of states, as defined in the seventeenth and eighteenth centuries, has always depended on their international recognition. The guarantee of non-intervention by other states allowed the consolidation of sovereignty in the state itself.

Also, although nation-states have seen their capacity for exclusive control of a *territory* enormously diminished, what is true is that they still have a central role in the control of the *population* of this territory, taking into account that it is much less mobile than either information or economic flows.For this reason, it seems that the issue under debate is not the avowed disappearance or reduction to a minimum of the role of the nation-state in a 'globalized' world, but rather the question of governance in a more integrated society at world level and the role of governments in this society.

There is no doubt that the nation-states have a vital role in this process: they still possess a great deal of the power and, in any case, maintain the legitimacy of representing the populations that live within their frontiers; and beyond having an unquestionable role as 'local' suppliers of certain public goods in the world context,

They are the natural interlocutors in intergovernmental organizations that can possibly make advances in the task of designing, proposing and maintaining standards (voluntary, agreed or legislated) for the functioning of international and/or global systems.

Although there may be other protagonists in the creation of framework conditions - multinational companies for example - it does not seem that they can claim a greater representation of the world's citizens, and the authentic multinational nature of many companies - which in reality are strongly established in one of the developed regions of the world and also have operations and subsidiaries in other countries and regions - is questionable.

In any case, it seems evident that the *second generation* tasks, to which the introduction of this chapter refers - the creation and strengthening of responsible international and global institutions in charge of these framework conditions - will in great part depend on the collaboration between nation-states and other major protagonists on a world level.

Within the area of tourism activity, and, as has been previously indicated, the transition from national policies almost exclusively quantitative in dimension (maximizing the number of tourists through promotion), to others stimulating competitiveness (quality and efficiency) in an international context, entails a change of traditional functions in the tourism public sector.

This change can be summarized as follows:

- First, the transition from a situation where the public sector owns and operates all types of tourism facilities and intervenes customarily in the direct provision of goods and services, to a role of coordinator of private and public actions in tourism.

- Second, the opening up of the goals and means of tourism policy, from an almost exclusive promotional content (generic advertising, trade missions and exhibits, publications, *etc.*), to a broad range of instruments to foster and facilitate the activities of tourism decision-makers.
- Finally, the evolution, from a philosophy of rigid regimentation of entrepreneurial activities, to deregulation and privatization of tourism.

This ties in well with the new role of the nation-state: international representation of populations (and enterprises) located within its frontiers, concordance of interests which are not always in agreement - through the stimulation of associative and cooperative activity - and the improvement of the quality of life within its territorial limits.The implications for the formulation of national tourism policies are clear:

- The objectives of these policies must refer to the creation of competitive frameworks on a local-regional-national scale which, by improving the conditions of the economic, social and environmental framework, achieve contributions of the tourism sector to the well-being of the citizens.
- Although the use of promotional instruments by tourism administrations (communication, publicity, *etc.*) continues to be requested by decision-makers in tourism, its importance is decreasing. On the other hand, the need to coordinate promotion with a wider range of instruments in tourism policy has become evident.
- The new public instruments for tourism development and management are not fundamentally different from those used in sectoral industrial policy. Essentially, they foster the competitiveness of existing tourism clusters and the adoption of strategies for success in international markets of emerging destinations or those which are in the process of restructuring.

Although a study of the budgets of national tourism administrations indicates that public expenditure in tourism is still greatly concentrated in promotional instruments, in the area of competitiveness and strategy there is a growing dedication to Porterian-type instruments. Specifically, the new tourism policies of countries such as France, Spain, Italy, Germany, Canada, Australia and South Africa concur in the use of the following instruments:

Strengthening supply conditions:

- Human resource development in tourism. Education and training which is more in line with the short, medium and long-term needs of the tourism employers. Awareness of the need to anticipate the upsurge of new tourism professions and the continuous training of professionals in the sector.
- Fostering innovation and development (R and D) specifically for use by tourism enterprises. Awareness of the need to give priority to

the R and D of tourism processes over the R and D directly applicable to products and services.

- Modernization of the productive plant, installations and infrastructure in tourism. Awareness of the need to make compatible the modernization of the supply of public and private goods and services, and to create lasting mechanisms to permanently (and not on a one-time basis) carry out this task.
- Impetus of diversification and specialization in tourism destinations, products and services, although taking into account that the competitive advantages are more easily achieved in the realm of tourism processes.
- Stimulus to the conservation of natural, cultural, urban or rural areas in which tourism is carried out, and of heritage sites sensitive to tourism use. Awareness that these areas form part of the consumer *tourism experience* and that there is no tourism product and destination quality without eco-tourism quality.
- Fostering a more even geographical distribution of tourism supply and demand, in support of other more generic objectives of public policy (*e.g.* an incomes policy for farming in disadvantaged areas). This has to be tightly coordinated with the responsible regional and local governments.

Strengthening the business fabric:

- Fostering of associative and cooperative initiatives between tourism enterprises and destinations. Awareness of the need to cooperate and not only compete at the intra-cluster and inter-cluster level in the context of a national tourism policy.
- Stimulus to give tourism activities an adequate dimensional scope. Awareness that this dimensional scope depends on the nature of niche-markets and the (changing) state of available technology. New information and communication technologies allow for new solutions in this respect.
- Public and cooperative contributions to sectoral and sub-sectoral information management, useful for decision-making at the enterprise, sectoral association, *cluster*, tourism destination level or even at a macro-national level.
- Adaptation of the judicial and institutional framework to give confidence and greater efficiency to business decision-making. Awareness of the need to make this framework flexible so that it continuously adapts to rapidly changing circumstances.
- Contribution of the tourism administration and sectoral cooperation institutions to *strategic*decision-making, beyond considerations of short-or medium-term quality and efficiency and the search for excellence in established market niches.

Strengthening demand conditions:

- In the context of the Porterian paradox that a better informed, exigent and sophisticated demand favours competitiveness and strategic positioning of enterprises.
- Obtaining and disseminating market information on consumer groups typology and communication channels for this purpose.
- Improving the promotion policy, from an instrument based on passive information on the positive characteristics of products, destinations and cultural and environmental amenities, to a means of forming and modulating the expectations and even the perceptions of the clients.
- Support to marketing efforts of tourism enterprises and destinations. Awareness of the role of new technologies and stimulus to innovation in tourism marketing processes.
- Improving the tourism information milieu in which consumers, workers, enterprises and tourism administrations move. Awareness that the cost of obtaining this information for the individual decision-maker may be high and that it is therefore preferable to approach this matter as the provision of a public good.
- To strengthen tourism training and qualifications, not only within the business context, but also in that of the consumer and host societies.
- Protection of the consumer-tourist, improving the applicable standards and the inter-administrative coordination. Awareness that today's tourist demands a high degree of confidence in the quality of the product and in his personal safety as an essential condition to increasing his loyalty to tourism products, services and destinations.
- Integral management of tourism quality to increase the level of consumer satisfaction and the well-being of receiving societies. Awareness that it is essential to have existing client loyalty to be competitive in tourism destinations, and that this cannot be achieved only through aggressive commercial promotion aimed at new clients.

Strengthening of linked industries and services:

- Stimulus to the creation and adequate functioning of related industries and services in tourism clusters and destinations. Awareness of their relevance, both in the horizontal (complementary) and vertical (suppliers, sub-contractors and client companies) sense to achieve competitiveness.
- Coordination of public administrations concerned with tourism, both in the horizontal (departments within an administration) and vertical (local, regional and national administrations) sense. Awareness that the public administration in general (and not only the *tourism* departments of the same) constitutes part of this institutional and business milieu essential for competitiveness in tourism.

- Stimulus to the re-engineering of the macro-processes within the tourism clusters and destinations. Awareness that it is possible to achieve the necessary quality objectives by improving the efficiency of the optional useable processes. Re-engineering of public administrative processes and their coordination with the private sector, improving their quality and dedication to service, usually is an important part of this instrument.

THE ROLE OF INTERGOVERNMENTAL ORGANIZATIONS IN TOURISM

In spite of abundant references in professional and academic literature to globalization in tourism, the fact is that the tourism business fabric is mainly made of sub-sectors with a large number of medium, small and micro industries, often of a marked local character.

The most notable exceptions are the air transport sub-sector in itself and the existence of some large enterprises in the hospitality (hotel chains), travel agency (certain tour operators) and entertainment (macro theme parks) sub-sectors. In fact, though, one of the best-known business lobbies in the sector, the World Tourism and Travel Council (WTTC), which defines itself as comprising the chairpersons and highest executives (CEOs) of the largest companies in the world, has only seventy-five members.

In addition, even when considering these large tourism enterprises, there is reason to question their status as *global* enterprises. Most frequently, they are strongly identified - by origin, business culture, major operations and decision-making strategies - with one of the countries of the G3 triad (North America, Europe and Japan), with their presence in other countries being as subsidiaries, franchises, *etc.*

For these reasons, it is difficult to agree with the statement that 'tourism is one of the most globalized industries'. The fact that many of the industry's clients have to cross borders to travel and that there are suppliers with products in several countries can grant it, at the most, a partially *international* character.

According to WTO estimates, only one in ten tourist movements is international, while the rest are domestic. Thus, although international tourism demand is already more than 650 million trips annually and is growing at an accumulative yearly rate of 4.3 per cent, most travel takes place within world-regions (Europe, North America-Caribbean, East Asia-Pacific) and within national borders. Additionally, tourism, unlike financial transactions or information flows, requires the physical transport of people, a characteristic which makes it highly controllable by the sovereignty, albeit residual, of nation-states. Thus, it seems reasonable to defend the premise that the tourism industry is still in a phase of international activity, although it is also true that tourism is, on the other hand, contributing to the worldwide dissemination of cultural and social habits, and is therefore in this regard, a *factor* in the globalization process.

However, the importance and growing expansion of international tourism, its contribution to the development of regions and countries, to income and employment creation, its status, which has already been mentioned, as a transmitter of cultural identity images, all justify the attention it has merited and still merits from institutions on a worldwide scale as well as the existence of an intergovernmental organization (WTO) specifically dedicated to international tourism policy.

Neither an analysis, nor an exhaustive inventory of the international institutions, which have had or do have influence, either direct or indirect on tourism flows, is attempted here; the list is too long and the analysis complex. Many international organizations and agencies, from the OECD, with a tourism committee whose existence is now at risk, to the World Bank, have given attention to some of the most relevant functions of tourism activity.

The European Union, in 1989 for the first time, granted responsibility for tourism policy to a specific department - its General Directorate XXIII - although the budgetary provisions given to the tourism unit were always minimal and the main part of the European budget had a much stronger impact on tourism activity through the structural funds, programmes for innovations and training or, in the case of third world countries, through development aid programmes.

Perhaps the most relevant issue, in the context of this chapter, is the substance of supranational intergovernmental action in tourism, *i.e. international tourism policy*, and the viability and pertinence of hypothetical global tourism policy. Justification of an international tourism policy, apart from the arguments already indicated, is also based on the growing importance of the knowledge factor in the production of tourism services and *experiences*.

Perhaps, somewhat paradoxically, the tourism industry, the origins of which tied it geographically to nature resources and/or historical or cultural heritage, has freed itself from these conditioning factors, to the extent where the most sought after tourism destinations at present are often totally artificial (man-made).

The use of communication in tourism, often tied to the leisure-entertainment industry, has shaped new consumer needs and created a demand for new tourism destinations in a process where communication-entertainment (the film industry, computerized games, the internet, television, publishing, *etc.*) has created expectations in potential tourists which are later satisfied (theme parks, theme hotels, dramatized tourism experiences, *etc.*) with major contributions from information-communication technology and the entertainment industry.

It is in this context, where one can see a rapid tendency towards globalization in the tourism industry, standardizing supply and demand and freeing them from the confines of stationary cultural or natural realities, and making it almost indistinguishable from the leisure industry, advancing towards a future of *virtual experiences* that could easily escape the control of the sovereignty of states. What should the substance of a contemporary international tourism policy be, and in what direction should this policy move, taking account of the previously mentioned tendencies towards future globalization?

The first issue should, without doubt, be to identify the players in tourism policy. If the globalization of tourism is not considered to have already happened, there is still time and the opportunity to identify those players who are more desirable and those who are less so. There is also time to favour the most sensible future scenarios, seen from the perspective of the contribution of tourism to the well-being of citizens, and their participation in the decisions as to what type of well-being they truly desire.

Far from accepting extreme positions on globalization - *i.e.* that it is already determined, that the decision-making power of multinationals/transnationals is above that of the traditional sources of governance - it is possible to determine explicitly the current players, and possibly future ones, of governance in general and tourism policy in particular:

- *Regional and local administrations*: Although their area of competence falls within the framework of higher level administrations, they have the effective advantage of being close to the citizen and the entrepreneurial units. They constitute the ideal public players to implement sectoral policies, which can be decided on occasion within the local and regional context or coordinated with the administrations having a wider scope of action. In the democratic context they are validated by the vote of their citizens.
- *National administrations*: They still have a wide magnitude of sovereignty. On occasion, they have devolved part of this to regional and local administrations and/or relinquished part to institutions or administrations with an international mandate. In the democratic context, they are endorsed by the vote of their citizens and frequently discharge this representation within international institutions. The consequent limitations (free circulation of capital, elimination of tariffs, *etc.*) are accepted in view of the benefits expected from a better distribution of resources on an international/world scale, but other objectives of national economic policies can be in contradiction with this self-limitation.
- *Supranational administrations*: Their historical origin lies in commercial agreements. The European Union is the most significant experience in this sense. The size of this type of administration enables economic, social, environmental and sectoral policy objectives to be set, which are out of the reach of national administrations, and

they can more successfully confront the undesirable aspects of the globalization process.

- Agreements between countries or even between blocks of countries (G3 or G7 type). These are established to confront specific problems (financial speculation, international crime, *etc.*) and sometimes lead to the creation of international legislation.
- International agencies and organizations created by a group of states to permanently handle specific issues arising from economic, social or environmental activities. In the field of tourism, the paradigmatic player in this category is the World Tourism Organization (WTO).

This final type of player is the one whose decisions on tourism policy are considered here, although the substance of the tourism policy which can evolve should be analysed within the context of other players in international governance.

Non-governmental organizations (NGOs) and private sector businesses and institutions are excluded here as principal players in governance, since they lack democratic representation, although their important role as partners or associates in governance by the previously mentioned players is obvious.The instruments which are useful to the international organizations usually belong to one of the following categories:

- *Legislation*: Agreements with a judicial scope to standardize the laws of member states and even of other states which may join the initiative. These agreements are directed at remedying the non-extraterritoriality of national laws and/or the lack of international legislation and/or the lack of enforcing bodies.
- *Agreements without a judicial scope*: Aimed at eliminating or lessening the repercussions of frontier restrictions by creating a framework for greater security in international transactions. These agreements have a technological, economic, social and/or ethical content. They are generally enforced through specific mechanisms to penalize infractions.
- *Voluntary quality standards*: These are proposed without the need of previous consensus, at the initiative of the organization in question or by a group of member states. They propose a model for conduct with regard to technological, economic, sociological and/or ethical matters. They do not usually have authority to penalize, but are intended rather to oversee or coordinate. They are accepted voluntarily due to the added value they give in terms of promotional image, facilitation in communication with other players in the market, interspatial and inter-temporal measurements, *etc.*

Given the demonstrated difficulty in establishing and developing the tourism policy instruments indicated in the first two categories, it can be said that international organizations specialized in tourism, and concretely WTO, are showing a growing tendency to use voluntary quality standard instruments.

This signifies, without doubt, an advance over the previous situation, where the insistence to establish legal agreements, or even simply enforceable agreements, led to a general impasse given the inability to achieve consensus or wide majorities because of:

- The diverse economic, social, cultural and political situations of the member states;
- The frequently heterogeneous nature of the member state's representation in the organization: Departments of Foreign Affairs, of Commerce and Tourism, of Culture and Tourism, of the Economy (Tourism Department), of Industry and Tourism, of Tourism, *etc.*;
- The variable importance of departments of tourism and of tourism affairs within governments of member states, where on occasion they play a minor role;
- With regard to legislative instruments, the difficulty that departments with competence in tourism have to influence sufficiently the deliberations and decisions of the national legislative powers.

The instruments in the voluntary quality standards category can point to models, of varying types, for flexible and rapid action, which can be gradually adopted by member states and even as a global voluntary standard. These models can successfully bring added value to international markets, which are potentially global, and can be adapted to different national situations.

Although the explicit adoption of a voluntary standard by a sovereign state facilitates its global establishment, this can be expedited, in the case of delay or a lack of will, if the standard is *de facto* adopted by the industry and/or citizens of the country in question. Furthermore, the standards proposed can also fail when their format is rejected or ignored by potential users.

Thus, in this context, it should be noted that the role of international organizations in tourism, and specifically that of WTO, is rapidly evolving, from the traditional one of a forum where countries meet, to that of serving as an information broker between the countries and of being responsible for carrying out economic development projects and giving specific assistance to countries, up to the present role of also serving as an institution where voluntary quality standards are created and implemented in such key areas of tourism as:

- The development of human resources for tourism - education, training, strategy, management and labour conditions;
- Statistical information;
- Market intelligence;
- Know-how in products, services and processes;
- Infrastructure, collective services and urban environments;
- Cultural and environmental aspects of tourism;

- Economic and social effects of tourism;
- Facilitation of international movements of travellers and tourists;
- Financing of tourism;
- Quality of products, services and tourism environments;
- Communication in tourism;
- Ethical aspects of tourism activity;
- Legislative processes and contents in tourism; and
- Coordination of administrations with competence in tourism - intra-administration, inter-administrations, and with the private sector.

The content of the tourism policy instruments being used in contemporary action is justified by the two major reasons for the existence of international organizations specialized in tourism (and that of the WTO itself):

- International and global public goods, externalities, market imperfections and merit and demerit goods.

To analyse the contemporary scope of this justification it must be realized that the foundations - *i.e.* the so-called resources - of tourism activity are rapidly changing. In principle, as has already been indicated, cultural and natural resources were those backing tourism development. The addition of financial capital and work efforts to these resources created tourism products. The comparative advantages of tourism destinations were based on the abundance and correct combination of these elements.

At present, the relevance of natural and cultural resources has diminished - except for world-class resources and in specialized niche markets - while the importance of financial capital and above all that of information, intelligence-creativity and know-how - used by human teams in business and organizational cultures prepared for competiveness and strategic success - has increased.

Given these circumstances, the role of international organizations specializing in tourism is clear:

- The provision of public goods which previously were the domain of the states, such as quality education and training, strategic information and basic know-how;
- The internalization of externalities in the planetary context, such as the costs of pollution or possible climate changes;
- The correction of imperfections in international markets such as the costs of information or the appearance of highly monopolized tourism operations; and
- The introduction of ethical criteria in carrying out tourism activity on an international scale (working conditions in tourism, sexual exploitation in tourism and the like).

This first justification of the activity of WTO or other international organizations clearly shows the differences between intergovernmental agencies or organizations - created by and responsible to a (large) group of states, and occupied with international governance - and other international organizations (such as NGOs, motivated by more specific aims), international business lobbies or large enterprises, whose objectives differ from, and on occasion are in conflict with, those mentioned above.

- The benefit to member states of exercising their sovereignty in optimal conditions and of supplementing it when it is questioned or proves inefficient in the globalization process.

This is where the traditional role of international organizations is evolving towards greater technical contents, which give depth and relevance to the member states' fora of discussion. Without assuming a conceptual breach with this traditional role, it is obvious that the use of a voluntary standard type of instruments, already mentioned above, gives greater flexibility and scope to the resolutions discussed and adopted in these fora, which are later subjected to a validation process - through an appraisal of their value in the market and society and their acceptance or not by businesses, institutions and the citizen.

The acceptance and establishment of these standards, when it takes place, represents a real step towards international and global governance for:

- It makes it possible to have truly global rules (standards), backed by states, which are more representative than businesses or other types of organizations;
- This acceptance happens only when the standards create added value for a large enough number of social and economic players;
- It reinforces the role of the organizations creating and overseeing these standards as well as the capacity of such organizations to adapt them to changing circumstances with greater democratic legitimacy.

Although the concept of globalization is broadly used in academic and professional literature, its exact definition, its measurement and its effects are far from being clear. The mere reference to phenomena affecting the world is still conceptually weak and cannot be used as evidence of globalization without being qualified.

Economic, technological or cultural internationalization processes are not new, and their present acceleration does not imply that globalization is inexorable. Historically these processes have stopped and reversed several times. It is also not evident that these processes and their future culmination in globalization imply the disappearance or impotence of the sovereignty of nation-states. This assumption on occasion responds to a highly ideological view of world society. States still have mechanisms to control large enterprises and to create new instruments for governance, guaranteeing democratic control of future scenarios compatible with the well-being of a majority of the citizens.

Multinational/transnational enterprises are not necessarily global, since their cultural and strategic bases and the greater part of their business volume are generally found in only a few countries, normally located in the area of the G3 (North America, Europe or Japan). The phenomena related to globalization affect tourism differently, depending on whether demand or supply are being considered. Demand shows clearer globalization tendencies as consumer preferences and expectatives converge, even though the *type* of holidays sought is becoming more diverse. On the other hand, tourism supply is still far from being global; thus, multinationals in tourism have not permeated the markets, with a few exceptions such as airlines, and hotel chains.

The business fabric in almost all tourism sub-sectors is formed by hundreds of thousands of small and micro enterprises. In addition, international tourism, although significant and rapidly growing, only represents a minor part of the total volume of the tourism business, in the most part domestic. As tourism implies the physical movement of people, the capacity of the states to exercise their sovereignty in this activity is obvious.

National tourism policy will remain a key factor in the development of tourism in a majority of countries for at least the next decade, although devolution to regional and local governments may change its role in some areas. The importance of tourism and its economic, social and environmental implications, which affect governance and broader scope economic policy, speak in favour of establishing explicit national tourism policy frameworks.

This sectoral policy may then be implemented by regional and local administration, which is closer to concrete tourism destinations and business clusters. The question is therefore one of reassigning tasks and it does not imply the automatic weakening of national tourism administrations.

The substance of tourism policy in key countries has been broadly in line with other economic sectoral interventions, particularly industrial policy. Emphasis has shifted, from almost exclusive concern with promotion, to a wider range of instruments acting on productive conditions as well. However, the specific characteristics of tourism supply ask for special attention being put in certain elements of competitiveness.

The comparative advantages (natural and cultural resources) which used to be the base for the success of tourism destinations are giving way to *competitive* advantages in a new business paradigm (the New Age of Tourism) where information, inteligence and know-how play a vital role.

These national tourism policies increasingly have a central theme: the use of Porterian style instruments to foster the competitiveness of tourism clusters (destinations, sub-sectors and/or groups of enterprises).

These instruments belong to one or several of the following types:

- Strengthening the supply conditions;
- Strengthening the business fabric;
- Strengthening the demand conditions;
- Strengthening of linked industries and services.

Even though it may be premature thinking of tourism as an already globalized activity, the importance and expansion of international tourism does justify the treatment of tourism matters in international-scope organizations and the existence of an intergovernmental institution (the WTO) specifically dedicated to international tourism policy.

The work programme of any intergovernmental institution committed to tourism, and, in particular, that of WTO, must respond to two types of rationale:

- The importance in tourism of international and global public goods, externalities, market imperfections and merit and demerit goods; and
- The benefit to member states of exercising their sovereignty in optimal conditions and of supplementing it when it is questioned or proves inefficient in the globalization process.

When in this context, tourism policy implemented by an intergovernmental organization represents a real step towards international and global governance.

International legislation or enforceable agreements are rather rigid instruments for international tourism policy. The evolution of national tourism policies - towards deregulation, privatization and a role coordinating public-private partnerships - leads the way to a more participative and less coercive kind of tourism policy.

The preferred type of instruments of such a policy is found in the realm of voluntary standards of quality; they can be very flexibly adopted by countries, destinations or the industry. These types of instruments adapt best to the difficulties found in developing international tourism policy given:

- The heterogeneous nature of government departments competent in tourism;
- The diverse economic, social, cultural and political conditions in nation-states;
- The variable importance of departments of tourism within governments of nation-states, where on occasion they play a minor role; and
- The difficulty that departments with competence in tourism have to sufficiently influence the deliberations and decisions of the national legislative powers.

The threats and opportunities characterizing the internationalization and globalization processes in contemporary society require, in tourism as well, responses beyond *ad hoc* legislation, treaties or agreements. International and global matters need international and global *institutions*.

The liberalization of trade and tourism, the removal of obstacles and the consequent improvement in the allocation of resources make for big improvements in the well-being of the peoples of the world. However, it is important to pay attention to the *actors* of the globalization processes. Multinational/transnational companies and non-governmental organizations are without doubt very relevant decision-makers in the new realities - but they cannot play the leading role in representative governance, which is a question of increasing concern at world level.

Tourism, because of its importance in the development of regions and countries and its capacity to convey images of cultural identity - so deeply needed in the configuration of global society - requires international and global *representative* organizations, to play a key role in world governance.

9

Tourism Demand and Competitiveness

Globalisation is already evident in most aspects of tourism activity. International tourism and hospitality enterprises have taken advantage of numerous factors to expand their operations globally. Globalisation has raised competitive pressures by bringing more entrants into the market and as a result enterprises have to compete within a much more complex environment. Emerging technologies enabled greater homogeneous control and operational systems as well as coordination with head office despite geographical location and distance.

Changes in the political and legal environment introduced greater freedom of trade and more specifically in travel deregulation of transportation and more flexible and adaptive international investment and development systems. A wide range of forms and arrangements is followed, from direct ownership, partnerships with local operators and/or governments, to franchising and marketing consortia. Labour mobility also enabled people to travel to different countries to manage properties and systems.

Perhaps more importantly the emerging multi-culturalisation of investors' employees generated through education and training, media reports, and extensive travelling experience developed a new breed of global enterprises which offer their products at a standard quality regardless of locality. As a result of the emerging globalisation new tools are required to manage processes, multi-ethnicity and culture and to support employees and enterprises in satisfying all their stakeholders. A whole range of changes in society and the global economy will need to be taken into consideration in planning and managing tourism destinations and enterprises in the era of globalisation.

This chapter concentrates on leisure tourism and identifies the main trends influencing demand. It illustrates that four main factors propel changes in the international tourism demand and explains that globalisation magnifies the scale and scope of the implications emerging.

The chapter illustrates that the most critical factors affecting demand are:

- Proliferation of technology both on transportation and information technology.

- Ecology and environmental concern.
- An increase of multicultural societies.
- A quest for edu- and enter-tainment, where education and entertainment merge to offer personal development opportunities.

The chapter suggests that tourism demand is going through a transformation which can be explained through the change of the 4Ss framework for seaside tourism: Sea-Sun-Sand-Sex; and the 4Ss framework for urban tourism; Sightseeing-Shopping-Shows-Short breaks, to Segmentation-Specialisation-Sophistication-Satisfaction. This framework should facilitate the interpretation of major demand trends in the international tourism arena in order to assist tourism managers to develop suitable solutions, which will delight, rather than just satisfy, all tourism stakeholders.

TOURISM DEMAND TRENDS AND GLOBALISATION

Tourism demand evolved rapidly in the 1990s altering conventional wisdom and changing a whole range of factors influencing tourism planning and management. Attempting to interpret tourism phenomena and forecast the future of international activity is similar to reading the 'crystal ball'. Tourism has grown enormously in the last half century and become the world's largest 'industry'. It has also developed a multidimensional and multidisciplinary character making the analysis of both demand and supply a complex task. The globalisation experienced alters the competitiveness of destination regions and provokes a whole range of new activities and requirements from the demand side.

Increasingly people are becoming more aware of their limited time and are looking for both value for time and value for money. Predicting international demand trends is therefore a very challenging task, as the dynamic nature of these developments clearly demonstrates that the only constant in tourism is continuous change.

Nevertheless, successful tourism management and planning will increasingly need to identify the factors changing demand trends. The industry should therefore offer meaningful tourism products and also provide strategic and operational tools, which can delight consumers and enhance the competitiveness of destinations and enterprises within the global market.

Workers have established their right for leisure time, dedicated to their recreation. Paid annual holidays of about four weeks are nowadays a right for most people in Western developed countries, and the rest of the world is gradually heading in this direction. Leisure time is also increasing gradually, as discussions are in progress in the European Union to reduce the working week to 35 hours and to establish a maximum of 48 hours per week. O'Brien (1996) explains that 'The West European leisure travel market is undergoing structural and cultural changes.

These changes are critical to the future demand for, and supply of, leisure products both to consumers and to intermediaries who distribute travel products.' The European market has experienced a certain level of maturity as the vast majority of North Europeans take annual holidays abroad. In contrast the majority of South European tourists as well as people in North America have traditionally consumed domestic tourism products for a variety of reasons.

A large proportion of these holidays is spent on international trips, especially during the summer season, when people from northern climates traditionally visit southern resorts in order to enjoy the warm weather and waters. These leisure products are widely referred to as the '4Ss', *i.e.* Sun, Sea, Sand and Sex. Leisure 4Ss products are packaged together and consumers purchase a combination of transportation, accommodation and activities packaged together by tour operators. In addition, several other types of demand emerge, especially for short-break holidays, which tend to concentrate on sports and educational activity, hobbies and visiting cultural attractions. This kind of tourism is generally domestic and often takes advantage of resources located in urban environments (such as theatres, cultural centres) or rural areas (*e.g.* agriculture or heritage) in close proximity to the main residence of consumers.

In recent years, however, tourism demand started changing towards a new type of activity where the individuality and independence of travellers are placed at the heart of the leisure activities. An environmental awareness is evident and consumers are actively selecting destinations which manage their environmental resources properly. Moreover, 'a return to nature and its pace, the search for a measure of isolation, the concern for hygiene and health, the taste for do-it-yourself, home handicrafts and sport' can be observed along with an increasing interest in cultural issues. In this sense 'people prefer to live their holidays rather than to spend them'.

As a result, Goodall suggested that 'the days of 4S's holidays are numbered'. Buhalis proposed that the traditional 4S's for tourism (sea-sun-sand-sex) be transformed in 'specialisation-sophistication-segmentation-satisfaction'. This process started in the late 1980s and it is expected to dominate the transformation of tourism demand as well as the re-engineering of the industry during the next century.

As a result, both tourism destinations and enterprises will need to appreciate demand trends as well as the factors that affect them in order to predict the needs and want of their travellers and develop satisfactory tourism products.

CRITICAL FACTORS AFFECTING TOURISM DEMAND

A wide range of forces from the external environment propel the changes in tourism demand. The ones that are more critical are summarised in the following points.

Table: Forecast Growth of Worldwide Travel 1995-2010.

Volume of travel	Actual 1985	Actual 1995	Fore cast 2000	Fore cast 2005	Fore cast 2010
Trips abroad excl. day trips (millions)	307	535	632	782	964
Short/medium haul (millions)	272	455	518	617	724
Long haul (millions)	35	79	114	165	240
Nights abroad (millions)	2,828	4,571	5,518	6,903	8,654
Spending abroad (US$bn at 1995 prices)	206	393	516	686	922
Travel charact-eristics					
Nights per trip	9.2	8.5	837	8.8	9.0
Spending per trip (constant 1995 US$ excl. fares)	671	735	816 .	877	956
Spending per night (constant 1995 US$-excl. fares)	73	86	93	99	107
Growth rates per cent					
Trips abroad excl. day trips		5.7%	3.4%	4.4%	4.3%
Short/medium haul		5.3%	2.6%	3.6%	3.3%
Long haul		8.5%	7.5%	7.7%	7.7%
Nights abroad		4.9%	3.8%	4.6%	4.4%
Spending abroad (US$ at 1995 prices)		6.7%	5.6%	5.9%	6.1%

Table: Forecast Trips Abroad by Destination Region 1995-2010.

Trips (mn) Excl. day trips	Actual 1995	Of world (%)	Forecast 2000	Forecast 2005	Forecast 2010	Of world (%)	Growth pa, actual 1985-95 (%)	Growth pa, forecast 1995-2000 (%)	Growth pa, forecast 2000-05 (%)	Growth pa, forecast 2005-10 (%)
Europe/Mediterranean	379.6	71.0	412.2	489.5	566.7	58.8	5.1	1.7	3.5	3.0
North America	58.3	10.9	75.0	95.2	121.8	12.6	5.1	5.2	4.9	5.1
Caribbean	8.0	1.5	12.8	18.4	27.0	2.8	7.1	9.8	7.5	7.9
Central/South America	29.7	5.6	47.2	63.1	84.5	8.8	6.6	9.7	6.0	6.0
Africa (excl. North)	5.0	0.9	5.8	7.4	9.7	1.0	8.0	3.2	4.8	5.6
Middle East	4.2	0.8	5.5	6.2	7.5	0.8	7.6	5.5	2.4	3.8
South Asia/Indian	4.0	0.8	6.0	8.9	13.8	1.4	12.4	8.2	8.4	9.0
Ocean										
South East Asia	18.8	3.5	30.9	45.5	66.4	6.9	13.8	10.4	8.0	7.9
Australia/New Zealand	4.5	0.8	7.5	12.7	22.7	2.4	13.0	10.7	11.3	12.3
Far East/Pacific	22.3	4.2	29.4	35.3	44.3	4.6	8.8	5.6	3.7	4.6
Total	534.4	100	632.3	782.2	964.4	100	5.7	3.4	4.4	4.3

TECHNOLOGY IN GENERAL AND INFORMATION TECHNOLOGY INPARTICULAR

Bradley, Hausman and Nolan illustrate the profound role of technology on the competitiveness of organisations in the global economy, as they claim that 'globalisation and technology are mutually reinforcing drivers of change'. In addition, Metakides asserts that the global information revolution obliges enterprises to 'act local and think global', while transforming dramatically both production and consumption patterns.

The technological revolution since the 1970s has facilitated tourism activity and has enabled consumers to travel further afield at a fraction of the cost and time required earlier on. The proliferation of jet engines, the ubiquitous motor car and new technology vessels and trains have not only reduced money and time required but has also provided the infrastructure for more people to travel.

Consumers are also empowered by information technology. They not only require value for money, but also value for time for the entire range of their dealings with organisations. This reflects people's shortage of time, evident in Western societies. The emerging Internet tools enable consumers to search on-line for information and to undertake reservations. Increasingly, IT and the Internet in particular, enable travellers to access reliable and accurate information as well as to undertake reservations in a fraction of the time, cost and inconvenience required by conventional methods. IT can also improve the service quality and contribute to higher guest/traveller satisfaction.

The availability of information on everything conceivable enables consumers to personalise their tourism bundles and to purchase only the most suitable products. The usage of IT on the one hand is driven by both the development of the volume and complexity of tourism demand, and on the other hand it alters their characteristics and enables individuals to select a much more personalised bundle of tourism products.

Nobody really knows how many consumers are currently connected to the Internet and how many of them buy products electronically. It was estimated that 150 million people or 2 per cent of the global population used the Internet in the late 1990s. Most Internet users match the profile of the most desirable market segments: they are well-educated professionals who travel frequently and have a higher disposable income, as well as a higher propensity to spend on tourism products.

The proliferation of the Internet revolutionised communications as it enabled organisations to demonstrate their offerings globally using multimedia interfaces. Suppliers have an unprecedented opportunity to communicate with their target markets globally, to develop their global presence and to establish direct relationships with consumers. The WTO (1985) argues that 'the key to success lies in the quick identification of consumer needs and in reaching potential clients with comprehensive, personalised and up-to-date information'.

The rapid growth rate and the expeditious increase of on-line revenue experienced in most industries, including tourism, illustrates that electronic commerce will dominate by the year 2005. This justifies massive investments by organisations to develop their electronic presence.

The Internet has revolutionised flexibility in both consumer choice and service delivery processes. Every tourist is different, carrying a unique blend of experiences, motivations and desires often as a result of previous experience, background and social status. Increasingly customers become much more *sophisticated and discerning*.

Tourists become demanding, requesting high quality products and value for both their money and - perhaps more importantly - time. Having experienced several products the new/experienced/sophisticated/demanding travellers rely heavily on electronic media to seek information about destinations and experiences, as well as to be able to communicate their needs and wishes to suppliers rapidly.

Tourists are increasingly frequent travellers, linguistically and technologically skilled and can function in multicultural and demanding environments overseas. The Internet empowered the 'new' type of tourist to become more *knowledgeable* and to seek exceptional value for money and time. New consumers are more culturally and environmentally aware and they often would like a greater involvement with the local society.

ECOLOGY AND ENVIRONMENTAL CONCERN

Ecology and environmental concerns are increasingly becoming more important and attract a higher degree of interest by consumers. 'Green consumers' especially in Scandinavia and North Europe lead a new movement where regions and products, which fail to demonstrate a certain degree of sustainability, are increasingly becoming unacceptable in the marketplace. In tourism, there is a gradual growth of an environmentally friendly tourist who is often referred to as 'green', 'responsible', 'eco', 'ethical', 'alternative', *etc.* A wide range of considerations are related to green tourism which can influence the selection of destination, transportation modes, activities undertaken and products consumed during the holiday. As a result, a growing number of consumers are attracted to natural areas and ecotourism has emerged as one of the more significant powers of change in the international tourism industry.

Different consumers have dissimilar tolerance levels. As a result, Swarbrooke and Horner illustrate that there are shades of green tourism from 'very green' to 'not green at all'. Nevertheless, consumers are becoming less tolerant to environmental damage and actively seek unspoilt areas to spend their holidays. Escaping from environmentally unfriendly urban regions holidaymakers often require sustainable environments where they can relax and play.

Middleton and Hawkins explain ‘there is overwhelming evidence of customer preference for product qualities that are unambiguously concerned with environmental quality at chosen destinations. Even more interesting is the clear evidence of growing preference among experienced travellers’. As a result, a new sector is emerging in the industry to offer green products and at the same time to preserve their sustainability.

However, the ability of destinations and enterprises to restrict themselves and to avoid overexploiting resources is questionable and often it is only a matter of time before greedy entrepreneurs and unwise planning procedures push a destination through the different stages of its life cycle to overdevelopment and oversupply forcing mass tourism. Nevertheless, environmental concern and preference will increasingly dominate consumer choice and it will also determine their willingness to pay as well-preserved destinations and facilities will be able to charge premium prices for the privilege.

MULTI-CULTURAL BACKGROUND

People increasingly live in a multi-cultural environment. A great labour mobility as well as immigration effectively means that societies are often composed of a multi-ethic population. Different cultural backgrounds often entail different customs and values which create dissimilar if not conflicting tourism needs and wants. Multi-culture is also promoted by the emerging global television channels, such as CNN, MTV, *etc.* which on the one hand broadcast global images and social behaviour paradigms, and on the other hand generate interest and curiosity for the ‘global village’. As a consequence.

Consumers become more aware of other places, their political situations and special conditions. In addition, the exposure of consumers to many cultures through previous travelling experiences provides plenty of examples for comparisons and a wealthy basis for building expectations. Globalisation effectively implies that increasingly tourists and the industry need to interact in a culturally diverse environment and to learn how to manage, negotiate and compromise with people from different cultural backgrounds and experiences.

A whole range of new skills are therefore required by the industry to communicate with the entire range of customers as well as to interact with all stakeholders.

EDU- AND ENTER-TAINMENT

Consumers are also increasingly using their leisure time for personal development. Instead of lying by the swimming pool, there is evidence that a greater percentage of tourists use their time at destinations to learn about other cultures, history and customs. Special interest and activity holidays are attracting larger numbers of holidaymakers not only because people lack time to undertake these activities whilst at home, but also because they assume a more active and participative style of holidays where they take the opportunity for personal development and exploration.

Several levels of activity can be identified. People may use the time to practise their favourite sport, such as skiing, tennis, *etc.*; explore an area for a specific interest, *e.g.* archaeology, architecture; learn a new skill, such as cooking, painting; or simply interact with local people to meet, understand and appreciate the local culture.

THE TRANSFORMATION OF TOURISM DEMAND

The development of mass tourism, since the early 1950s, has been based on a combination of 'sea-sun-sand-sangria-sex' products for summer and sea-side holidays and on 'sightseeing, short breaks, shopping, shows, scotch whisky' for urban-based tourism. Holidaymakers from northern/cold regions traditionally 'escape' for a certain period to southern/warmer destinations in order to relax, 'recharge their batteries', restore their physical and mental strength for another heavy winter and hard work at home. Tourists largely enjoyed a 'mass, standardised and rigidly packaged' holiday product, which enabled them to consume tourism products at reasonable prices due to economies of scale.

Recently, however, a shift can be identified in the marketplace, which takes customers away from the traditional tourism demand prototypes to the new era of tourism. The inclusive tour sector in the UK, for example, is set to experience the first decline since 1980, not just simply due to short-run factors or airport congestion and increased prices. A structural shift in consumer preference towards independent or semi-independent trips, and away from perceived mass tourism destinations can be observed.

Other Europeans, and particularly Germans and Danes, also move away from traditional mass destinations and select new, environmentally-friendly and more authentic regions for their holidays. O'Brien (1996) illustrates that across the West European market the estimated ratio of independent to package-booked travel is in the order of 70:30, with the majority of the French, Spanish, Italian and Greek markets arranging their travels themselves. In addition, consumers take a larger number of short holidays.

Consequently, they normally spend a couple of weeks away during the summer and also have two or three short breaks throughout the year. Holidays are not only regarded as opportunities to escape from the daily routine, but also as a personal development opportunity, where tourists can explore cultures and develop new skills, interests and hobbies. WTO (1985) claims that 'this non-mainstream tourism presently accounts for no more than 5per cent of the total tourism demand, but it is growing much more rapidly than traditional resort-based or round-tour tourism.

A ceiling of 10per cent of total tourism is forecasted by the travel trade for this new type of tourism, though this may rise over time as alternative becomes standard'. Traditional destinations have been victims of their own success. They grew to attract a large amount of people and inevitably have become overcrowded. The development of facilities and services, which cater for the mass markets, has forced them to lose parts of their character and has reduced their appeal. Operating on low margins also prevented principals from reinvesting and regenerating their products. Hence, mass tourism products are often regarded as responsible for both the aesthetic and environmental degradation of various destinations. Failure to control tourism development and practices has had disastrous impacts on well-known resorts.

Thus, traditional tourism products and destinations have become outdated and have lost their ability to attract their intended market segments. Instead, they can attract consumers by reducing their prices and by developing a volume based product. Hence, they jeopardise their resources further and are unable to generate the positive impacts attributed to tourism. Marketing can therefore assist the management of tourism behaviour at the destination. Marketing should encourage a responsible attitude towards local resources.

FROM SEA-SUN-SAND-SEX-SANGRIA

The transformation of tourism demand follows a wide range of trends and developments, which propel several differences in consumer behaviour. The summer/sea-side holiday is changing due to a wide range of environmental and climatic reasons. Firstly, the *sea* in well-established resorts has often been polluted by sewage, waste leaked by leisure boats and litter left behind by holidaymakers. In addition, pollution caused by other industrial sectors as well as accidents in oil tankers, has also degraded the quality of the water environment.

A number of diseases and viruses can also be transformed through the sea, causing serious health problems. Examples include the algae in the Adriatic in 1989 and the pollution of the sea in several British seaside resorts. As modern tourists are reluctant to tolerate environmental pollution, the sea becomes less attractive at destinations that have failed to protect the natural environment.

Although the *sun* has been a prime motivation for sun-lust tourists, it becomes under attack as the Green House Effect and the Ozone Layer Loss have increased temperatures to uncomfortable levels. In addition, skin cancer from sun overexposure reduces its appeal as a tourism motivator, while Poon claims that 'the sun sets on tourism'.

Wall suggests that 'the Greenhouse Effect and the likely climate changes to which it will give rise will likely impinge upon tourism at a global scale and may lead to diverse and profound consequences of global climate change for tourism'. Consequently, these phenomena will probably change tourism demand patterns in the next century and lead tourists towards northern and cooler climates.

Sand has similarly been degraded since masses of tourists are normally packed into a limited space on beaches, and spoil the environment. Poon (1993) claims that 'degradation of beaches and soil erosion from construction too close to the shore line, for example, some hotels and resorts in the Caribbean region are experiencing a loss of sand and bathing area as the sea begins to reclaim some of the area, exposing ugly building foundations'.

In addition, sand has been identified as responsible for the transformation of various diseases and hence future tourists may avoid being exposed to the sand. Thus, excessive numbers of holidaymakers and tourism overdevelopment eventually destroy both the environment and the 'escape' element for consumers. In addition, the transformation of various diseases from sand starts being another negative factor against attracting tourists.

Sangria symbolises the tendency of traditional holidaymakers to consume great quantities of alcohol. New consumers use holidays as a form of personal development and hence alcohol will increasingly be less important. Excessive alcohol consumption is not only unhealthy and often responsible for accidents and injuries, but it also creates a range of social problems at destination areas. Frequently hooliganism and conflicts between locals and tourists are also attributed to excessive consumption of alcohol. New tourists will therefore need less alcohol in order to enjoy themselves.

Sex and romance have always been an important, but often untold, element of leisure and tourism activities. It may be one of the major motivations for 'sex-tourists', especially for some 'specialised' destinations or part of the sightseeing experience. Eroticism accompanies almost all tourism activities, and it has been extensively used for advertising purposes. Specific products have been developed to accommodate this type of demand.

For example holidays in particular clubs (*e.g.* the 18-30 Club or the Club Med.) traditionally had the image of the wild, care-free bachelors looking for companions while on holiday; various destinations (*e.g.* Amsterdam, Mykonos) are prime destinations for homosexuals; some Far East and African destinations have developed a prostitution industry which caters for wealthy Western tourists; whilst 'romantic' destinations fiercely target the 'couple/honeymooners' market. However, modern diseases (*i.e.* Aids) have increased public concern and have reduced sexual activity with non-regular partners during holidays.

This is influencing the tourism demand patterns. Destinations where sex is a primary activity or areas with a large Aids-sufferers population might face a decline in arrivals. In contrast, 'romance' destinations might gain a greater market share; tourism enterprises like the Club Med. have altered their image significantly and target different segments (*i.e.* family or sportive markets); while other clubs (*e.g.* Sandals) emerged to cater exclusively for couples.

It is quite apparent therefore, that the sex element in the traditional holiday patterns is also changing radically and it will influence the decision-making processes of future holidaymakers. As a consequence of the above trends, Mediterranean destinations lose some of their market share and appeal. Trips from main European countries to this region are projected to fall from 45 per cent in 1995 to 38 per cent in 2010.

A combination of short breaks, sightseeing, shopping, shows and Scotch whisky has dominated urban tourism in the past. Often urban tourism is closely related with business travel (characterised by MICE [Meetings, Incentives, Conferences, Exhibitions]) as business travellers usually consume some leisure tourism products or they may stay for a few more days to enjoy the local resources.

Hence, urban tourism is often characterised by *short breaks*, sometimes combined or as an extension of business trips. Leisure tourists also tend to be curious to visit metropolitan centres which they are familiar with through the media. They also take advantage of the large amount of cultural and heritage resources often found in urban destinations, such as museums, galleries, theatres, cathedrals, monuments, *etc.* A wide range of facilities such as hospitals, centralised government agencies and educational establishments also act as attractions for consumers.

Often urban tourism is consumed through organised *sightseeing,* which aims to pack as many attractions as possible into the limited time available at the destination. Sightseeing is facilitated through transfers and guided tours. However, sightseeing programmes are often characterised by their rapidity and inflexibility. Consumers take specific interest in fewer but more personalised attractions and use their leisure time to concentrate on their interests.

They will be more interested in experiencing elements of the destination, rather than tick them off their 'must see' items. This will be particularly the case for repeat visitors to destinations who become familiar with local resources and people. Hence future tourists will need a greater flexibility and control over their time at the destination in order to explore in detail and experience resources of their choice. Thus they will need tailor-made sightseeing programmes which will enable them to increase their flexibility.

Shopping has dominated urban tourism as people from peripheral areas were lured by a great variety and often cheaper prices in urban centres. The proliferation of shopping malls out of city centres and the globalisation of manufacturing and retailing, as well as the distribution of products through the electronic media are expected to reduce the appeal of shopping as an attraction to urban destinations. Instead, shopping will be integrated with other attractions and experiences at the destination. Perhaps tourism shopping will be themed in relation to the local tourism product.

Another element of urban tourism has traditionally been shows of any kind, such as theatre, opera, cinema, circus, *etc.* Only cities have the infrastructure as well as the critical mass of consumers required in order to stage performances. However, the growth of electronic media and the development of facilities in peripheral regions as well as the maturity of the market demonstrate that it will be difficult to impress consumers in the future.

Even shows and entertainment activities will need to be customised to suit the feelings of consumers during their holiday. Similarly with sea-side tourism, *Scotch whisky* symbolises the contribution of alcohol to the urban tourism product. It can be observed that, although alcohol has been playing a significant role in urban tourism, health considerations as well as other life style influences discourage tourists from consuming large quantities of alcohol.

As a result, alcohol will be themed with the overall experience rather than being a stand-alone product. Examples of that can be demonstrated by the expansion of Irish pubs where Irish food and drinks can be consumed within a themed environment.

TOWARDS SOPHISTICATION-SPECIALISATION-SEGMENTATION-SATISFACTION-SEDUCTION

The shift of demand towards quality and value-for-money products is increasing rapidly in the tourism industry. Tourists demand higher quality products and services and real experiences during their holidays. The traditional annual family holiday in a seaside resort will play a less dominant role in the future. Multi-interest travel is therefore replacing part of the present bread and butter products of the industry. Future products will probably combine beach holidays with pleasure and special interest of some kind or culture. Future tourists will 'prefer to live their holidays rather than to spend them', and they do so by engaging in cultural, physical, educational and spiritual activities (WTO 1985).

Rigidly packaged tours are not in line with trends towards individual expression. As a result, the independently organised tourism segment emerges rapidly whilst there is a decline of the relative importance of packaged tours. O'Brien (1996) suggests that 'Growth in the inclusive tour market will continue, though at a much slower rate, but in the larger summersun markets, particularly Germany and the UK, the major IT operators will develop a wider product range to ensure that sales remain buoyant.'

One of the most important obstacles in organising individual tourism packages hitherto is the lack of economies of scale and bargaining power, which will enable the reduction of the individual package prices to affordable levels. WTO (1991:18) suggests that packaged tours are not in line with trends towards individual expression.

As a result, the decline of the relative importance of packaged tours is expected in favour of independently organised tourism. Bentley (1991:57) states that 'tour operators in the 1990s will seek to combine inclusive tour elements with individual variations, in order to satisfy the desire for an individual experience, but at a cost lower than an individually arranged holiday'.

Meanwhile, the tourism industry is moving towards the accommodation of activity/adventure/wildlife/culture/independent/special interest holidays. The new generation of tourists is more educated, experienced, sophisticated, knowledgeable and demanding. This is reflected in the kind of travel experiences they seek, their behaviour and preferences whilst at the destination and also in the information they require in travel decision-making.

The WTO (1985) estimates that 'ecotourism (or nature based tourism) is growing by 25-30 per cent per year while culture-based tourism is recording annual expansion of 10-15 per cent. Endemic tourism (based on the individual character of the locality or community) is expected to become an important means of differentiating tourist destinations and appealing to the 'new' types of tourism'.

SOPHISTICATION

Tourists in the post-industrial era are better prepared for living in an international world. Modern people are able to work and function in a demanding environment. They are often familiar and capable to cope with foreign languages, customs and cultures and as a result a 'new global lifestyle is emerging', often as a result of the globalisation of the media as well as the extensive travelling experiences of consumers.

The enhancement of the media, and especially television, has reduced the distances and increased the eagerness of modern people to approach and experience remote cultures and foreign areas. Bennett (1992:87) states that: educational improvements, together with enhanced communications have led to more sophisticated requirements from holidaymakers who are now looking for new activities to fill their leisure time and satisfy their cultural, intellectual and sporting interests. Increased linguistic ability among the younger generations, communication and financial services have made travel easier.

Hence, sophistication is a major element in the 'new types' of holidays and the products emerging to satisfy modern demand. Holidaymakers take advantage of their education as well as the availability of information through the new media and plan their holidays in advance. They are eager to approach and experience remote cultures and foreign areas in order to 'live their leisure time' and satisfy their cultural, natural, intellectual and sporting interests.

The linguistic abilities of younger generations (both hosts and tourists), as well as the prevalence of communication and financial services at a global level have made travel more accessible and easier.

Extensive travelling has also increased the required sophistication of the tourist product. As many modern travellers have been in several countries and treated by several tourism enterprises, they have developed a set of assessment criteria, which they utilise in order to compare their tourism experiences. Moutinho (1992) illustrates that the 'sophistication of the customer will have an impact on all product development throughout the industry. There will be an increased requirement for high standards of product design, efficiency and safety'. Thus, people will seek more varied, personal and authentic experiences, while a wide range of new, imaginative, tourism products will be demanded.

In addition, personal development and special interest travel are expected to provide rewarding, enriching, adventuresome experiences. Not only is mass tourism less able to satisfy a large proportion of the marketplace, it is also regarded as environmentally unacceptable and thus 'politically incorrect'. Moreover, Cooper and Ozdil (1992:378) suggest that:

In particular the realisation of the negative impacts of tourism on host environments and societies has prompted a search for alternative forms of tourism and a move away from 'mass' tourism. Indeed, this movement is largely consumer rather than industry driven and may lead to 'politically correct' or acceptable forms of tourism which will be chosen by the consumer in preference to more damaging forms. Thus, adventure and green tourism are driven by consumer requirements at the expense of mass and environmentally threatening tourism.

Tourist product sophistication should probably aim to deliver the appropriate product, at the appropriate time, at the appropriate price. The amalgamation of tourism products and the delivery of seamless travel experiences are increasingly important. Information technology facilitates the development of suitable businesses and communication networks for achieving these purposes. Modern travellers demand customer convenience in all aspects, while 'total consumer satisfaction' and enrichment of the holiday experience are required; all these at a competitive and fair cost.

The anticipated sophistication of the consumer will have an impact upon product development as well as on customer retention throughout the industry. Not only will there be an increased requirement for high standards of product design, efficiency and safety, but also the tourist will be more critical of the product and will have the experience to compare offerings. Tourists' requirement for sophistication has recently initiated the demand for specialised products. Tourism motivation is a very complicated set of needs and desires, which differ for various people. Several motivators are consistently rated in a variety of consumer behaviour surveys.

However, tourism researchers are generally unable to identify the motivators and determinants of tourism activity with accuracy, as a result of the diversified needs, desires and decision-making criteria used by each individual consumer each time s/he selects a tourism product.

Hitherto, tourism products used to be general, unspecialised, with almost identical characteristics and have been traded as commodities rather than services for the satisfaction of specific needs. The mass tourism philosophy, where tourism products should appeal to all different tastes and should be as cheap as possible, in order to attract customers of all purchasing abilities and achieve economies of scale, used to dominate the marketplace. These products become less attractive as consumers are exceedingly conscious and keen to explore the cultural, social, gastronomical, political, and environmental aspects of destinations.

They are expected therefore to organise more independent activities, adventure and sport holidays and devote their holidays to special interest activities. As a result tailor-made travel arrangements are expected to grow at a faster pace than pre-packaged holidays over the next decade. Kotler (1988) suggests that 'each buyer is potentially a separate market because of unique needs and wants'. This statement could not be more valuable in any other industry than tourism. Technology makes possible more tailored products to meet individual tastes and hence we turn from mass production of all kinds to customisation.

One-to-one marketing initiatives emerge gradually to take advantage of expressed consumer requirements and to develop individualised product solutions. Long-term customer segmentation will be based on the feeling of individual consumers at each particular moment, rather than on broad segmentation variables.

This will enable enterprises to offer instantaneous tourism products to satisfy the needs of consumers at each moment. Hence, the competitiveness of tourism organisations and destinations will depend on their ability to differentiate their product and serve individual consumer needs.

New specialised tourism products are marketed and distributed differently from ordinary offerings. Advertising will primarily be carried out in specialised media, while direct selling and relationship marketing will be utilised for understanding the consumer needs and promoting specialised products. The Internet and technology in general will facilitate one-to-one marketing, as specialised products will be distributed directly to the right market segments.

Offering specialised products on-line will not only improve the specialisation of the industry, but it will also enable the reduction of the brochure used for the promotion of tourism products, reducing both the printing cost as well as the environmental damage caused from the production and distribution.

Apart from including special interest activities in traditional holiday brochures, a wide range of new programmes emerge to cover these markets. New programmes such as 'Battlefields', 'Italian Cooking', 'Dutch Bulb-fields', *etc.* address specific interest markets and aim to provide a thematic tour. These new products are based extensively on activities that are undertaken during holidays, while accommodation and transportation arrangements are given less importance. Themed leisure activities are also expected to increase in order to satisfy the demand for specialisation. In the catering industry, for example, restaurants used to be specialised only in national cuisines (*e.g.* French, Chinese, Greek restaurants).

New themes are rapidly emerging based on the food served (*e.g.* Steaks: Aberdeen Steak House; Hamburger: McDonald's; Chicken: Kentucky; Pizza: Pizza Hut); on the entertainment provided (*e.g.* Hard Rock Café or Planet Hollywood); the surrounding environment (*e.g.* Country pub: Bass Pubs or Rainforest Café); or on the life style and preferences (*e.g.* vegetarian or game restaurants) are continually emerging.

As a result, Lickorish (1990) predicts that the importance of the 'mini market segments' will increase rapidly. Independent holidays increase their market share in the international arena. In the UK for example they increased their contribution to 45 per cent of the total holidays abroad in 1994, from 37 per cent in 1983. Thus, Moutinho (1992) suggests that 'tourist innovation is more likely to be about un-packaging rather than packaging, providing more individual attention within a number of price bands'.

Eventually tourism marketing will move even further from one-to-one relationship marketing to the level of marketing towards how a person is feeling at a particular moment. This will be facilitated with the development of intelligent agents and push technology which will assess the situation and mood of a person and will promote the most appropriate products for that particular moment.

As a result, specialisation is expected to be a dominant element of holidays in the future. People will be able to select numerous specialised holidays all over the world. Both destinations and tourism enterprises should therefore identify their competitive advantage in offering specialised products and develop integrated and themed tourist experiences. For example, France could develop gastronomic themed activities, while Greece could emphasise themes based on archaeology-philosophy-culture. Orlando and Las Vegas in the USA, which are strongly themed towards Disneyland visitors and gamblers respectively, are good examples of specialised/themed tourism products which attract a large volume of visitors based on these attractions.

SEGMENTATION

Specialisation of tourism products entails a need for segmentation of tourism markets. Since tourists no longer have single, standardised and rigidly packaged wants, segmentation offers the opportunity to provide appealing tourism products to well-defined markets.

Market segmentation can be defined as the grouping of individuals according to their preference or reaction to specific elements of the marketing mix, *i.e.* product, price, distribution and promotion or according to their characteristics. WTO (1991) claims that 'segmentation is the process by which a travel vendor, whether an airline, hotel or destination, identifies and attracts consumers who will be satisfied by the product or service the vendor offers'.

Traditionally, tourism marketers have been using geographic and demographic criteria in order to describe their markets, probably because these categories offer objective tangible and measurable variables.

However, as a number of phenomena could not be explained and interpreted, additional segmentation categories and methods have been added. Consequently, psychographics and behavioural criteria are used nowadays, in tourist segmentation, in order to provide detailed customer profiles, identify tourist motivations, needs and determinants, and offer an appropriate tourist product mix. Thus, life-style segmentation has gained ground in modern tourism marketing.

'Lifestyle is a way of living, characterised by the manner in which people spend their time (activities), what things they consider important (interests) and how they feel about themselves and the world around them (opinions)'. Although life-style segmentation is probably the most difficult and subjective method, it provides the best prediction and understanding of tourist activities.

Tourism destinations, enterprises and organisations will need to undertake thorough segmentation in order to ensure that they design suitable tourist products, use proper communication media and charge acceptable prices. Moreover, segmentation is essential for treating seasonality problems, as well as for mitigating tourism impacts at destinations. Segmentation is also critical in bringing together the right types of consumers/tourists, as their interaction during the travel experience is largely responsible for the delivery and perception of tourism products.

For example, the demographic changes worldwide demonstrate the development of a new market segment of older/retired but active people who have plenty of time and often money to spend. Several operators currently develop suitable products for this market segment.

The UK company Saga Holidays specialises with holidays for the over 55s, while a new style of club is currently being developed by Mr Trigano, the ex Club Med. Chairman. The required sophistication and specialisation of tourism can only be offered to small segments of the market with very similar needs and motivations. Hence, customer satisfaction will largely depend on proper segmentation and achievement of a suitable customer mix.

SATISFACTION

Consumer satisfaction is the essence of most developments in tourism demand. Satisfaction 'occurs when consumer expectations are met or exceeded' and can be defined 'as an evaluation that the chosen alternative is consistent with prior beliefs with respect to that alternative'. Increasingly customer satisfaction will be inadequate for the fiercely competitive environment and thus 'delighting the customer' should become the target for all enterprises. Tourism satisfaction should be one of the strategic directions of every tourist enterprise, destination or organisation. This can be achieved by offering:

- At least the quality promised;
- Undertaking consumer research and formulating innovative tourism products;
- Improving services constantly;
- Adjusting tourism products to customer needs and feelings;
- Enriching the tourist experience; and
- Offering value for money.

Satisfying consumers, as well as providing sufficient value for both money and time, are also ethical obligations and responsibilities of tourist destinations and organisations. Satisfying consumers also makes financial/business sense.

- First, satisfied tourists are normally very loyal. The increasing sophistication of travellers, and the fierce competition in the international market make repeat business difficult to maintain. Therefore, it should be extremely welcome and appreciated by the tourism industry.
- Second, satisfied customers are always the best, most reliable and cheapest promotional medium, as they usually recommend tourist destinations/enterprises to friends through word of mouth. In contrast, dissatisfied travellers spread their complaints to potential customers. Bearing in mind that most people get advice for their travel plans from friends and relatives, the image of the destination depends heavily on the description of the previous visitors.
- Third, providing adequate services and satisfying the tourist will eliminate enterprises and destinations from potential legal actions and suits against them. Consumerism and consumer protection are international movements forced by various private and governmental organisations. The European Community Package Travel Directive, especially on the package and timeshare holidays, is expected to have major impacts on tourism enterprises in the near future.

Due to the fact that the tourism product is an amalgam of many products and services, which formulate the 'tourist consumption chain', each trip is assessed as a total experience. Hence, the satisfaction of tourists normally depends on the harmonic delivery of the product throughout the chain.

As destinations represent the 'raison d'être' for tourism, travel experience tends to be appraised at a destination level. Consequently, an integrated approach should be employed, by all enterprises and organisations involved at a destination level, in order to ensure that consumers are satisfied by the whole range of products consumed during their travelling experience. Thus, all tourist enterprises should consider the needs and wants of their customers before, during and after the delivery of their own products to ensure that everybody involved in the tourism product delivery chain offers satisfactory services. The ultimate measurement of tourist satisfaction is probably hidden in the answer of two critical questions:

- Would the customer come back?
- Would the customer recommend the product/destination to his/her friends?

SEDUCTION

Tourism providers need to 'seduce' tourists through the development and delivery of offerings and marketing mixes which reflect consumers' feelings at a particular moment and satisfy their entire range of needs and wants. The inconsistency and unpredictability of tourism consumers, which is emerging due to the dynamic nature of modern life and the overexposure of consumers to the media, illustrates that tourism marketing will become much more difficult for the future.

Tourism destinations and organisations that manage to seduce consumers will need to make them feel special at each stage of their travelling experience. Offering tailor-made tourism products and caring for the individual needs and wants of consumers will be one of the most critical attributes tourism organisations will need to have in order to attract and satisfy tourists in the future.

Extensive marketing research, using psychology methodologies will enable tourism organisations to explore consumer feelings and requirements whilst on holidays. Data mining on the information available through loyalty clubs, Passenger Name Records (PNRs), guest history, and other sources of information should be exploited in order to assess the needs and wants of particular consumers.

Complex models of behaviour can then be developed in order to predict consumer requirements and develop instantaneous products before consumers require them. Developing relationship marketing will enable tourism organisations to establish a closer partnership with consumers. Destinations and organisations who manage to seduce their consumers will be able to increase the value added they offer and achieve high levels of customer retention and loyalty.

This chapter attempts to explore the trend of the tourism demand by providing a framework of analysis. It is argued that the traditional tourism products will no longer be adequate for the recreation of the new generation of tourists emerging. Instead, a more individualised product is expected to dominate demand in the near future. Tourism demand trends can be illustrated in a framework of five new S's, namely sophistication-specialisation-segmentation-satisfaction-seduction.

Emerging tourism products need to be sophisticated in order to delight the new, experienced, and demanding consumer. Moreover, a certain degree of specialisation is required in order to cater for the individual needs and wants.

This can only be achieved by detailed segmentation of the market where all cluster segments are identified and offered tailor-made products. The ultimate aim should be the total customer satisfaction before, during and after the consumption of the tourist product, which is underlined by both ethical and business motives.

Tourism organisations and destinations which achieve the above will 'seduce' their clientele and achieve sustainable competitive advantages. A thorough understanding of this transformation framework as well as the utilisation of marketing and information technology tools will be essential for all players involved in the tourism industry. Enterprises and destinations which fail to appreciate these developments and modernise their offerings will be marginalised in this century.

10

Global Policies and the Tourism Industry

In the last decade, global environmental policies have made substantial progress in institutional development, international cooperation, public participation and private sector action. National governments and the private sector have developed stronger legal frameworks, market-based environmental incentive instruments, environmentally sound technologies, and cleaner production processes. Consequently, several countries report significant progress in controlling environmental pollution and slowing the rate of resource degradation as well as reducing the intensity of resource use (UNEP 1997).

The tourism industry, arguably the world's largest, bears a great responsibility in the effort to move towards sustainable development. The economic importance of tourism is undeniable. A study sponsored by the World Travel and Tourism Council (WTTC) and conducted by Wharton Econometric Forecasting Associates (WEFA) found that the tourism industry generates 11.7 per cent of global gross domestic product (GDP) and nearly 200 million jobs worldwide.

These figures are forecast to total 11.7 per cent global GDP and 255 million jobs in 2010 (United Nations Economic and Social Council 1999). While the economic development potential of tourism is substantial, there is also strong evidence of the negative environmental impact of tourism development. Nevertheless, tourism may be a more sustainable option for economic development because, unlike other natural resource based industries, it is based on enjoyment and appreciation of local culture, built heritage, and the natural environment which provides a powerful economic incentive to conserve these valuable assets (United Nations Economic and Social Council 1999).

The potential for tourism development to be a sustainable - that is for it to *meet the needs of the present without compromising the ability of future generations to meet their own needs* - has resulted in support for environmentally sustainable tourism development from both the public and private sectors at the national and international levels.The United Nations and its associated organisations, the World Bank, and regional development banks are attempting to 'green' their loan programmes and assistance mechanisms.

They are also supporting the development of environmentally sustainable tourism directly and indirectly through a variety of means, including sustainable tourism product identification, infrastructure development, environmentally sound hotel financing, and ecotourism development in protected areas.

The Commission on Sustainable Development (CSD) - an intergovernmental forum to coordinate and monitor the progress of Agenda 21's implementation - has produced a number of policy recommendations for stakeholders involved in the sustainable tourism development following their annual meetings in 1999.

These recommendations were broken down into private sector, public sector, non-governmental organisation, and international community policy challenges. The following section summarises these recommendations (United Nations Economic and Social Council 1999).

PRIVATE SECTOR POLICY CHALLENGES

The key challenges facing the tourism industry are to:

- Promote wider implementation of environmental management, particularly in the many small and medium enterprises that form the backbone of the tourism industry, and spread initiatives to all sectors of the tourism industry;
- Use more widely environmentally sound technologies, in particular to reduce emissions of CO and other greenhouse gases and ozone-depleting substances, as set out in two international agreements;
- Address the key issues of siting and more eco-efficient design of tourism facilities;
- Raise the awareness of tourism clients of the environment and social implications of their holidays, and of opportunities for their responsible behaviour;
- Develop a better dialogue with the local communities in travel destinations, and promote the involvement of local stakeholders in tourism ventures;
- Work with governments and other stakeholders to improve the overall environmental quality of destinations; and
- Report publicly on environmental performance.

Public sector policy challenges:

Governments need to further develop and implement the legislative and policy frameworks for sustainable development. In particular, they need to:

- Ratify, if they have not already done so, and work towards the effective implementation of, international and regional environmental conventions;
- Integrate more fully tourism development into the overall plans for sustainable development and develop participatory approaches;

- Develop more widely land use planning, and protect the coastline through building restrictions (for example, legislation in France, Spain, Denmark and Egypt forbids building within a defined distance from the coast);
- Identify and adopt the most appropriate mix of regulation and economic instruments, and, in many cases develop economic instruments to address environmental issues; and
- Work towards the effective enforcement of regulations and standards.

Governments need to raise awareness, build capacity and promote effective action for sustainable tourism.

This requires that they strive to:

- Improve the understanding of the benefits and burdens of tourism in environmental, social and economic terms, for the areas under their jurisdiction;
- Strengthen capacity for the management and control of tourism in their sphere of responsibility, and establish and maintain procedures for cooperation and coordination with neighbouring authorities, and with relevant state authorities;
- Provide support through pilot projects and capacity development programmes, including capacity development at the local government level;
- Ensure the participation of all stakeholders affected by or involved in tourism and its development, especially indigenous and local communities;
- Ensure that tourism makes a positive contribution to economic development, and that the economic benefits of tourism are equitably shared;
- Encourage and catalyse industry initiatives for sustainable tourism across all sectors of tourism, including accommodation, land, air and sea transportation, tour operators, travel agents, attractions sectors, *etc.*; and
- Promote changes in consumer behaviour in both tourist-originating countries and destinations towards more sustainable forms of tourism.

Governments will also need to develop monitoring of progress towards sustainable tourism. It is important to develop activities to monitor, control and mitigate adverse effects that may arise from tourism activities and development.

NON-GOVERNMENTAL ORGANISATIONS POLICY CHALLENGES

The key environmental policy challenges that face non-governmental organisations are to:

- More specifically voice their views in tourism policies and strategies;
- Contribute to the development and implementation of environmental standards for tourism;

- Develop or participate in raising awareness and education activities for sensitising tourists towards improving guest consumption patterns; and
- Assist in monitoring tourism activities and development and progress towards more sustainable tourism.

INTERNATIONAL COMMUNITY POLICY CHALLENGES

The key challenges facing the international community are to:

- Assist and support governments in the development of national strategies or master plans for the sustainable development of tourism, and of environmental land use and building regulations and standards for tourism;
- Raise awareness and build capacity of all stakeholders by providing information on best practices for sustainable tourism;
- Encourage the private sector to develop and apply codes and guidelines, and environmental management systems, and promote the development of the use of environmental reporting by companies in the various branches of the tourism sector;
- Assist in assessing the environmental effectiveness of existing voluntary initiatives in the various branches of the tourism sector, and make recommendations accordingly;
- Promote the transfer of environmentally sound technologies (ESTs), practices and management tools adapted for the tourism sector, and disseminate information on ESTs to governments and the tourism industry;
- Work with other stakeholders to establish and disseminate lessons from best practices projects on sustainable tourism;
- Provide support through provision of information and capacity development programmes, particularly on the costs and benefits of tourism development, the use of economic incentives to promote sustainable tourism, and on destination management; and
- Assist in the establishment of monitoring of progress towards sustainable tourism.

THE ROLE OF THE INTERNATIONAL COMMUNITY AND GLOBAL ENVIRONMENTAL INITIATIVES

Some other notable international environmental institutions that support sustainable tourism initiatives include:

The world bank group: Despite its formal distancing from the tourism sector in the 1970s, the Bank's focus on economic development and its private sector capacity, particularly in the International Finance Corporation, makes it technically well placed to address the pressures of a global tourism industry.

Its now strong environmental capacity also makes it well placed to address the impacts of the tourism sector on biodiversity.

The united nations development programme (UNDP): A United Nations organisation whose mission is to help countries in their efforts to achieve sustainable human development by assisting them to build their capacity to design and carry out development programmes in poverty eradication, employment creation and sustainable livelihoods, the empowerment of women and the protection and regeneration of the environment, giving first priority to poverty eradication.

The united nations environmental programme (UNEP): The environmental voice of the United Nations, responsible for environmental policy development, scientific analysis, monitoring, and assessment. *The global environment facility* (GEF): A financial mechanism that addresses the incremental costs that developing countries face in responding to selected global environmental problems. The World Bank, UNEP and UNDP implement GEF projects.

New international environmental conventions and agreements are being adopted, older treaties are being improved, and new approaches to international policy are being developed and implemented. Four important international environmental conventions and treaties that are particularly relevant to the tourism industry include the following:

RIO DECLARATION ON ENVIRONMENT AND DEVELOPMENT (AGENDA 21)

The plan of action adopted by governments in 1992 in Rio de Janeiro provides the global consensus on the road map towards sustainable development.

Agenda 21 is grouped around a series of themes - comprising 40 chapters and 115 separate programme areas, each of which represents an important component in the overall strategy towards global sustainable development. The Agenda identifies three core tools to be used in achieving sustainable development goals:

1. Introduction of new, or strengthening of existing, regulations to ensure the protection of human health and the environment.
2. Use of free market mechanisms through which the prices of goods and services will reflect the environmental costs of resource inputs and process outputs.
3. Industry-led voluntary programmes that deliver environmentally responsible products and services.

In 1996, WTTC, the World Tourism Organisation and the Earth Council joined together to launch 'Agenda 21 for the Travel and Tourism Industry: Towards Environmentally Sustainable Development', making the tourism industry the first industrial sector to develop an industry specific action plan based on Agenda 21. WTTC has now introduced an addition to this programme - The Alliance for Sustainable Tourism - which invites public and private sector tourism organisations to record their Agenda 21 based activities on a central Internet site and encourage cooperation with other local partners.

THE CONVENTION ON INTERNATIONAL TRADE IN ENDANGEREDSPECIES OF WILD FAUNA AND FLORA (CITES)

CITES is an international convention banning commercial international trade in an agreed list of endangered species and by regulating and monitoring trade in others that might become endangered. The international wildlife trade, worth billions of dollars annually, has caused massive declines in the numbers of many species of animals and plants.

The scale of overexploitation for trade aroused such concern for the survival of species that an international treaty was drawn up in 1973 to protect wildlife against such over-exploitation and to prevent international trade from threatening species with extinction (World Conservation Monitoring 1998).

THE UNITED NATIONS FRAMEWORK CONVENTION ON CLIMATE CHANGE

In the 1992 United Nations Framework Convention on Climate Change (UNFCCC), finalised for the Earth Summit in Rio de Janeiro, Brazil, the world's nations agreed on voluntary actions to reduce greenhouse gas emissions. Negotiations on the Kyoto Protocol to the UNFCCC were completed on 11 December 1997, committing the industrialised nations to specified legally binding reductions in emissions of six 'greenhouse gases'.

During negotiations that preceded the December 1997 meeting in Kyoto, Japan, little progress was made, and the most difficult issues were not resolved until the final days - and hours - of the Conference. There was wide disparity among key players especially on three items:

- The amount of binding reductions in greenhouse gases to be required, and the gases to be included in these requirements.
- Whether developing countries should be part of the requirements for greenhouse gas limitations.
- Whether to allow emissions trading and joint implementation, which allow credit to be given for emissions reductions to a country that provides funding or investments in other countries that bring about the actual reductions in those other countries or locations where they may be cheaper to attain.

The convention on biological diversity:

A convention adopted as part of the 1992 UN Conference on the Environment and Development with the goals of:

- maintaining biodiversity;
- using its elements sustainably; and

- sharing in a balanced and fair way the advantages springing from the exploitation of genetic resources.

The Convention on Biological Diversity (CBD) is the major and most visionary global biodiversity agreement. Now ratified by almost all the countries in the world - with the notable exception of the United States, the CBD is attempting to develop a global framework for the management of biodiversity.

It is striving to meet the trinity of biodiversity objectives - conservation, sustainable use and equitable benefit sharing - through globally agreed policies and procedures for managing biodiversity. These policies and procedures are also intended to support the overall goal of sustainable development and the corollary objective of poverty alleviation. But given the tradition of biodiversity management, the CBD has understandably yet to address the pressures of globalise commerce directly.

There is, however, an increasing recognition that the private sector must be an active player in managing biodiversity, but this recognition has yet to be articulated into clear roles and responsibilities for the private sector and global market processes.

CRITICAL WEAKNESSES IN THE GLOBAL ENVIRONMENTAL POLICY STRUCTURE

While global policy structures and international environmental solidarity are growing in strength, they remain too weak to make significant progress a worldwide reality. As a result, the gap between what has been done thus far and what is needed is widening. From a global perspective, the environment has continued to degrade during the past decade, significant environmental problems remain, and the outlook is, unfortunately, pessimistic.

Internationally and nationally, the funds and political situation are not sufficient to halt continuing global environmental degradation or address the most pressing environmental issues, even though the technologies and knowledge are available to do so.

The recognition of environmental issues as necessarily long-term and cumulative, with serious global and security implications, exists but the will to act remains limited. The continued preoccupation with immediate local and national issues and a general lack of sustained interest in global and long-term environmental issues remain major impediments to environmental progress internationally.

*According to the CSD's report on:*Tourism and the Environment, there are several important emerging issues with regard to tourism and environmental protection that must be addressed in order to overcome these impediments. These include:

Developing partnership: For sustainable tourism, the involvement and commitment of all stakeholders is essential. However, public, private and academic sector partnerships are still underdeveloped and therefore need to be encouraged.

Involvement of the banking and insurance sectors: Banks and insurance companies could greatly expedite the progress of sustainable tourism by incorporating environmental and social criteria into assessment procedures for loans, investments, and insurance.

They could help to finance environmentally sound technologies and provide incentives for sustainable tourism. This approach has worked well in other contexts. Widespread involvement of the banking and insurance sectors should be sought.

Use of economic instruments: The tourism industry consumes increasingly scarce natural resources. The costing of energy and water in particular could expedite greatly eco-efficiency in the tourism industry and raise revenue for the improved management of those resources. Governments should consider the development and widespread use of economic instruments for sustainable tourism.

Involvement of tourism boards: Often, marketing strategies and messages are not in line with the principles of sustainable tourism. There is a need to better involve tourism boards in sustainable tourism efforts.

Capacity-building of local government: In many countries, local governments have important responsibilities regarding tourism development. Capacity-building programmes should be implemented to help them understand those responsibilities, develop integrated and participatory approaches, and define and implement policies for sustainable tourism.

Greater focus on transport: There is a continued development of long-haul travel. Economic, technological and management approaches should be developed to reduce emissions, waste and pollution resulting from tourism transportation. Changing consumption patterns should also be considered.

Emerging types of tourism: Tourism is rapidly diversifying. Emerging forms of tourism should also develop according to sustainability criteria. The increase of cruises and the current trend towards mega-ships necessitate that the cruise ship industry develop a socially and environmentally responsible approach.

Improve monitoring: Careful monitoring of impacts and results, as well as the adoption of corrective measures, are conditions for sustainable tourism. All stakeholders at all levels should thus develop monitoring programmes. As previously stated, the private sector should develop monitoring and public reporting of its activities. Local and central governments should develop monitoring tools, such as indicators, and should incorporate the results into their decision-making process.

Where appropriate, participatory approaches should be used. Monitoring is currently uncommon and that should be made a priority (United Nations Economic and Social Council 1999).

SUSTAINABLE TOURISM AT THE NATIONAL AND REGIONAL LEVEL

While the global policies and international donor organisation priorities discussed above are important because they tend to act as positive drivers towards environmental sustainability, particularly in the developing world, it is the national and regional policies within individual countries that are the key to sustainable tourism development strategies.

ENVIRONMENTAL MANAGEMENT SYSTEMS AND THE TOURISM INDUSTRY

Within the last two decades the concept of quality management systems emerged in an effort to gain consistent performance in meeting specified standards (initially in military equipment procurement and operations). The best-known QMS in the commercial world is the ISO 9000 standards of the International Standards Organisation. The implementation of a QMS is intended to provide consumers with an assurance that a company's products and services will be of consistent quality.

As the importance of environmentally-friendly private sector operations grew (as reflected generally in the industry sponsored sustainable development principles described previously), the conceptual model of QMS was applied to industry operations that impacted on the environment. (An EMS can be defined as a management system that incorporates management commitment, organisational structure, operational practices and procedures, and resources into a documented and implemented environmental policy.)

The implementation of an EMS represents the basis by which an organisation can exercise control over its impact on the environment by systematically gathering and coordinating knowledge about those impacts. Implementing an EMS demonstrates a strong commitment to Agenda 21 principles.

Typically, a private sector EMS most often conforms with the International Standards Organisation ISO 14001 standard, although the European Union's Eco-Management and Audit Scheme (EMAS) is a valuable reference because of its rigorous parameters. It is important to note that all of the preceding material regarding QMS/EMS and ISO14001 is actually intended for use by private businesses or perhaps certain public sector agencies.

It is not designed for use with a tourism destination that comprises many different types of organisations from the public and private sector; but it does lay a foundation of terminology and processes that will be used in discussing EMS for tourism destinations.

The application of the EMS process to tourism destinations is an emerging area of interest, and while there is not yet a substantial amount of direct anecdotal or documentary evidence to examine we can look to recent work by groups like the World Travel and Tourism Council's Green Globe Alliance and others for case studies that illustrate the potentials and pitfalls of the destination-based EMS process. The rationale behind applying the EMS process to tourism destinations is simple and logical.

The natural environment is an extremely valuable resource for most tourism destinations and the aggregate impact from many different sectors of the travel and tourism industry - transportation, accommodations, and tour operations - tends to have a negative environmental effect. Coupled with this assumption is the fact that the public sector is responsible for many functions that should minimise negative environmental impacts - waste management, land use planning, transportation infrastructure, biodiversity conservation, *etc.* - but often fails to meet this challenge adequately.

Proponents of the destination-based EMS believe that truly sustainable destination management requires a public/private sector partnership in the form of a cooperative management structure that deals proactively with environmental issues. With this in mind, we will be looking closely at methodologies and processes that can be used in the creation of a strategically designed EMS with broad public/private stakeholder support.

The benefits of such an EMS will include:

- Providing a systematic framework for public and private sector cooperation on environmental issues;
- Improving compliance with regulatory requirements and industry codes of conduct;
- Reducing public and private sector operation costs as greater energy/resource savings are achieved;
- Increasing competitive advantage in the market for 'green' tourism destinations; and
- Creating a practical mechanism for pursuing the Agenda 21 principles of sustainable development.

PROPERTY-BASED ENVIRONMENTAL MANAGEMENT SYSTEMS

The creation of property-based EMSs to guide site audits and monitoring processes and in which to anchor certification processes is a new phenomenon in the hospitality industry and, to date, one without a defined standard. This is generating a mounting confusion within the industry over what environmental standards, which criteria, and whose certification programme to use.

The advent of EMSs into tourism is based on the success of EMS operations in other industries, the perceived market benefits of independent certification of environmental standards for individual tourism enterprises, and a demonstrated growth in demand for environmentally friendly or 'green' tourism destinations in major outbound markets. EMSs are desirable because their adoption can reduce operation costs through energy and resource savings, improve internal management methods, reduce liability/ risk from environmental deterioration, improve a property's image in the area of environmental performance and compliance with regulatory requirements, and open opportunities for profit in the emerging market for 'green' tourism destinations. The overall benefit of a properly designed and administered EMS, then, is its ability to provide credible and objective assurance to inbound markets that the environmental conditions in a particular property or destination are of a higher quality than those of competing locations.

THE GROWTH OF ECO-LABELS IN THE TOURISM INDUSTRY

The creation of environmental management systems for the tourism industry is a new phenomenon that is looking to build on three important trends:

- The success of EMS operations in other industries.
- The perceived potential market benefits of independent certification of environmental standards for individual tourism business.
- The demonstrated growth in demand for environm-entally friendly or 'green' tourism destinations in major outbound markets.

A number of organisations are currently certifying tourism providers as 'environmentally friendly', including Green Globe, Green Seal and HVS Ecotel. The primary benefit, to date, of conforming with the various EMS standards developed for the tourism industry is the cost savings achieved through various operational efficiencies. It is anticipated, however, that as awareness of environmental certification within the tourism industry is raised, there will be an increased competitive advantage to being independently certified as environmentally friendly.

The hope is that as consumer consciousness of environmental issues increases, more people will choose tourism service providers and, indeed, destinations, based on their environmental performance. As indicated previously, though, there is not yet quantitative evidence to indicate that consumers make these types of choices based on their perception of environmental factors. While there is not currently a defined standard for an EMS that deals with a destination as a whole, organisations like Green Globe, Green Seal and others are examining the best method to institute such a standard. Destinations are looking into adopting an EMS system for many of the same reasons individual businesses choose to create an EMS:

- Reduction in operation costs as greater energy/resource savings are achieved;
- Improved internal management methods;
- Reduction in liability/risk from environmental deterioration;
- Improvement of a destination's image in the area of environmental performance; and compliance with regulatory requirements; and
- Desire to profit in the market for 'green' tourism destinations.

ECOLABELLING AND CERTIFICATION PROGRAMMES

The tourism industry is dependent on the environment for its sustainability and makes extensive use of the natural and cultural resources in its area of operation. The industry's prosperity is thus dependent on the conservation and responsible use of the environment.

Several organisations, including government organisations, not-for-profit industry organisations and non-governmental organisations, have addressed the issue pertaining to environmental conservation and best practices within the tourism industry by introducing ecolabelling and green certification schemes.

Each certification programme defines criteria and standards that enhance efficiency and reduce overuse and wastage. Each scheme is unique in that the certification period varies and may range from one to three years. Some schemes such as the PATA Green Leaf require the industry operator to merely sign the PATA Code, whereas others have more detailed application procedures. Evaluation methods also vary from scheme to scheme.

Though there is abundant information on the criteria required to participate in these schemes, there is a shortage of information on the evaluation mechanisms and duration period of each scheme. The following section discusses the individual certification programmes in greater detail. The majority of this information was obtained through personal communication or taken from the United Nations Environment Programme (UNEP) report entitled 'Ecolabels in the Tourism Industry'.

PATA GREEN LEAF (ASIA PACIFIC)

This is a green certification scheme developed by the Pacific Asia Travel Association, which is an industry association. It was launched in 1995 and requires that participants officially accept and abide by the PATA principles of conduct listed below. The PATA Code urges Association and Chapter members and their industry partners to:

Adopt the necessary practices to conserve the environment, including the use of renewable resources in a sustainable manner and the conservation of non-renewable resources.

Contribute to the conservation of any habitat of flora and fauna, and of any site whether natural or cultural, which may be affected by tourism.

Encourage relevant authorities to identify areas worthy of conservation and to determine the level of development, if any, which would ensure those areas are conserved.

Ensure that community attitudes, cultural values and concerns, including local customs and beliefs, are taken into account in the planning of all tourism-related projects.

Ensure that assessment procedures recognise the cumulative as well as the individual affects of all developments on the environment.

Comply with all international conventions in relation to the environment.

Comply with all national, state and local environmental laws.

Encourage those involved in tourism to comply with local, regional and national planning policies and to participate in the planning process.

Provide the opportunity for the wider community to take part in discussions and consultations on tourism planning issues insofar as they affect the tourism industry and the community.

Acknowledge responsibility for the environmental impacts of all tourism-related projects and activities and undertake all necessary changes to those practices.*Foster* environmentally responsible practices including waste management, recycling and energy use.

Foster in both management and staff, of all tourism-related projects and activities, an awareness of environmental and conservation principles.

Support the inclusion of professional conservation principles in tourism education, training and planning.

Encourage an understanding by all those involved in tourism of each community's customs, cultural values, beliefs and traditions and how they are related to the environment;

Enhance the appreciation and understanding by tourists of the environment through the provision of accurate information and appropriate interpretation; and *establish* detailed environmental policies and/or guidelines for the various sectors of the tourism industry.

TYROLEAN ENVIRONMENTAL SEAL OF QUALITY (AUSTRIA AND ITALY)

Tirol Werbung and Suditirol - public authorities operating in the area of accommodation and catering - promote this scheme. It was launched in 1994 and sets mandatory criteria pertaining to waste prevention, waste utilisation, energy, soil and transportation for businesses operating in the lodging industry. These include the hotel trade, the catering trade, private lodgings and farm holidays, camping sites and alpine refuges. The standards include but are not limited to the following:

WASTE PREVENTION

No portion packages in the catering and sanitary areas; no sales of beverage cans; refundable deposits instead of dispensers with disposable containers; no dispensers for beverages in disposable containers; no disposable tableware or cutlery; use of recycled paper or chlorine-free paper in the office, advertising and sanitary areas; drawing up of refuse concept guidelines.

TRANSPORT

Providing, hiring or arranging for guest bicycles (where terrain permits); advising visitors of best public transport connections (rail and bus) for arrival and departures; transfer service for guests arriving by public transport; facilities for storing winter sports equipment over the summer or between holidays.

GREEN GLOBE (INTERNATIONAL)

The World Travel and Tourism Council, which is an industry association, promote the Green Globe certification programme, which focuses on all industries within the tourism sector.

It was launched in 1994 and requires that the participating agents comply with the Green Globe minimum standard requirements, which are as follows:

WASTE MINIMISATION, REUSE AND RECYCLING

The company shall undertake a detailed assessment of the source and content of the waste produced.

The company shall ensure that all treatment of all waste is conducted in accordance with best industry practice and according to legislative requirements.The company shall identify opportunities to reduce, reuse and recycle waste, and develop an action plan for implementing appropriate action.

ENERGY EFFICIENCY, CONSERVATION AND MANAGEMENT

The company shall undertake a detailed assessment of energy use throughout the company, establish the type of energy required for all activities, and monitor and review use on a regular basis. The company shall set targets for reducing energy use throughout the company.

The company shall ensure that energy efficiency is a key consideration in the purchasing of new or replacement equipment and in the design of new buildings or facilities. The company shall encourage energy efficiency among staff, residents, guests and business partners. The company shall research alternative, environmentally benign methods of energy generation, such as solar, wind or biomass power.

MANAGEMENT OF FRESHWATER RESOURCES

The company shall undertake a detailed assessment of water use throughout the company and monitor water use on a regular basis, installing sub-meters where necessary. The company shall set targets for reducing water consumption and ensure that its water requirements do not adversely affect the water supplies for nearby communities.

The company shall identify opportunities to reduce and reuse water and take action accordingly. The company shall minimise the wastage of water by undertaking regular maintenance checks. The company shall where possible, install water saving devices in new and existing buildings. The company shall ensure that water efficiency is a key consideration when purchasing new and replacement equipment, and is built into the design of new buildings and facilities.

WASTEWATER MANAGEMENT

The company shall dispose of waste water responsibly, by ensuring that all effluent is treated to match existing minimum standards for the area. The company shall establish emergency procedures to ensure that the aquatic environment is protected from disasters within the facility.

The company shall avoid products containing potentially hazardous substances that may eventually find their way into the water system.

Traditional 'command and control' governmental approaches are not currently capable of developing the greatest value from investments in sustainable tourism. A special report by the World Tourism Organisation (WTO) emphasised the importance of the changing government role in tourism and the need to re-examine traditional activities undertaken by the public sector. These changes have been particularly evident in Europe and North America where government owned assets have been divested and privatised. Governments have also created public-private partnerships to market their countries as international travel destinations.

Successful sustainable tourism initiatives require the active and concerted involvement of the public and private sectors. This involvement can and must occur at a variety of levels. At the most general level, we observe that the core resources that attract tourists are national patrimony - the cultural and resources that make a country, region or people distinctive or even unique.

As national patrimony, these resources tend to be owned and managed (or at least directed) by the government. Tourism also requires the active participation of private sector entrepreneurs to develop services that make enjoyment of those assets possible (such as hotels, restaurants, tour companies, transportation providers). However, these services are largely meaningless if there is no infrastructure to permit tourists to enter an area or support the entrepreneurs. Airports, roads, potable water and other basic services are generally provided by the public sector.

At a more operational level, public-private partnerships can take many forms: such as concessions or outsourcing contracts to manage public assets; joint ventures to develop tourism attractions; agreements to develop and operate paid infrastructure such as roads, ports and water systems; user fee systems to support common objectives such as resource protection; and other simpler forms of cooperation such as agreements between governments and the private sector to support shared objectives with human and financial resources. The principal objective of these mechanisms is to leverage investment capital. The governments provide the core assets, necessary investment conditions and the 'licence' to invest in activities that have a much greater impact than the government alone is capable of achieving.

For example, these mechanisms are used to help advance tourism development in local areas near major protected areas. Declining government budgets and other financial difficulties have led to weak governmental mechanisms to care for national parks. Local governments are requesting the private sector and non-governmental organisations to assume management responsibility for most of the nation's parks.

This form of public-private partnership allows for greater management agility, lowers government budget obligations and provides the parks with more flexibility to enter into agreements with donors, tour operators and the local hospitality sectors. However, the only thing public about the parks is the land itself; the public sector is not necessarily participating in the management of these areas. In many countries, government rules greatly restrict the options for generating park revenue and entering into alliances with the private sector. While not necessarily the ideal long-term strategy, the current arrangement offers numerous advantages over a purely public park system.

Additional public-private cooperation will be needed to protect the natural and cultural assets that attract visitors. National governments will need to work with the private sector to identify common objectives and opportunities for producing revenue to protect the parks and protected areas of the region, ensuring the sustainability of these core attractions into the future. User fees, room taxes, environmental performance bonds for new tourism development and a variety of other mechanisms could be considered.

In addition to providing revenue, these types of mechanisms provide assurances to tourists that the destination is serious about the quality of its attractions.

Effective public-private partnerships can accomplish other desirable sustainable development goals, such as providing greater opportunities for smaller enterprises to participate in tourism development, and reducing 'leakage' of tourism revenues out of the country. Overall, tourism development decision-making could be improved by enhanced collaboration of the private sector in land use planning and environmental impact assessment and more transparent use of permitting and zoning.

11

Tourism Industry in India

THE BOOMING TOURISM INDUSTRY

India's tourism industry is thriving due to an increase in foreign tourists arrivals and greater than before travel by Indians to domestic and abroad destinations. The visitors are pouring in from all over the world: Europe, Africa, Southeast Asia and Australia. At the same time, the number of Indians traveling has also increased.

Some tourists come from Middle East countries to witness the drenching monsoon rains in India, a phenomenon never seen in desert climates. Domestic tourists are also fueling the industry's revival. Many of them escape from the summer heat on the plains to resorts in the Himalayan Mountains. One of the major beneficiaries this year is Kashmir, where a cease-fire between India and Pakistan has reduced violence, if not completely, at least enough to help revive the state's sagging tourism industry.

The year 2004-05 saw tourism emerging as one of the major sectors for growth of Indian economy, the foreign exchange earnings increased from ₹. 16,429 crore to 21,828 crore up to December, 2005. Similarly in the last year, tourism industry registered a growth rate of 17.3 per cent in foreign tourist arrivals, which has been the highest in last 10 years. Foreign exchange earnings grew at an even higher rate 30.2 per cent. Among the most favoured tourist destinations in India, Kerala for its scenic beauty, Agra for Taj Mahal, Khujraho for its sculptures and temples, Goa for its beaches and some pilgrimages are the most important.

Interesting feature of this growth is that it has come even as global tourism has dropped, due to the September 11 terrorist attacks in the United States, the outbreak of Severe Acute Respiratory Syndrome in East Asia, and the Iraq war. Even the disastrous tsunami didn't affect India's tourism industry, as tourist arrivals in India rose 23.5 per cent in Dec 2004 and tourist arrivals crossed 3 million mark for the first time in 2004. The disaster was expected to have a negative impact on India's tourism in terms of large-scale cancellations of tourists to India but nothing of that sort was seen.

Many Reasons of this Boom

There could be several reasons for the buoyancy in the Indian tourism industry. First, the upward trend observed in the growth rate of Indian economy has raised middle class incomes, prompting more people to spend money on vacations abroad or at home. Also, India is booming in the information technology industry and has become the IT center. Aggressive advertising campaign " Incredible India" by the government has also had contribution in changing India's image from that of a land of snake charmers, and sparking new interest among overseas travellers.

Manor Role in The Indian Economy

Tourism contribution to the Indian economy is major. Tourism is among India's important export industries. Even with comparatively low levels of international tourist traffic, tourism has already emerged as an important segment of the Indian economy. Tourism also contributed to the economy indirectly through its linkages with other sectors like horticulture, agriculture, poultry, handicrafts and construction. Foreign exchange earnings from tourism during 2003-04 were US $ 3,533 million (₹. 16,429 crore). Besides being an important foreign exchange earner, tourism industry also provides employment to millions of people in India both directly and indirectly (through its linkage with other sectors of the economy.) It is estimated that total direct employment in the tourism sector is around 20 million.

INDIAN TOURISM 2001

India has significant potential for becoming a major global tourist destination. The country witnessed foreign tourist arrivals of 2.75 million in 2001. The industry is waking up to the potential of domestic tourism as well, with an estimated 4.7 billion domestic trips in 2001. Tourism spending within India in 2001 was US$ 22 billion. There is considerable government presence in the travel and tourism industry. Each state has a tourism corporation, which typically runs a chain of hotels/motels and operates package tours, while the central government runs the India Tourism Development Corporation. Divestment of these state-run tourism corporations have either already taken place or are in process. Incoming foreign tourist arrivals have shown a 6per cent compounded annual growth rate over the last 10 years. The government has realised the potential and has advanced several incentives to promote infrastructure growth in the tourism sector.

Tourism Policy Initiatives

The Tourism Policy, released in May 2002 has outlined the following policy initiatives for the tourism sector:— 1. This policy was built around the 7-S Mantra of Swaagat (welcome), Soochanaa (information), Suvidhaa (facilitation),

Surakshaa (security), Sahyog (cooperation), Sanrachnaa (infrastructure) and Safaai (cleanliness). 2. The focus of this policy was on making tourism a catalyst in employment generation, wealth creation, development of remote and rural areas, environment preservation and social integration. Its aim was to spruce up economic growth and promote India's strengths as a tourism destination that is both safe and at the same time exciting.3.

The policy proposed the inclusion of tourism in the concurrent list of the Constitution so as to enable both the central and state governments to participate in the development of the sector. 4. No approval was required for foreign equity of up to 51 per cent in tourism projects. Enhanced equity is considered on a case-to-case basis. NRI investment was allowed up to 100 per cent.5. Approvals for Technology agreements in the hotel industry are available on an automatic basis, subject to the fulfilment of certain specified parameters.6. Concession rates on customs duty of 25 per centfor goods that are required for initial setting up, or for substantial expansion of hotels.7. 50 per cent of profits derived by hotels, travel agents and tour operators in foreign exchange were exempt from income tax.

The remaining profits were also exempt if reinvested in a tourism related project. 8. Approved hotels were entitled to import essential goods relating to the hotel and tourism industry up to the value of 25 per cent of the foreign exchange earned by them in the preceding licensing year. This limit for approved travel agents/tour operators was 10 per cent.Hotels located in locations other than the four major metro cities were entitled to 30 per cent deduction from profit, for a ten-year period. The expenditure tax had been waived in respect of hotels located in the hills, rural areas, places of pilgrimage or specified place of tourist importance.

INDIAN TOURISM IN 2004

During 2004, India for the first time breached the three million mark and the number of tourists who came to this country stood at 3.37 million reflecting an increase of 23.5 per cent over 2003. Foreign exchange earnings did better with ₹ 21,828 crore, up by 32.9 per cent and this momentum has continued during the first half of 2005.

Till May end, arrivals have increased to 1.52 million, a growth of 23.5 per cent over the corresponding period in 2004 and foreign exchange earnings touched ₹ 10,571 crore, an increase of 26.7 per cent. Mr Anil Bhandari, Managing Director, International Travel House Ltd, said that domestic tourism has continued to be upbeat. During 2004, domestic visits, according to provisional figures crossed the 360 million mark compared to the 2003 record of 309 million. Mr. Bhandari pointed out that more Indians are travelling abroad also, much more than inbound travellers. During 2003, the number of Indians going abroad was 5.3 million but this grew to 6.2 million in 2004 according to provisional estimates showing a growth of 15.2 per cent. For instance, the number of Indian visitors to Malaysia in April 2004 was 10,480; this went up by 47.5 per cent in the corresponding period in 2005 to 15,464.

People increasingly have been looking at the Net to plan their leisure travel for both international and domestic sectors. This trend is on the rise with growing Internet penetration (about 5 million) in the country. In India, most of the booking is still done through travel agents though the airlines are now ready with e-ticketing platforms. The travel trade in India has understood the importance of the Net and now has comprehensive information on fares, packages and other travel related matter on their Web sites.

In the field of tourism another trend is that more families are travelling together. This is because family get-togethers are getting rarer as family members find it difficult to take time off to visit parents and siblings. Family groups consisting of 30 and more, along with grandparents, from places such as Hyderabad, Bangalore and even interior Tamil Nadu have opted to travel overseas. Short stays are another new travel trend. Executives employed in high pressure jobs, which do not allow them to take long vacations, are more likely to take short holidays, closer to their place of work. Sri Lanka, Singapore, Maldives are some such getaways.

Sri Lanka Tourist Board holds the opinion that India topped the list of arrivals into Sri Lanka in April 2005 at 9,024 compared to the 5,784 in April 2004. The dynamics of the Indian travel scene has changed with the coming of the low-cost airlines. The low fares have changed the way people look at air travel. Air travel is no longer considered a luxury but a necessity. The advent of low-cost carriers has created a new boom in the Indian travel scene offering more options for the Indian traveller, who now has access to better and cheaper air connectivity plus attractive package deals for new destinations. Leisure traffic to India is yet to pick up in a big way.

A Federation of Hotel and Restaurant Association survey shows that more than 50 per cent of the occupancy in hotels comes from corporate travellers. The average room rate (ARR) from corporate occupancy is higher than that of the leisure travellers. India ranks 50th in the global growth ranking by the World Travel and Tourism Council, below Malaysia which is ranked third and China which is ranked 11th. To fall in line with internationally benchmarked tourism models, India needs at least 90,000 more rooms (in the five star segment) and therefore an investment of ₹ 80,000 crore. India also needs to increase inbound traffic from 3.3 million to at least 10 million in the next six to seven years.

EASIER INVESTMENT IN INDIAN TOURISM

India requires considerable investment into infrastructure which could only be met with foreign direct investment. The shortage of rooms in Delhi is adversely affecting the flow of tourists to the capital as well as to other destinations. The accommodation constraints in Delhi will have serious implications on the arrangements for the 2010 Commonwealth Games. It is estimated there will be a requirement of about 40,000-50,000 rooms in the budget category for the tourists visiting Delhi and surrounding areas during the Games. The issue of giving tax benefit, under section 80 IA of Income Tax Act by declaring them as infrastructure projects for three and four star hotels, which are constructed prior to 2010, has been taken up with ministry of finance. Tourism industry is approximately a $200-billion industry and India doesn't even touch eight per cent of this. We are looking to get a larger chunk of it. The government of India was considering offering tax incentives for attracting attract investment into building convention centres and halls. Pointing out the country was facing severe shortage of hotel accommodation in the wake of its preparation for 2010 Commonwealth games, The government has outlined plans to facilitate land procurement by hoteliers in order increase number of budget hotels, bed and breakfasts (BandBs) and self-service apartments.

STEPS TAKEN TO PROMOTE TOURISM

Recently, Indian government adopted a multi-pronged approach for promotion of tourism, which includes new mechanism for speedy implementation of tourism projects, development of integrated tourism circuits and rural destinations, special capacity building in the unorganized hospitality sector and new marketing strategy.

A nation wide campaign, for creating awareness about the effects of tourism and preservation of our rich heritage and culture, cleanliness and warm hospitality through a process of training and orientation was launched during 2004-05. The aim was to rebuild that sense of responsibility towards tourists among Indians and re-enforces the confidence of foreign tourist towards India as a preferred holiday destination. More than 6500 taxi drivers, restaurant owners and guides trained under the programme.

Government also took several other initiatives to promote Indian tourism industry and increased the plan allocation for tourism *i.e.* from ₹ 325 crore in 2003-04 to ₹. 500 crore in 2004-05. Road shows in key source markets of Europe, Incredible India campaign on prominent TV channels and in magazines across the world were among the few steps taken to advertise Indian tourism. In addition a task force was set up to promote India as prominent health tourism destination. However, in order to attract more visitors, India still needs to upgrade its airports, roads and other infrastructure to global standards. Even with the recent surge, tourist arrivals are just a mere percentage of those in such popular Asian destinations like Bangkok and Thailand.

12

Tourism in Afghanistan

Kabul

Tourism and Sightseeing

Kabul, is the capital and largest city of Afghanistan with a population close to 3 million. The population city proper is 2,994,000 and the Kabul metro area reaches almost 4 million. It is an economic and cultural center strategically situated in a narrow valley along the Kabul River, high in the mountains before the Khyber Pass. Kabul is linked with Ghazni, Kandahar, Herat and Mazari Sharif via a long beltway (circular highway) that stretches across Afghanistan. It is also linked with Pakistan in the south and Tajikistan in the north by a highway, and is approximately 1,800 metres (5,900 feet) above sealevel.

Kabul's main products include ordnance, cloth, furniture, and beet sugar, though continual war since 1979 has limited the economic productivity of the city. Kabul's population is multicultural and multi-ethnic, reflecting the diversity of Afghanistan, with Pashtuns, Tajiks, Uzbeks, Hazaras and others all comprising the bulk of the city's population. Kabul is in the process of being rebuilt following decades of war and devastation, so accurate census counts remain difficult and only rough estimates are available.

The old part of Kabul is filled with bazaars nestled along its narrow, crooked streets. Cultural sites include the Afghan National Museum, notably displaying an impressive statue of Surya excavated at Khair Khana, the Mausoleum of Emperor Babur, the mausoleum of Mohammad Nader Shah, the Minar-i-Istiklal (column of independence) built in 1919 after the Third Afghan War, the mausoleum of King Timur Shah, and the very huge Id Gah Mosque (founded 1893). Bala Hissar is a fort destroyed by the British in 1879, in retaliation for the death of their envoy, now restored as a military college. The Minaret of Chakari, destroyed in 1998, had Buddhist swastika and both Mahayana and Theravada qualities.

Other places of interest include Kabul City Center, which is Kabul's first shopping mall, the shops around Flower Street and Chicken Street, Wazir Akbar

Khan district, Kabul Zoo, Babur's Gardens, Shah Do Shamshera and other famouse Mosques, the Afghan National Gallery, Afghan National Archive, Afghan Royal Family Mausoleum, the OMAR Mine Museum, Bibi Mahroo Hill, Kabul Christian Cemetery, and Paghman Gardens.

Tappe-i-Maranjan is a nearby hill where Buddhist statues and Graceo-Bactrian coins from the 2nd century BC have been found. Outside the city proper is a citadel and the royal palace. Paghman and Jalalabad are interesting valleys north and east of the city.

- General
  - Flower Street
  - Chicken Street
  - Chelsea Supermarket
- Attractions
  - Kabul City Center
- Parks
  - Boghi Babur (Babur's Gardens)
  - Boghi Bala (High Gardens)
- Mosques
  - Grand Mosque (Under Construction)
  - Id Gah Mosque
  - Pulli Khishti Mosque
  - Shah Do Shamshera Mosque
- Mausoleums
  - Mausoleum of Emperor Babur
  - Mausoleum of King Timur Shah
  - Mausoleum of Mohammad Nader Shah
  - Mausoleum of Amir Abdur Rahman
  - Mausoleum of Tamim Ansar
- Museums
  - Afghan National Museum
- Hotels
  - Serena Hotel — Safi Landmark Hotel
  - InterContinental Hotel — Heetal Plaza Hotel
  - Hyatt Regency (2007)
- Banks
  - AIB Bank — Kabul Bank
  - Azizi Bank — Habib Bank
  - Punjab National Bank — Western Union
- Communication
  - Afghan Wireless — Roshan
- Districts
  - Shar-e-Naw (The New District)

— Shir Pul
— Shar-e-Dawlati (Governmental District)
— Mecroyan
— Shar-e-Barq (The Light District)-Under Construction; see the City of Light Development
— Wazir Akbar Khan
— Dost Muhammad Khan
— Shar-e-Askar (The Soldier's District)
— Istiqhal
— Villuerbanne (Shar-e-Azade or the Peacful District)

13

Tourism in Australia

Australia, officially the Commonwealth of Australia, is a country in the Southern Hemisphere comprising the mainland of the world's smallest continent and a number of islands in the Southern, Indian, and Pacific Oceans. Neighbouring countries include Indonesia, East Timor and Papua New Guinea to the north, the Solomon Islands, Vanuatu and the French dependency of New Caledonia to the northeast, and New Zealand to the southeast.

The mainland of the continent of Australia has been inhabited for more than 42,000 years by Indigenous Australians. After sporadic visits by fishermen from the north and by European explorers and merchants starting in the seventeenth century, the eastern half of the mainland was claimed by the British in 1770 and officially settled through penal transportation as the colony of New South Wales on 26 January 1788.

As the population grew and new areas were explored, another five largely self-governing Crown Colonies were successively established over the course of the nineteenth century.

On 1 January 1901, the six colonies became a Federation, and the Commonwealth of Australia was formed. Since federation, Australia has maintained a stable liberal democratic political system and remains a Commonwealth Realm. The capital city is Canberra, located in the self-governing Australian Capital Territory. The current national population is around 20.6 million people, and is concentrated mainly in the large coastal cities of Sydney, Melbourne, Brisbane, Perth, and Adelaide.

Australia's main tourist attractions are Sydney, the Great Barrier Reef, the Gold Coast of Queensland and Uluru (Ayers Rock), in the rugged outback of the Northern Territory. Other attractions in the continent range from the wild flowers of Western Australia to the vineyards of the Barossa Valley, and from Western Australia's ghost towns to the remarkable wildlife on the island of Tasmania.

It is possible to visit the relatively undisturbed Aboriginal communities on Bathurst and Melville Islands, about 80km (50 miles) north of Darwin, providing valuable insights into the continent's ancient indigenous culture. The

Australian coastline has thousands of miles of beautiful beaches. Information on resorts, excursions, places of interest, sports and activities within Australia is given under each individual State section.

Barbados

Barbados is an independent island nation located in the western Atlantic Ocean, just to the east of the Caribbean Sea, found at roughly 13° north of the Equator and 59° west of the Prime Meridian. Located relatively close to South America the nation of Barbados is around 434.5 kilometres (270 miles) northeast of the South American nation of Venezuela.

The closest island neighbours to Barbados are Saint Lucia and Saint Vincent and the Grenadines both located to the westTrinidad and Tobago to the south and Grenada to the south-west. Barbados is part of Lesser Antilles.

Barbados possesses a land area of around 430 square kilometres, (166 sq. mi), and is primarily low-lying, with some higher regions in the island's interior. The organic composition of Barbados is thought to be of non-volcanic origin and is predominantly composed of limestone-coral. The island's atmosphere is sub-tropical with constant trade winds off the Atlantic Ocean and some undeveloped areas contain marshes and mangrove swamps. Other parts of the island's interior contributing the island's agricultural sector are dotted with large sugarcane estates and wide gently sloping pastures with many good views down to the sea.

Barbados has one of the highest standards of living and literacy rates in the developing world and, according to the United Nations Development Programme (UNDP), Barbados is currently the No. 4 most developed of all developing countries in the world. Despite its small geographical size, Barbados constantly ranks in the top 30 (or 31) countries in the HDI (Human Development Index) rankings. The island is also a major tourist destination.

Characteristics and Tourist Information

The island of Barbados has a single major airport, the Sir Grantley Adams International Airport (GAIA) (IATA identifier BGI). The Grantley Adams Airport receives daily flights by several major airlines, from points around the globe, as well as several smaller regional commercial airlines and charters. The airport serves as the main air-transportation hub for the Eastern Caribbean. The airport is currently under-going a US$100 million upgrade and expansion.

The island is well developed and there are many local quality-hotels known internationally which offer world-class accommodations. Timeshares are available, and many of the smaller local hotels and private villas which dot the island have space available if booked months in advance. The southern and western coasts of Barbados are popular, with its calm light blue Caribbean sea and fine white and pinkish sandy beaches. Along the island's east coast the

Atlantic Ocean side are tumbling waves which are perfect for light surfing, but a little bit risky due to under-tow currents. The 'Soup Bowl' near to Bathsheba is a very popular spot with surfers all year round.

Shopping districts are another treat in Barbados, with ample duty-free shopping. There is also a festive nightlife available in mainly tourist areas like the Saint Lawrence Gap. Other attractions include wildlife reserves, jewelry stores, scuba diving, helicopter rides, golf, festivals (the largest being the annual crop over festival July/Aug), sight seeing, cave exploration, exotic drinks and fine clothes shopping.

14

Tourism in Botswana

Botswana, officially the Republic of Botswana (Tswana: Lefatshe la Botswana), is a landlocked nation in Southern Africa. Formerly the British protectorate of Bechuanaland, Botswana adopted its new name after becoming independent within the Commonwealth on September 30, 1966. It is bordered by South Africa to the south and southeast, Namibia to the west, Zambia to the north, and Zimbabwe to the northeast. The economy, closely tied to South Africa's, is predominated by mining (especially diamonds), cattle, and tourism. The country is named after its largest ethnic group, the Tswana.

TOURISM

Tourism plays a role in Botswana. A number of national parks and game reserves, with their abundant wildlife, are a top draw for tourists. United States President George Bush once stated that he visited a park in Botswana. Botswana is the setting for the popular mystery series by Alexander McCall Smith, The No. 1 Ladies' Detective Agency, and was also the location for the 1980 movie "The Gods Must Be Crazy".

15

Tourism in Bulgaria

Bulgaria is a country in southeastern Europe. It borders the Black Sea to the east, Greece and Turkey to the south, Serbia and the Republic of Macedonia to the west, and Romania to the north, mostly along the Danube.

Bulgaria is an active member of NATO and will join the European Union on January 1, 2007. The country has been a member of the UN since 1955, and a founding member of the OSCE. Bulgaria has a base in Antarctica, and as a Consultative Party to the Antarctic Treaty takes part in the governing of the territories situated south of 60° south latitude.

TOURISM IN BULGARIA

During the winter months, Borovetz, Bansko, Pamporovo and Vitosha are popular ski resorts. During the summer season Bulgaria welcomes steadily increasing numbers of tourists to its numerous resorts along the Black Sea coast. Popular summer resorts include Sozopol, Nessebur, Golden Sands, Sunny Beach, Albena, St. St. Constantine and Helena and many others. Bulgaria has become an attractive destination because of the quality of service and the affordable prices of accommodations that the country offers. Bulgaria has enjoyed a substantial growth in income from international tourism over the past decade. Beach resorts are popular with tourists from Germany, Russia and Scandinavia. The ski resorts are a favorite destination for English tourists.

Besides the traditionally developed forms of tourism new types are also gaining popularity. Ethno tourism is one such kind, where tourists explore living among local people, particularly in small mountain villages far from five star hotels and luxury shops.

Bike tourism and mountain hiking have also shown strong growth in popularity among foreign tourists. The mountains of Rila, Pirin and the Balkan attract climbers. Hikers enjoy the mountains of Vitosha and the Rhodopes. Bicycling is popular, Bulgaria is one of only six countries to annually host official 1200km Randonnees - ultra-marathon bicycle rides patterned after Paris-Brest-Paris. Historical tourism is undeveloped in Bulgaria. The country is situated at crossroads linking East and West. It has been home to many civilizations, including the Thracians, Slavs, Romans, Byzantines, Proto-Bulgarians, and Ottomans.

Although the country is rich in historical ruins, museums and monasteries those are not properly advertised and maintained. Some are not tourist-accessible due to poor infrastructure. This underdevelopment is regarded as desirable by some tourists who prefer to experience history first-hand rather than look at artefacts behind glass.

Popular Destinations

- Summer Resorts
  - — Albena — Ahtopol
  - — Balchik — Dyuni
  - — Elenite — Golden Sands
  - — Kiten — Lozenets
  - — Nessebar — Obzor
  - — Pomorie — Primorsko
  - — Riviera — Rusalka
  - — Sinemorets — Sozopol
  - — St. Constantine — St. Vlas
  - — Sunny Beach — Tsarevo
- Winter Resorts
  - — Bansko — Chepelare
  - — Borovetz — Pamporovo
  - — Uzana— Vitosha
  - — Rousse — Kardzhali
- Hiking
  - — Balkan Mountains— Pirin Mountains
  - — Rila Mountains — Rhodopi Mountains
  - — Strandzha Mountains — Sakar Mountains
  - — Vitosha Mountains
- Paragliding
  - — Central Balkan Mountains
- Monasteries
  - — Rila Monastery — Rozhen Monastery
  - — Bachkovo Monastery — Drianovo Monastery
  - — Pomorie Monastery — Sokolsky Monastery
  - — Troyan Monastery
  - — The Assumption Monastery in Kardzhali town

16

Tourism in Burundi

Burundi is a small country in the Great Lakes region of Africa. The former name was Urundi-Ubrundi-Bruwanda. Urundi is the shortened form of "Urundi Rwanda" ("The other Rwanda"), as the Belgian colonial powers formerly referred to the territory. It is bordered by Rwanda on the north, Tanzania on the south and east, and the Democratic Republic of the Congo on the west. Although the country is landlocked, much of its western border is adjacent to Lake Tanganyika. The country's modern name is derived from its Bantu language, Kirundi.

Geographically isolated, facing population pressures and having sparse resources, Burundi is one of the poorest and most conflict-ridden countries in Africa and in the world. Its small size belies the magnitude of the problems it faces in reconciling the claims of the Tutsi minority with the Hutu majority.

17

Tourism in Chile

- Santiago
- Around Santiago
  — Maipo, Valparaiso, Casa de Isla Negra, Vina del Mar
- Northen Chile
  — Ovalle, La Serena, Elqui Valley, Copiapó, Caldera, Pan de Azucar National Park, Antofagasta, Calama, Chuquicamata, San Pedro de Atacama, Iquique, Arica, Putre, Lauca National Park
- Southern Heartland
  — Rancagua, Pichilemu, Curicó, Talca, Chillan, Concepción, Los Ángeles, Laguna del Laja National Park, Angol, Nahuelbuta National Park
- The Lake District
  — Temuco, Conguillio National Park, Villarrica, Pucon, Huerquehue National Park, Villarrica National Park, Lican Ray, Panguipulli, Valdivia, Osorno, Puyehue National Park, Puerto Octay, Frutillar, Puerto Varas, Vicente Perez Rosales National Park, Puerto Montt, Alerce Andino National Park
- Chiloe
  — Ancud, Castro, Dalcahue, Chonchi, Chiloe National Park, Quellón
- Carretera Austral
  — Chaiten, Futaleufu River, Queulat National Park, Coyhaique, Lago General Carrera, Laguna San Rafael National Park
- Magallanes
  — Punta Arenas, Puerto Natales, Cordillera del Paine, Bernardo O'Higgins National Park
- Juan Fernandez Islands
  — Robinson Crusoe Island — Easter Island
  — Hanga Roa, Rapa Nui National Park

18

Tourism in China

- Beijing • Chengdu
- Dalian • Great Wall of China
- Hainan Island • Nanjing
- Qingdao • Shanghai
- Silk Road • Xian

Tourism in Hong Kong

- Aberdeen Harbour
- Country parks and hiking trails
- Causeway Bay • Mai Po Marshes
- Cheung Chau • Peng Chau
- Lamma • Repulse Bay and other
- Lantau beaches
- Mong Kok • Stanley Market
- Po Lin Monastery • Tai O
- Sai Kung • Victoria Peak
- Star Ferry
- Victoria Harbour

Tourism in Macao

- Canidrome • Casino Lisboa
- Grand Prix • Museum of Macau
- Macau Tower • Racecourse
- Ruins of Saint Paul's Cathedral

Tourism in Colombia

- Bogota
  — North of Bogota — Tunja
  — Villa de Leyva — San Gil
  — Barichara — Bucaramanga
  — Giron — Cúcuta
- Caribbean Region

— Santa Marta— Ciudad Perdida
— Cartagena — Barranquilla
— Santa Cruz de Mompox

- San Andres and Providencia Department
  — San Andres — Providencia Island
- Northwest Colombia
  — Medellin — Santa Fe de Antioquia
  — Pereira
- Southwest Colombia
  — Cali — Isla Gorgona
  — Popayan — Silvia
  — San Agustin— Tierradentro
  — Pasto — Ipiales
- Amazon Basin
  — Leticia
  — Amacayacu National Park

19

Tourism in Costa Rica

- San Jose
- Central Valley and Highlands
  — Alajuela, Poas Volcano National Park, Heredia, Barva, Braulio Carrillo National Park, Cartago, Turrialba Volcano
- Northwestern Costa Rica
  — Monteverde and Santa Elena, Canas, Palo Verde National Park, Lomas de Barbudal Biological Reserve, Rincón de la Vieja Volcano National Park, Santa Rosa National Park, Guanacaste National Park, Penas Blancas Wildlife Refuge, Ciudad Quesada, Cordillera de Tilaran
- Nicoya Peninsula
  — Playa del Coco, Las Baulas National Marine Park, Santa Cruz, Nicoya, Barra Honda National Park, Ostional Wildlife Refuge, Paquera, Montezuma, Cabo Blanco Absolute Natural Reserve
- Northern and Caribbean Lowlands
  — Cano Negro Wildlife Refuge, Puerto Limón, Tortuguero National Park, Tortuguero, Barra del Colorado Wildlife Refuge, Cahuita National Park
- Southern Costa Rica
  — Chirripo National Park
- Osa Peninsula and Gulf of Dulce
  — Corcovado National Park, Golfito, Ciudad Neily
- Central Pacific Coast
  — Puntarenas, Carara National Park, Jacó, Quepos, Manuel Antonio National Park, Dominical, Isla Uvita, Ballena National Marine Park

20

Tourism in Cote d'Ivoire

- Abidjan
- East Coast
  - — Grand-Bassam — Assinie
- West Coast
  - — Jacqueville — Dabou
  - — Tiagba — Grand Lahou
  - — Assagny National Park — Sassandra
  - — Gaoulou National Park — Monogaga
  - — San Pedro — Taï National Park
  - — Tabou
- The West
  - — Man — La Dent de Man
  - — Mount Tonkoui — Touba
  - — Danane
- The Centre
  - — Yamoussoukro — Marahoue National Park
  - — Bouake — Tanou-Sakassou
  - — Katiola
- The North
  - — Korhogo — Niofouin
  - — Boundiali — Kouto
  - — Odienne — Ferkessedougou
  - — Bouna — Kong
  - — Comoe National Park

21

Tourism in Croatia

- Zagreb, the capital of Croatia, with its attractive old town, among the other
- Inland Croatia
  - — Kumrovec, the birth place of the Josip Broz Tito, with his house and Ethno museum
  - — Karlovac, the fortress town
  - — Gorski Kotar mountain region, with its breathtaking wild nature
  - — Bjelolasica, ski resort in the Gorski Kotar
  - — Osijek, the beautiful old town with its fortress

  Slavonski Brod, town of the old baroque fortress and monastery
  - — Kutjevo, famous wine producing place
  - — Vinkovci
  - — Vukovar, ancient city on the river Danube
  - — Sljeme, ski resort on the mountain near Zagreb (FIS World Cup - Snow Queen Trophy)
- Istria
  - — Rovinj
  - — Pula, with its famous Roman Arena
  - — Motovun, a cute medieval village of central Istria
- Kvarner Gulf

  Rijeka — Opatija
  - — Krk Island — Cres Island
  - — Pag Island
  - — Senj, the ancient medieval town with strong Nehaj fort
- Dalmatia
  - — Zadar, the remarkable old coastal town with numerous monuments
  - — Kornati
  - — Sibenik, with its renaissance cathedral
  - — Split, home town of the Roman Emperor Diocletian's palace

— Solin
— Trogir, with its old monuments (especially Cathedral)
— Hvar Island
— Dubrovnik, the jewel of the Mediterranean
— Cavtat — Brijuni
— Plitvice Lakes — Rab Island
— Makarska — Vis Island
— Velebit mountains, including the national park

22

Tourism in Cuba

Havana

- Havana Province
  — San Antonio de los Banos, Artemisa, Bejucal, Batabanó, Santa Cruz del Norte, Jibacoa
- Pinar del Rio Province
  — Pinar del Rio, Vinales, Guanahacabibes Peninsula
- Isla de la Juventud and Cayo Largo del Sur
  — Nueva Gerona, Canarreos Archipelago, Cayo Largo del Sur
- Matanzas Province
  — Matanzas, Varadero, Cardenas, Zapata Peninsula, Bay of Pigs
- Cienfuegos Province and Villa Clara Province
  — Cienfuegos, Castillo de Jagua, Escambray Mountains, Santa Clara, Caibarien
- Sancti Spiritus Province
  — Sancti Spiritus, Trinidad
- Ciego de Avila Province and Camaguey Province
  — Ciego de Ávila
  — Camaguey, Morón, Cayo Coco, Cayo Guillermo, Nuevitas
- Las Tunas Province and Holguin Province
  — Las Tunas, Holguin, Gibara, Guardalavaca, Moa
- Granma Province
  — Bayamo, Sierra Maestra, Manzanillo
- Santiago de Cuba Province
  —Santiago de Cuba — Guantanamo, Baracoa
- Guantanamo Province

23

Tourism in Germany

- Berlin
- Brandenburg
  — Potsdam, Sachsenhausen concentration camp
- Saxony
  — Dresden, Leipzig, Gorlitz
- Thuringia
  — Erfurt, Weimar, Eisenach
- Saxony-Anhalt
  — Magdeburg, Quedlinburg, Wernigerode, Dessau, Lutherstadt Wittenberg, Halle, Naumburg
- Mecklenburg-Western Pomerania
  — Schwerin, Wismar, Rostock, Warnemunde, Stralsund, Rugen Island, Hiddensee Island
- Bavaria
  — Munich, Augsburg, Romantic Road, Wurzburg, Bamberg, Nuremberg, Regensburg, Passau, Bavarian Alps
- Baden-Wurttemberg
  — Stuttgart, Heidelberg, Baden-Baden, Black Forest, Neckar River, Freiburg, Danube River, Ulm, Lake Constance, Konstanz, Meersburg, Lindau, Friedrichshafen, Freiburg im Breisgau, Tubingen, Ludwigsburg
- Rhineland-Palatinate
  — The Moselle Valley, Trier, Rhine Valley, Koblenz, Mainz
- Saarland
  — Saarbrucken
- Hesse
  — Frankfurt, Marburg, Rudesheim
- North Rhine-Westphalia

  — Cologne, Dusseldorf, Aachen, Munster
- Bremen
  — Bremen
- Lower Saxony
  — Hanover, Gottingen, Goslar, Harz Mountains, Hamelin, Hildesheim
- Hamburg
- Schleswig-Holstein
  — Lubeck, Kiel, North Frisian Islands, Heligoland

24

Tourism in Greece

- Athens
  — Parthenon
- Around Athens
  — Piraeus
- The Peloponnese
  — Patras, Diakopto-Kalavryta Railway, Corinth, Acrocorinth, Nafplion, Epidavros, Mycenae, Sparta, Mystras, Monemvasia, Gythio, Mani Peninsula, Olympia
- Central Greece
  — Delphi, Meteora
- Northern Greece
  — Igoumenitsa, Ioannina, Zagori, Vikos-Aoos National Park, Thessaloniki, Halkidiki, Mount Olympus, Alexandroupolis
- Saronic Islands
  — Aegina, Poros, Hydra, Spetses
- Cyclades
  — Mykonos, Delos, Paros, Naxos, Ios, Santorini, Sifnos, Milos
- Crete
  — Iraklion, Knossos, Phaestos, Lasithi Plateau, Rethymno, Hania, Samaria Gorge, Lefka Ori, Paleohora, Sitia
- Dodecanese
  — Rhodes, Karpathos, Symi, Kos, Patmos
- Northeastern Aegean Islands
  — Samos, Chios, Lesvos
- Sporades
  — Skiathos, Skopelos, Alonnisos
- Ionian Islands
  — Corfu, Ithaki, Kefallonia, Zakynthos, Lefkada

25

Tourism in Italy

- Rome • Vatican City
- Lazio
  — Ostia Antica, Tivoli, Tarquinia, Cerveteri
- Liguria
  — Genoa, The Riviera
- Alps
- Piedmont
  — Turin
- Lombardy
  — Milan, Mantua, Lake of Como
- Veneto
  — Venice, Verona, Padua
- Emilia-Romagna
  — Bologna, Ferrara, Ravenna, Rimini
- The Dolomites
  — Cortina d'Ampezzo, Canazei, Val Gardena, San Martino di Castrozza
- Tuscany
  — Florence, Pisa, Siena, San Gimignano, Certaldo, Cortona, Maremma
- Umbria
  — Perugia, Assisi
- Marche
  — Ancona, Urbino
- Campania
  — Naples, Sorrento, Capri, Amalfi Coast, Paestum, Ischia, Procida
- Basilicata
  — Matera, Potenza

- Apulia
  — Bari
- Calabria
  — Catanzaro, Reggio Calabria
- Sicily
  — Palermo, Aeolian Islands, Taormina, Mount Etna, Syracuse, Agrigento
- Sardinia
  — Cagliari, Cala Gonone, Alghero, Costa Smeralda

26

Tourism in Malaysia

Peninsular Malaysia

- Kuala Lumpur
- Perlis
  — Kuala Perlis
- Kedah
  — Alor Setar, Pulau Langkawi
- Penang
- Perak
  — Ipoh, Lumut, Pulau Pangkor, Kuala Kangsar, Taiping
- Selangor
  — Kuala Selangor
- Putrajaya
- Malacca
  — Malacca Town
- Johor
  — Johor Bahru, Mersing
- Pahang
  — Bukit Fraser, Cameron Highlands, Pulau Tioman, Kuantan, Kuala Lipis, Jerantut, Taman Negara National Park, Tasik Chini, Cherating
- Terengganu
  — Pulau Kapas, Kuala Terengganu, Tasik Kenyir, Merang, Pulau Redang, Pulau Perhentian
- Kelantan
  — Kuala Besut, Kota Bharu

East Malaysia

- Western Sarawak

— Kuching, Batang Rejang, Sibu, Kapit, Belaga, Bintulu

- Eastern Sarawak
  — Niah Caves National Park, Lambir Hills National Park, Miri, Marudi, Gunung Mulu National Park, Kelabit Highlands, Limbang, Lawas
- Western Sabah
  — Kota Kinabalu, Tunku Abdul Rahman National Park, Tambunan Rafflesia Reserve, Tambunan, Beaufort, Labuan, Tenom, Kota Belud, Ranau
- Eastern Sabah
  — Kudat, Kinabalu National Park, Poring Hot Springs, Sandakan, Sepilok Orang Utan Sanctuary, Kinabatangan River, Semporna, Pulau Sipadan, Tawau

Bibliography

Jack Randall.: *Agriculture Tourism*, Discovery Publishing House, Delhi, 2011.

Jagmohan Negi and Gaurav Manoher.: *Project Report Preparation : Hospitality Management and Tourism Development*, Aman Publications, Delhi, 2010.

Jagmohan Negi and Gaurav Manoher.: *Travel Agency Operations: Concepts and Principles (With Examination Questions*), Kanishka Publications, Delhi, 2003.

Jagmohan Negi, Gaurav M.J., Suniti and Ritushka.: *Communication Skills for Hospitality Management*, Kanishka Publication, Delhi, 2012.

Jagpradeep.: *Hotel Management*, Murari Lal & Sons, Delhi, 2008.

Jitendra K. Sharma.: *Contemporary Tourism and Hospitality Management*, Kanishka Publication, Delhi, 2006.

Krishan K. Kamra and Mohinder Chand.: *Basics of Tourism: Theory, Operation and Practice*, Kanishka Publication, Delhi, 2002.

Lalita Sharma.: *An Introduction to Ecotourism*, Centrum Press, Delhi, 2003.

M C Metti.: *Advertising and Hotel Management*, Anmol Publication, Delhi, 2008.

M C Metti.: *Catering : Housekeeping and Hotel Management*, Anmol Publication, Delhi, 2008.

M C Metti.: *Customer Service and Hotel Management*, Anmol Publication, Delhi, 2008.

Manohar Puri and Gian Chand.: *Travel Agency and Tourism*, Pragun Publications, Delhi, 2006.

R.K. Arora.: *Heritage Tourism Management,Problems and Perspectives*, Mohit Publications, 2007.

Rabiranjan Biswas and Gautam Kumar Mallik.: *Heritage Tourism An Anthropological Journey to Bishnupur*, Mittal Publication, 2009.

Rajesh Singh.: *HRM in Travel and Tourism Industry*,Sonali Publications, Delhi, 2011.

Ramesh Mathur.: *International Tourism,* ABD Publications, Delhi, 2007.

Ratandeep Singh.: *Indian Ecotourism , Environmental Rules and Regulations*, Kanishka Publications, Delhi, 2003.

Ravee Chauhan.: *Heritage and Cultural Tourism*,Vista International,Delhi, 2006.

Ravindra Verma.: *Hotel Management and Tourism*, Centrum Press, Delhi, 2010.

Robinet Jacob; Sindhu Joseph and Anoop Philip.: *Indian Tourism Products*, Abhijeet Publication, Delhi, 2007.

Romila Chawla.: *Impacts of Tourism*,Sonali Publications, Delhi, 2006.

S K Anand.: *Historial Development of World Tourism,* Sumit Enterprises,Delhi, 2007.

S.P. Singh.: *International Tourism Development*, ABD Publications, Delhi, 2005.

Shambhu Dayal.: *Handbook of Tourism Ethics*,Akansha Publcation, Delhi, 2006.

Sunil Sharma.: *Hospitality and Tourism Management Strategies*, Akansha Publication, Delhi, 2005.

Sunil Sharma.: *Hospitality and Tourism Marketing*, Akansha Publications, Delhi, 2005.

Swadesh Sinha.: *International Tourism and Sustainable Development*, Random Publications, Delhi, 2012.

Varinder Singh Rana.: *Hospitality and Tourism Management Strategie,* Centrum Press, Delhi, 2011.

Vikas Choudhary.: *International Tourism And Sustainable Development*, Centrum Press, Delhi,2010

Vinod Kumar Singh.: *Historical and Cultural Tourism in India*, Book Enclave, Delhi, 2008.

Vivek Verma.: *Hospitality and Tourism Marketing*, Centrum Press, Delhi, 2011.

Yogendra Bali and R.S. Somi.: *Incredible Himalayas Environment, Culture, Tourism and Adventure* : Indus Publications, Delhi, 2005.

Index

A

Access 241
Allocation 42, 67
Alternative Action 87
Alternative Development 12, 13
Alternative Tourism 9, 12, 14, 15
Analytical Tools 24
Another Time 128
Attributes 60
Authenticity In Tourism 15

B

Brand Loyalty 47

C

Civil Society 92
Community Policy 223
Creating and Delivering 39
Cultural Tourism 107
Customer Equity 45, 46
Customer value
39, 40, 59, 60, 61, 67, 68
Customer Rate 39, 40, 42, 46

D

Dark Past 125
Design Link 63
Development Debate 86

E

Economic Trends 6
Emphasized 57
Enter-Tainment 201, 206
Execution Link 62
Expectations Link 59
Experience Drives 43

G

Guests Value 43

I

Indian Tourism 237, 238, 239
Inherent 65
Innovative 55

L

Liable 44, 62
Lifetime Costs 52
Lifetime Revenues 48, 52
Lifetime Value 49
Local Claims 121
Local History 123
Location and Price 43

M

Mainstream Tourism 6
Maximizing Lifetime Value 50
Meaning in Development 15

O

Operational 67
Organizations in Tourism 190, 206
Organizing Concept 20
Orientation 57, 59, 60

P

Perceptions
57, 58, 59, 60, 63, 64, 65, 66
Perhaps 39, 40, 48, 54, 58, 63, 67
Policy Challenges 221, 225, 226
Policy Implementation 29, 33
Political Economy 89
Political Support 94
Prioritized 62
Priority 62
Psychological 42

R

Recovery 42, 53, 63
Referral Value 50, 51
Relations and Tourism 95
Right Customer 47

S

Satisfaction 211, 213, 214
Satisfaction Data 66
Segmentation 201
Selecting and Attracting 39
Singaporean Society 102
society Relations 95, 102
Susceptible 53

T

Tangibles 63, 65
Tourism and Politics 93
Tourism in Singapore 95
Tourism Spaces 100
Tourist Industry 132
Travel Elements 133